Soviet Film Music

Contemporary Music Studies

A series of books edited by Peter Nelson and Nigel Osborne, University of Edinburgh, UK

Soviet Film Music

An Historical Survey

Tatiana K. Egorova

Translated by
Tatiana A. Ganf and Natalia A. Egunova

harwood academic publishers
Australia • Canada • China • France • Germany • India
Japan • Luxembourg • Malaysia • The Netherlands • Russia
Singapore • Switzerland • Thailand • United Kingdom

Amsteldijk 166
1st Floor
1079 LH Amsterdam
The Netherlands

British Library Cataloguing in Publication Data

Egorova, Tatiana

 Soviet film music: an historical survey. – (Contemporary music studies; v. 13)
 1. Motion picture music–Soviet Union
 I. Title
 781. 5'42'0947

ISBN 3-7186-5911-5

CONTENTS

INTRODUCTION TO THE SERIES

The rapid expansion and diversification of contemporary music is explored in this international series of books for contemporary musicians. Leading experts and practitioners present composition today in all aspects — its techniques, aesthetics and technology, and its relationships with other disciplines and currents of thought — as well as using the series to communicate actual musical materials.

The series also features monographs on significant twentieth-century composers not extensively documented in the existing literature.

Nigel Osborne

LIST OF ILLUSTRATIONS

PREFACE

The interrelation of music and cinematography became the subject of considerable interest as soon as the silent film acquired its musical accompaniment. At first it remained off-screen and had the utilitarian function of illustrating the episodes represented: nevertheless, its ability to intensify the expressiveness of film sequences and contribute to their rhythmic organization captured the attention of both the theoreticians and the practitioners of this new kind of art. An extensive set of methods of musical arrangement for silent films was developed, including the use of compilation techniques—the preparation of special tables and lists of well-known fragments from the classical repertoire which might be usable for cinematic art. Subsequently the film directors felt an urgent need for original music to be created and composers started being included as members of their shooting teams. But the status of the composer in the cinema was ultimately determined by the advent of sound cinematography.

This new development gave added impetus to the process of turning music from simple background accompaniment into an important dramatic component of screen synthesis. At the same time, the growing functional potential of film music made it the subject of vehement debate among composers, sound producers and film directors, as well as among musicologists and cinema critics. The appraisal of its aesthetic value was not always positive, due to a preference for the retention of established musical stereotypes. However, the subject of film music provoked the appearance of quite a number of fundamental works, such as: A. Helman, *Rola muzyki w filme*, Warsaw, 1964; Z. Lissa, *The Aesthetics of Film Music*, Moscow, 1970; R. Manvell and J. Huntley, *The Technique of Film Music*, London–New York, 1975; and W. Thiel, *Filmmusik in Geschichte*, Berlin, 1982. These works helped destroy the false idea that film music was inferior to traditional kinds of compositions. Most writers, however, in analyzing film music and its characteristics, devoted their studies mainly to developing universal systems of musical function in various genre categories. Having carefully considered the importance of a theoretical approach to this problem, I nevertheless decided to follow John Huntley's example in his book *British Film Music* (London, 1947; New York, 1947, 1972) and focus attention on the history of that unique and mysterious fusion of cinematic and musical art, Soviet film music.

This volume covers a long, specific period, from the October revolution of 1917, when the communist regime came to power, until 1991, the time of the disintegration of that once mighty socialist empire, the Soviet Union. In spite of unfavourable conditions and the controlling pressure of the State and Party authorities who carried out Lenin's directive on the priority of cinema in the Soviet hierarchy of arts, there were great achievements in the music created for that sphere. Perhaps in no other country were so many outstanding composers involved — Sergei Prokofiev, Dmitry Shostakovich, Isaak Dunayevsky, Georgy Sviridov, Aram Khachaturian, Alfred Schnittke, Nikolai Karetnikov, Edward Artemyev, Edison Denisov and Sofia Gubaidulina — all of whom succeeded in raising the quality of film music to a high professional level. Their cooperation with cinematographers, parallel to their work in academic music genres, resulted in close contacts between film music and autonomous music. Moreover, many composers readily accepted directors' invitations, because they considered the cinema to be a perfect laboratory for testing the latest devices and means of expression which their techniques could absorb; they saw in it a proving ground for experiments in the synthesis of musical and non-musical sound structures, for modelling artificial timbres, etc. Here, too, the concepts and themes of future operas, symphonies, oratorios and other large-scale compositions were frequently born.

Another remarkable characteristic of Soviet film music was the appearance of stable director–composer collaborations, such as the famous 'duets' of Eisenstein–Prokofiev, Kozintsev–Shostakovich and Tarkovsky–Artemyev. The fruitfulness of their cooperation contributed to the progress of Soviet film music; they helped understand the nature of sound-visual cinematography, create essentially new types of musical dramaturgy and master the methods of the polyphonic interaction of music and representation.

The present volume is the first attempt at a historical analysis of Soviet film music — a unique and fully formed phenomenon. As a kind of borderland of creative activity, film music was influenced by both music and cinematography: it passed through periods of triumph and crisis, of serving the totalitarian regime and surging up toward man's ideals of humane art. Now that its last word has been said, we can calmly and objectively assess its merits and demerits, and analyze its development over more than sixty years and its place in the world of cinematic expression. Finally, we have good reason to maintain that, being an experimental ground for composition, Soviet film music stimulated the quest for non-standard solutions and new ideas which were later successfully applied in various genres of autonomous music.

ACKNOWLEDGEMENTS

No serious research is ever carried out in complete isolation, without support from other people and organizations which possess the necessary information and materials on the subject chosen by the author. There are not many specialists in my field, because some professionals still adhere to the old prejudice of film music being 'second-rate' as compared to autonomous music composition.

I am therefore particularly grateful to Professor Mikhail Tarakanov, my teacher, who has always regarded my work with genuine interest and attention and who helped me become a researcher.

I also wish to thank Doctor of Arts Ludmila Korabelnikova, Nonna Alikhanova, the editor of *Muzykal'naya Zhizn'* (*Musical Life*), and the composers Edward Artemyev, Marina Krutoyarskaya and the late Nikolai Karetnikov, for the practical help they have given me. Further, I am very grateful to the publishers of *Muzyka* (*Music*), *Iskusstvo* (*Art*) and *Kompositor* (*The Composer*), who allowed me to make use of their musical and photographic material, as well as to the staff of the libraries of the Cinematographers' Union in Moscow and St Petersburg and of the music library of the State Cinema Symphony Orchestra, who made it possible for me to study both scores and rare archival materials on the history of Soviet cinema. Finally, I could hardly have written this book without the care and support of my sister, Ludmila Krasnoshchokova, who has always been, and still is, my guardian angel.

My heartfelt thanks to all those who have treated my work with kindness and understanding.

Part 1

1917–1941

1

Music and silent cinema.
The alternative: pianist versus composer

Scarcely a week had passed after the October Revolution in Russia, when on the 1st (14th) of November the First Conference of Proletarian Culture and Education Organizations was held in Petrograd. This Conference passed a unanimous resolution, stressing the necessity of creating proletarian cinema.

The Russian pre-revolutionary cinema had been the only one of its kind, there being no other national cinema in the Russian Empire. It appeared ten or twelve years later than did those in France, England, Germany and America. Nevertheless, by the beginning of the First World War, Russia had become one of the leading countries among those which possessed a well-developed and effective cinema and film industry (for example, within the period of 1914–1917 over two hundred feature films had been released). Thus, the young Soviet Republic inherited more than two thousand picture houses, about ten film studios, a number of laboratories for developing negatives and producing positive copies and, above all, trained and well qualified creative and technical workers. However, many of the owners of picture houses, studios, etc. found themselves in strained and hostile relations with the representatives of the new authorities who wished to take the contents and the subject-matter of released films under their own complete control, and to recast them in the spirit of the revolution.

By the middle of 1919, these unceasing efforts, to submit film manufacturers to certain conditions and continuously charge them with anti-Bolshevist tendencies in their films, led to a mass emigration of the owners and managers of film factories and studios. Emigrants would take away or destroy film equipment, reels and pictures. To stop this process and to preserve the basis of the film industry, the Soviet of People's Commissars passed a resolution, according to which the film industry was declared to be national property. On the 27th of August, 1919, Lenin signed a decree which placed all of the photo and film trade and industry under the jurisdiction of the People's Commissariat of Education. Later this date was celebrated in the USSR as the birthday of Soviet cinema.

The first two decades of the 20th century saw the flowering of silent cinema. True, it was not really silent, for films were accompanied by music. It was played in the auditorium during film shows and was considered indispensable. There were particular reasons for this. One of these was purely technical. According to the German film theoretician, K. London, film music was introduced 'because of the necessity to drown the zooming of the apparatus rather than for aesthetic reasons'[1]. Another explanation may be that in the early period of its development this new 'machine art' was regarded by part of the audience as a comic spectacle, an unusual and fascinating attraction which helped one spend one's free time pleasurably. It is, therefore, quite possible that the directors and producers of silent films started to get them 'wired for sound', with music acting in Z. Lissa's opinion, 'according to the same principle of noise damping as it does in the circus, in a café or at a fair'[2]. A similar view was held by Victor Shklovsky, a well-known specialist in literature and a film critic. As early as the mid-twenties he had a talk with Vladimir Messman, who, in collaboration with S. Bugoslavsky, had written the leading manual on music compilation for silent film. He tried to convince Messman that 'film music is of the same significance as music in a restaurant'[3].

This estimate of film music was supported by the fact that silent films were, as a rule, shot to the accompaniment of pianists. It seemed reasonable to suppose that, if music helped actors *perform* by emphasizing the expressiveness of their movements and gestures, it could in the same way help the audience *watch* the film. Anyhow, it was soon clear, both to the theoreticians and practicians and the common cinema-goer that 'music enhances the impressive effect of silent sequences' (S. Krakauer)[4]. In the end, the pianist and the cinema operator were taken on the cinema staff. Moreover, in March 1917, the first trade union of cinema operators and pianists was organized in Moscow. In January 1918 (i.e., already under Soviet rule) it was renamed and became the Union of Cinema Workers.

There was nothing paradoxical in this uniting of people so different by profession. On the contrary, it was consistent with the real state of affair, since neither the cinema operator nor the musician took part directly in the work of the film team, being mere 'mediators' between the picture and the audience, and providing the technical and, partially, the aesthetic conditions for watching. Thus, the picture recorded on the screen had no analogous musical accompaniment recorded: it was each time re-created anew and thus there existed a great number of contradictory variants in the individual musicians' improvisations. There seemed to be only one way to free silent film music from its dependence on the will or whim of these pianists: it was necessary that, besides the film director, the script writer, the camera-man and the actors, there should be a composer who, instead of selecting musical fragments to illustrate one or another sequence, should *compose* music intended only for one particular picture.

The need to create original music scores for silent films became especially acute in the later half of the 1920s; it was connected with the fact that a considerable number of cinemas in the large towns of the country had symphony orchestras at their disposal. Using orchestral accompaniment to silent films had become a tradition almost everywhere in Russia at the beginning of the century. Little by little pianists had to retreat, and were replaced by trios, quartets, quintets and small orchestras. By the year 1913, large orchestras of 24 and more would gather by the cinema screen not only in St. Petersburg and Moscow but also in the provinces. It is known, for instance, that at the famous Shander cinema palace in Kiev there was an orchestra of 60 musicians, who played whole symphonies during the shows, regardless of what was represented on the screen. (For some reason or other, preference was given to the later symphonies of Tchaikovsky.)

The October revolution and the civil war suspended this process for some time. In 1922, however, orchestras appeared again in the most respectable cinemas. Specially appointed members of the Association of Revolutionary Cinematography (as a rule, they were managers in the musical-artistic department of the cinema section) hurriedly compiled 'recommendation lists' and 'film albums', and collected fragments of 'old imaginative music', as the classical music of the past centuries was called.[5] For the same purpose, thousands of guidebooks and manuals were published, which contained recommendations and suggested the most typical devices for musical illustration of silent films; there were also the so-called 'tables of moods' which made it easy to decide what kind of music (should be performed) and at what moment, depending on the genre of the film and the contents of the particular sequence. Music examples were given in each case. Later, professional classes for the training of sound engineers were organized, while in the Moscow and Petrograd conservatoires optional courses were arranged. The next stage was the writing of music scripts ordered by the studios, indicating the musical fragments to be used, with strict limits on their time lengths. Afterwards such strict timing became one of the characteristics of sound film music.

The transition from improvisation and compilation to an original music score marked an entirely new phase in understanding the peculiarity of film music. No attempts at perfecting the technique of piano accompaniment, or replacing the pianist by an orchestra, or using records during the film show, etc., could stop this process. The complicated polyphonic dramaturgy of the montage cinema of the '20s, which required a thoroughly rhythmical treatment and organization of all cinematic techniques and, above all, the powerful art of Sergei Eisenstein, Vsevolod Pudovkin, Alexander Dovzhenko, FEKS[6], Lev Kuleshov, Dziga Vertov, which was revolutionary in spirit and in its very method of imaginative thinking — all of this by far surpassed the limits of the modest 'repertoire' of music designers, which consisted of a collection of popular song and dance melodies and fragments of classical music, turned into endless harmonic sequences and tremolo. Instead, the young Soviet cinema was in need of quite a different kind of music, which would not just illustrate the contents of separate scenes but would unite them dramatically; it had to be in keeping with those stormy times of the breaking up of the old order and the strengthening of the new ideology.

The following example shows the earnest and responsible attitude of directors towards silent film music, and their understanding of its role in the cinema: in July 1925, Vsevolod Meyerhold and Sergei Eisenstein were present at a conference held by the Commission of the USSR Central Executive Committee, where, at Eisenstein's request, a resolution was passed 'to ask comrade Meyerhold during his trip abroad[7], to meet the composer Prokofiev and to have preliminary talks with him about his return to the USSR to prepare a film-symphony, and notify the Commission of his terms'.[8] The film-symphony mentioned in the resolution was to be music for a monumental picture about the revolution of 1905 which Eisenstein was then going to shoot. This was an unprecedented episode in the history of the pre-sound cinema: not only did the director think it necessary to have original music for his film — he also tried to get a famous composer engaged for its creation. Unfortunately, this intended meeting of these two great artists of the 20th century did not take place. They finally met in 1938 in Paris, and agreed then and there to work together on the film *Alexander Nevsky*.

As for this great idea for a picture about the first Russian revolution, it was not to be realized. Parts of the material were used in *Battleship 'Potemkin'* (1925), for which special music was actually written. When this film was on in Berlin, the German composer Edmund Meisel approached Eisenstein with an offer to write music for it. The artistic effect surpassed all expectations: Meisel's music formed such an organic unity with the visual sequence of the picture that Lion Feuchtwanger, shaken by what he saw, devoted a whole chapter of his novel *Erfolg* (Success) to a description of the effect produced by both the representation and the music in *Battleship 'Potemkin'* upon thousands of Berliners. Afterwards, when analyzing his film, Eisenstein confessed that *Battleship 'Potemkin'*, though shot as a silent film, 'had much of what can be achieved by a sound picture'. The effect achieved was greatest in the scene where the battleship encountered the whole squadron, and 'music of the machines' ruled supreme: 'in style, this film already overstepped the limits of "a silent picture illustrated by music" and passed into the new province of *tone-film...*'[9]

Another example of a purposeful, specifically dramatic use of original music in this pre-sound cinema of the '20s, which anticipated the achievements of sound cinema, was *The New Babylon* (1929), a film by the Leningrad directors Kozintsev and Trauberg. This picture is significant not only because it was the beginning of the long-lasting and fruitful work in the cinema of composer Dmitry Shostakovich: the music of *The New Babylon* was the opening page in the biography of Soviet film music.

Of course, there were some other attempts at writing original music scores for silent films besides *The New Babylon*. Thus, according to Block and Bugoslavsky, over ten such film compositions were available in the USSR in 1929[10]. Only a few of them were of much interest, such as the musical illustrations by Belza to that classic example of Soviet silent film, *The Arsenal*, directed by Dovzhenko (1929), Arkhangelsky's music to *Polikushka*, filmed by Sanin (1919), Astradantsev's to the pictures by Chervyakov *A Golden Beak* (1929) and *Cities and Years* (1930). However, to a great extent, the musical accompaniment to these films had its prototype in a pot-pourri of operatic, song and dance melodies, embellished by unpretentious devices of sound expression. On the whole, music of this kind has not left any significant trace or memory in the history either of the country's cinema, or the country's music, except for the music score by Shostakovich for the above-mentioned film of Kozintsev and Trauberg, *The New Babylon*.

Accepting the director's invitation to write music for their new film, the young but already well-known composer did not feel himself to be a novice in the cinema. In his student days he had been obliged to take up jobs to support himself, and for two years he had worked as accompanist in one of the Leningrad cinemas, which was situated at the corner of Nevsky Prospekt and Herzen Street (now Bolshaya Morskaya) and bore the name *Bright Reel*. Later Shostakovich took over the pianist's job at the then luxu-rious cinema *Splendid Palace* during the incumbent's illness, and in February 1925 got permanent work in the cinema *Piccadilly*. All of this helped him acquire necessary practical skills and knowledge of the technical side of creating silent film music. He put his experience to use when writing his score for *The New Babylon*, though what the directors required from him was far from conventional. First, according to the film makers' idea, music should not just illustrate or copy the action, it was to participate actively in the action. Secondly, its role was, like that of the action, to be a powerful, emotional and ideological influence upon the audience. 'Therefore', one of the directors recollected, 'we at once came to an agreement with the composer that the music was to be connected, not with the exterior action but with its purport, and develop in spite of the events, regardless of the mood of the scene'[11].

Before he started working, Shostakovich carefully studied the arrangement of the film sequences and asked for timings of each scene. Then he looked through all the material once or twice, and only then set to work. He himself admitted that in writing the music he did not follow the principle of illustration, but assumed as a basis the contents of *the main* sequence in each series of several interconnected sequences[12]. Hence, many scenes in the film, which showed the tragic love of the Versailles soldier Jean and a shopgirl from a fashionable Paris shop, Louise, were 'read' by the composer not according to the exterior, factual aspect of the action, but in accordance with its inner subtext; special attention was paid to revealing the emotional state of the characters. The scene set in a restaurant where Jean comes in search of his beloved may serve as an example of this method. The bourgeoisie, having recovered from its panic, is noisily celebrating its victory, while by the walls of the Bastille the captive Communards, Louise among them, are being shot. The composition of the scene is based on a contrasting montage of sequences, representing the drunken revelry of the victors and the execution of the rebels, which alternate with a close-up of Jean's face; in his eyes we see inconsolable anguish and despair. But revelation comes too late: Louise is dead. Jean's inner state gave Shostakovich a clue to the treatment of the whole episode. The gloomy, dramatic music which accompanied it was in a complicated contrapuntal interaction with the representation, and persistent in attracting the spectator's attention to the man's tragedy, to his soul's drama.

The music of *The New Babylon* contains many ingenious and witty 'findings' which put one in mind of Shostakovich's grotesque comic opera *The Nose* (after Gogol). For example, the scene representing the rehearsal of an operetta was accompanied by Hanon's piano exercises. Depending on what was shown on the screen, these monotonous passages acquired nuances, causing now boredom, now gaiety, and sometimes a sense of danger. Similarly unusual and stereotype-breaking was the use of a large quotation from *The Child's Album* by Tchaikovsky (*An old French Song*) to characterize cold and haughty Versailles, hostile to rebellious Paris.

As a whole, the musical dramaturgy of *The New Babylon* was a mosaic structure, and resembled a suite. It contained several developed symphonic items with montage insertions of melodic and rhythmic dance sequences of the time, fragments of folk and revolutionary song ('Carmagnole', 'Ça ira'), and quotations from Offenbach's operettas *La belle Hélène* and *Orphée aux enfers*. But the strongest impression in the film was, perhaps, produced by its metamorphosis of the revolutionary song 'La Marseillaise', which was turned into a formal hymn of the bourgeois republic and a leitmotiv of Versailles. It not only lost its original meaning in the film, but also appeared in quite an opposite sense, as a hypocritical 'werewolf' theme, skilfully

Figure 1 *The New Babylon*

disguised behind the masks of other genres (can-can, waltz, galop). Its true essence was ruthlessly revealed in the restaurant scene, where an actress, with a tricoloured banner in her hands, jumped up on a table and, addressing the soldiers, sang the 'Marseillaise', but suddenly went off key and danced the frivolous can-can from Offenbach's *Orphée aux enfers*.

A similar device of genre transformation, of multifaceted leitmotiv themes symbolizing the forces of evil, hatred, animosity, would be used by Shostakovich in all his subsequent work in the cinema, especially in his 'Shakespearean' films of the 1960–1970s.

His specific and creative approach to music as dramatically significant instead of being a neutral background accompaniment to a silent film, and his attempt to create an integral musical-visual conception of film composition, raised Shostakovich's music for *The New Babylon* to a higher level than other examples of original silent film music. However, his initiative, which was warmly supported by the directors of the picture, cinema critics and composers, met with energetic opposition and protest on the part of musicians who worked in cinema. This technically complicated score, which was symphonic and required much rehearsal and preparation, as well as virtuosity. The orchestral musicians, who were used only to playing polkas, galops and 'sentimental' romances, proved unable to cope with it. They could think of nothing better than to accuse the composer of lacking professional skill. In answer, the critic Vainkop wrote in the *Rabochii i Teatr* (The Worker and the Theatre): 'This traditional method of 'laying one's own fault at somebody else's door" should meet with a proper rebuff, especially because this accusation is supported by many cinema conductors, who have lost their fee for musical compilations since there is a specially written score. Shostakovich's music for *The New Babylon* is not only the first experiment in creating special music for a given film, not only an attempt to infuse a fresh spirit into the stale atmosphere of musical film tradition: it is also itself of great immediate value'[13]. Of course, there were also different opinions concerning this music which was by some reviewers (including Ioffe) criticized for its formalism, constructivism and its shift of accent from the tragedy of the proletariat into a parody of the bourgeoisie: socialist realism, which was actively propagated in the country, began to yield results. As a consequence, after two extremely careless and faulty performances (the orchestra was constantly at variance with the screen representation) the music for *The New Babylon* was cancelled and forgotten. At one time it was considered lost. It was re-discovered by the conductor Gennady Rozhdestvensky in the archives of the State Centre of Musical Culture in the early '70s.

After long years of oblivion, the reunion of this music and *The New Babylon* took place in a retrospect of old films at the First Paris Film Festival. In January, 1983, it was performed at a showing of *The New Babylon* in London by a London orchestra conducted by Omri Handari.

In spite of its dramatic fate, this music, even though misunderstood and rejected, had done its part: just before the advent of sound film it had laid a firm foundation for the connection of film music with traditional academic genres of musical art, first and foremost with operatic and symphonic ones. For many years afterwards they would interact, thus enriching both their imaginative and expressive means. Finally, the appearance of the music for *The New Babylon* gave an irrefutable answer to the question of whether a composer or an accompanist is wanted in the cinema. Hence the technique of illustration and compilation gradually became a thing of the past, and so did the profession of cinema pianist.

2

Evolution from the silent to the sound film.
The duality of music during this transitional period in film history

The appearance of sound cinema was keenly anticipated all over the world. The Soviet Union did not keep aloof from discussing the problem of what a sound film should be like. At the end of the '20s, a heated discussion was carried on in the press. Some critics insisted upon a 'talking' (speech) film, others considered it to be a purely sound (that is, 'noisy') one, still others thought of it as a new 'film-opera'. The debates grew ever more vehement until, in 1928, an important document, *The future of the Sound Film: a Declaration*, was published. The authors were three leading directors, Eisenstein, Pudovkin and Alexandrov. Contrary to current predictions of the inevitable ruin of cinema as art, which would be caused by the introduction of sound, they solemnly announced the beginning of a new era.

One of the main items of this *Declaration* was its call for the use of sound as *a counterpoint* in relation to visual montage: in the authors' opinion, this should provide 'new possibilities for montage development and perfection'. Therefore, the directors maintained, '*the first experiments on working in sound should be aimed at its sharp divergence from visual images.*

It is such an "assault" that can alone give the necessary impetus which will lead to the creation of the new orchestral counterpoint of visual and sound images.'[14]

Proceeding from this thesis, Eisenstein, Pudovkin and Alexandrov came to this bold conclusion, which was later confirmed in practice: 'This new technical discovery is not a mere chance in history but a natural way for the cultured cinema avant-garde to emerge out of numerous blind alleys which have seemed quite hopeless...

'Sound interpreted as a new montage element (as an independent component of a visual image) will certainly introduce new means of great power for the expression and solution of very complicated problems which have oppressed us because of our inability to cope with them, using the imperfect methods of a cinema which had only visual images at its disposal.'[15]

Thus, even before the idea of sound film was practically realized in the USSR, the authors of the *Declaration* saw in sound a powerful means which could radically change the future fate of cinema, give it a multilayered structure, and discover new perspectives in building up a sound-visual film image.

The transition to sound film was accompanied by an intensive search for the functional potentials of sound in all of its hypostases. In earlier experimental sound films, devoted mostly to the theme of enthusiastic work and the country's industrialization, particular attention was paid to polyphonic interaction of word, music and sound effects, the latter being often shot on location, synchronically with the picture representation, and then music was superimposed. Such a principle of organizing the sound-track was used in the documentary *The Donbass Symphony (Enthusiasm)* by Dziga Vertov, with music by Timofeyev; in the film-programme *The Five Year Plan (The Plan for Great Works)*, directed by Abram Room, with the participation of composers Avraamov, Rimsky-Korsakov, Timofeyev, and Malakhovsky; in the feature film *Deeds and People* by director Alexander Macheret and composers Shebalin, Germanov and Kriukov. In the latter picture, which represented the construction of Dneproges, i.e. the state power station on the Dnieper (1932), dozens of 'noise-makers' produced all kinds of sounds, imitating cranes, trains, wind, tramping of people, etc. As for the music as such, it did not simply accompany the sounds but was born, or arose from them, as it were. A well-known Soviet film director, who worked on Macheret's picture as sound assistant, left an interesting description of the ways in which the sound score of the film had been created:

'I remember a symphonic étude for the picture: first, some girls thrashed mud with mallets, imitating the rhythmical tramping of the workers kneading concrete. This was joined by the clanging of chains, and then the orchestra entered gradually and a concrete symphony began.'[16]

However, the daring sound experiments in the 'industrial' film of the late '20s and early '30s, which had something in common with the innovatory constructivist symphonies with their 'sound effects', composed by Mosolov and Deshevov, were not given their due. The sound film, according to the French critic Goléa, 'had taken the place of the ancient tragedy and the medieval mystery' and determined the fate of the new music, making it dependent 'upon the quality of the film music of today and of the future'[17]; thus the sound film followed a beaten track, building on the silent film's experience in creating original musical compositions and autonomous programme music. Dmitry Shostakovich was the first to set the fashion in his music for one of the earliest sound pictures, *Alone* (1931), shot by Kozintsev and Trauberg.

The plot of this film was based on a short newspaper report about a village teacher who had lost her way in a snow storm. Frozen almost to death, she had fallen seriously ill, and, there being no doctor in the vicinity, a plane was sent by the Government to take her where she could be placed under medical care. In 1930 this seemed to many an event of great significance, as a practical demonstration of the humaneness of the new social order. Kozintsev wrote: 'A bare newspaper report set one thinking on many things. Man's fate had become an object of general care; this showed the utmost importance — even at a national level — of a single human life'.[18] The idea to make an individual, and not a collective hero or a number of personages, the leading character of the film had prompted the title, which occurred to the directors even before the script was written.

It should be mentioned here that this picture, in spite of the directors' wish to make a sound film, must be considered as work of a transitional period: shot in 1931 according to the rules of silent cinema, it was fitted for sound later. [19] No wonder sound was used in it very carefully, the noises of everyday life were hardly present, while the characters' remarks were as often as possible replaced with music.

This attempt to entrust music with the functions of other sound components was a result of the imperfection of sound recording technique rather than the director's inexperience. The fact was that, of all sound elements, only instrumental music and singing could be recorded clearly and precisely, while speech and noised were 'slurred' and indistinct. Therefore, irrespective of what the directors, the composer and the sound operator might have wished, music still played the primary role in conveying sound information in the film.

The picture opened with a great instrumental number which expressed the idealistic notions of a young graduate from a teachers' college about her future life. Her walks in town in company with her handsome husband, the cosiness of her excellent kitchen, a joyful concert of streets and shopwindows, ending in a tram taking off towards the sky — all of this throbbed with a cheerful, elastic toccata rhythm. But these romantic daydreams were suddenly destroyed by life's realities. Having graduated from college, the young girl was assigned by the Committee of People's Education to work as a school teacher in a far-off Altai village. From this moment both the style of the film and the music which accompanied it underwent a sharp change. The heroine entered an entirely different world, strange and even hostile, steeped in the darkness of ignorance and wild prejudice. Idyllic images were replaced by sharply grotesque ones.

A mocking *glissando* of trombones, imitating a yawn or stifled abuse — this is how the composer characterizes one of the characters, the chairman of the village council, a fat and indifferent bureaucrat and obedient puppet in the hands of a rich local Bey (a rich landowner in Central Asia). The scene of a confrontation between him and the young teacher, which is built up by means of operative techniques, is especially original and daring as to the role and the style of music. The teacher comes to the chairman's house to plead for her pupils, who have been sent by the Bey to shepherd his flocks. The scene is based on the contrast between the plastic performance of the actors, and the sound which personifies a power terrible in its heartlessness. The scene is developed against the background of the chairman's snoring, in which the teacher's words and appeals are drowned, and which grows ever louder until it gradually turns into a slow and heavy musical movement, the whole of the symphony orchestra joining in.

No less expressive in the music of the film *Alone* is the character or, more exactly, the 'voice' of the Bey, created with the help of the piercing timbre of the flute and the powerful, resolute phrases of the bassoon's solo. While in this sequence the actor stresses the senile feebleness of the character the music effectively dispels this impression in the above scene with the teacher, where in the Bey's 'voice' aggressive, menacing intonations are suddenly heard, typical of a man who is used to being implicitly obeyed.

Like an opera, the film also possessed a leitmotiv of its own, a simple-hearted, enthusiastic phrase: 'How good and beautiful life will be!' — a theme which revealed the heroine's naive idea of happiness among her clean, shining crockery, side by side with her husband playing the cello. But as she came face to face with real life, the character and the views of the young teacher gradually changed, and the spoilt girl, who had grown up in Leningrad and was used to a life of comfort, became an active participant in the process of collectivization in the village. These inner changes were reflected in the melodic variation of the leitmotiv, in which derisive, ironical notes were now heard. Some of the leitmotiv passages would for a moment reappear, like echoes of a half-forgotten dream, in the dramatic-climax of the film, a large picturesque scene of the snow storm in which the teacher was caught, having lost her way in a wilderness. In fact, for this episode Shostakovich composed an elaborate programme piece for symphony or-chestra. However, the illustrative elements proper played a secondary role, while the main theme expressed the heroine's feelings of fear, anger, misery, and despair.

In developing the sound dramaturgy of the film *Alone*, the directors used rather complex combinations of original and documentary music with natural noises, which made the general development extremely dynamic. One scene, showing the heroine's arrival in the village, is of great interest. The girl is trying to make herself at home, she is unpacking and arranging her things. Suddenly an alarm-clock starts ringing, and on this sound is superimposed the tune of a street-organ which used to wake her up every morning in Leningrad. But the cheerful melody of a galop (for greater resemblance to the timbre of the street-organ it had been specially recorded on a cylinder) is immediately broken into by the harsh strokes of a tambourine, the hoarse shouts of a *shaman* (genuine recording) and other noises which are later superimposed by the theme — the Bey's 'voice'.

On the whole, in spite of a number of interesting discoveries timbre dramaturgy, polyphonic sound montage and the new sound-track method of music technology in the cinema, Shostakovich was not pleased with the results of his work. Its main defect was, in his opinion, lack of a continuous line of symphonic development. Hence the items were musically isolated, each enclosed in its own structure. An attempt to overcome this defect was made in the next sound reel *Mountains of Gold*, filmed by Yutkevich (1931)[20], in which Shostakovich achieved a type of musical dramaturgy which was to become one of the leading types in the Soviet feature film of the '30s and was termed 'symphonic'.

3

General characteristics of the main types of musical dramaturgy in the 1930s and early '40s

The appearance of sound cinema brought about an essential change in the interrelation between screen action and music which had existed off-frame in the silent film. In a sound picture, music was introduced into the artistic structure of the film; moreover, it had become a competent element of screen synthesis, with the following demarcation between its off-frame and on-frame functions, as well as the ways of its presentation. As a rule, the off-frame music (expressing the director's standpoint in treating the subject) served as generalization and 'worked' for the idea of the film, governing the processes of perception and evoking a certain emotional response from the audience to the actions and conduct of the characters. The on-frame music (documentary — realistic) was meant to specify the place and time of screen events, and to reveal the social status of the characters and their ideological world-outlook.

The appearance of sound film gave rise to a natural process of differentiation of sound elements, whose interrelations were sometimes complicated. Music, speech, noises, which now existed all in the same space, had to be coordinated most precisely, for the inaccurate accentuation or retouching of one of the items of the sound track might result in technical defects, or even in the distortion of the meaning of a scene, and thus of the whole film. Besides, music, being recorded, lost its openness to various interpretations. A particular interpretation was fixed in the recording studio, which then was tested for its compatibility with the picture recorded.

One of the specific qualities of Soviet film music, which showed itself already at an early stage of the cinema's development, was a striving for self-expression: the fact is that the best creative forces in the realm of young multi-national Soviet music were engaged in cinema. It was in the 1930s that the names which soon became widely known appeared in the credits of the film shown in the country. These were Dunayevsky, Shaporin, Kabalevsky, Shebalin, the Pokrass brothers, Alexandrov, Popov, Khrennikov, Bogos-lovsky, Khachaturian, Balanchivadze, Kiladze, Tuskiya. New, unexpected

aspects of their talent were revealed in the art of two of the greatest composers of the 20th century, Shostakovich and Prokofiev, during their work
in the pre-war cinematograph. Moreover, creating film music helped many
of the above-mentioned composers discover new means and methods of
expressiveness as to timbre and intonation, and techniques of musical
composition based on sharp 'montage joins' of heterogeneous subject
material and on complicated associative interconnections of seemingly
remote themes and images. The fruitfulness of contact with the cinema was
apparent in the musical adaptation of particularly cinematic devices such as
'superimposition' and 'rapid' cross-cutting which later came to be also used
in opera and symphonic genres. Besides, the popular and democratic character of the young art gave the composers access to the multitudinous
cinema audience, within which an essentially new phenom-enon, the mass
spectator, was forming (the product of the growth and development of mass
media), who was able not only to submit to influence but also to foist on
others his own tastes and predilections.

The peculiarities of Soviet film evolution in the pre-war decade led
to the formation of two basic types of musical dramaturgy, a symphonic
type and a song type. The former was more frequent in films of historical,
historico-revolutionary, and dramatic content, where the main accent fell
upon off-frame (i.e. 'composed') music. The latter type of dramaturgy was
used particularly in the musical film comedy. And it so happened that the
progenitor of both was one and the same man — composer Dmitry
Shostakovich.

4

The symphonic type of dramaturgy

The appearance of the symphonic type of dramaturgy is thought to have been connected with the music composed by Shostakovich for the film *Mountains of Gold* (1931), shot by Yutkevich at the same time as *Alone*. But, unlike the film of Kozintsev and Trauberg, *Mountains of Gold* was a full-fledged sound reel containing speech dialogues, noises, and music, whose former power was already to a great extent lost due to a highly developed verbal element. But, strange as it may seem, it was just this discrete character of the musical material that made the composer search for an effective means of coping with thematic fragmentation and mosaicity, and establishing the dramatic integrity of the theme. The leitmotiv proved to be the best means for this purpose.

In building the musical conception of this film, Shostakovich used two leitmotivs, both of which were waltzes and had ironical implications: this was most distinguishable in their image transformation. One of the leitmotivs, the graceful waltz by Waldteufel 'Little Spring Flowers', was associated with negative characters, the factory owners and their assistants. True, today such a 'class' interpretation of the somewhat sentimental waltz melody seems naive and forced, but in those days nobody doubted that it was just the kind of music which would be played by an engineer who cringed before his masters, and that the same melody, but in a 'dollish' style, could be produced by the clock, which the worker Piotr Petrovich was given as a reward by the factory owners. And when this half-literate man, formerly a peasant, who had moved to the town to earn his living, divined the true meaning of their benevolence, his eyes opened to the fact that the expensive present was really his masters' attempt to make him betray his comrades: this was at once reflected in the leitmotiv. It seemed as if something had broken in the well-regulated clock mechanism: the waltz melody was distorted by false notes, its rhythm became irregular and the coordination between the melody itself and its accompaniment was lost.

The second leitmotiv, the popular romance 'Should I have mountains of gold...', personified Piotr Petrovich's naive dream of wealth. He had heard it at an inn, sung in a dashing manner to the accompaniment of an accordion by a factory labourer, Boris, and had been deeply impressed. Sung in the film more than once, the theme of the romance sounded more and more idealistic and sugary, reaching the culmination of its development in the scene of Piotr Petrovich's dream: in his sleep he saw himself young and strong, returning proudly to his native village, leading a beautiful horse by the bridle. Thus, quite distinct from Waldteufel's refined waltz, the dynamic movement of the song 'Should I have mountains of gold' had an opposite tendency, i.e. it was not a means of parodic lowering but served the purpose of an ironical elevation of the unpretentious street-organ theme.

It is curious that the romance 'Mountains of gold', like the waltz 'Little Spring Flowers', was not the composer's own creation: it was borrowed by him from urban, 'street' folklore. The connection between the music of silent cinema and that of the early sound film had not yet been severed, and composers working for the cinema still included popular melodies from the current repertoire and of 'the days of czarizm' to characterize the milieu, and especially the social status and ideological views, of the characters.

On the whole, the area of leitmotiv-use in the picture *Mountains of Gold* proved to be rather limited, since the main emphasis was on the unfolding symphonic episodes, associated with the representation of the rising struggle of the proletariat for its liberation. The culmination point of this main theme of the film was an extremely expressive scene built on a parallel, intersecting montage of sequences dealing with a strike of the proletariat in Petrograd and in Baku. To intensify its emotional effect, Shostakovich made use of fugue[21]. A resilient fugal theme carrying a tremendous charge of explosive energy, impetuously seizes the sound sphere within a two-octave range. In it, one can almost visually sense the beating of the pulse of revolutionary times, which urged into action vast masses of people in various parts of the Russian Empire, and threw them together in a unanimous protest against slavery and injustice.

Ex. 1 The theme of the proletarian strike, from the film *Mountains of Gold*

The complicated, untraditional combination of musical and visually plastic polyphony demonstrated in the strike scene by the makers of *Mountains of Gold* was to a great extent an experiment, associated with an innovatory search for a synthesis of music and representation. It appeared that not only spectators but also critics were not ready to understand and appreciate such a discovery. When in the '30s, a specialist in the problems of film music, Cheremukhin, found that the use of fugue in a film was 'not entirely successful'[22], the well-known specialist in art, Ioffe, also accused the composer of two things at once: first, that for the fugal theme he had chosen 'an abstract dramatic melody' (?!) instead of a revolutionary song; and secondly, of attempting a constructivist solution to the problem of combining music and subject-matter by revealing a formal analogy between them[23]. Further, when analyzing the music for the picture, Ioffe reproached the composer for his superfluous enthusiasm, for creating large and closed musical episodes which were only formally connected with the contents of the film and reminded one in their organization[24] of the suite form. However, there was nothing criminal in the fact that Shostakovich, when writing music for *Mountains of Gold*, resorted to composition techniques borrowed from opera / symphonic and chamber music: in those days film music was looked upon as a definite variant of a dramatic musical genre based on a literary script or a programme. Later Shostakovich resumed his most energetic attempts to assimilate academic music into film. His *Requiem*, written for the film *A Great Citizen* by Ermler (1937–1939, 2 parts), may serve as an example. It is based on a symphonic development of the melodies of well-known revolutionary songs. It is interesting that, some decades later, this idea was further developed in one of Shostakovich's most remarkable creations, his Eleventh Symphony (*The Year 1905*).

Among other films in the making of which Shostakovich took part, and in which the symphonic type of musical dramaturgy was used, the following pictures are worth mentioning: *Love and Hatred* by Gendelstein (1934), *The Girlfriends* by Arnshtam (1936), *Volochayevsky Days* by the Vasiliev brothers (1937)[25], *Man with a Gun* by Yutkevich (1938) and, above all, the *Maxim*, trilogy by Kozintsev and Trauberg (1934–1938): the latter was series of films treasured by and popular in the Soviet Union in the pre- and post-war years[26].

As a matter of fact, though the (action) of the trilogy abounded in all kinds of daily accessory musical material, the composer's functions were reduced to those creating a background accompaniment to each particular scene, without a subsequent outlet to the generalizing dramatic conception. The number of items written by Shostakovich was small. They included: the musical prologue to the first of the series, *Maxim's Youth*, a peculiar pot-pourri of 'hits' popular in 1910 (the 'Oira' dance, the chansonette 'I am a football player, I play football', and, as Kozintsev put it, a 'devil-may-care' galop); a waltz, an episode in the billiard-room, and the scene where a peaceful demonstration of workers is dispersed by the police, with a tragic funeral march at the end; in the second series, he wrote *Maxim's Return;* and, finally, in the third part of the trilogy, some orchestral fragments built on resilient, march-like, heroical themes, *Vyborgskaya Storona (The Vyborg side)*. Such diminution of the composer's function, unexpected in films made by Kozintsev and Trauberg, could be explained by the directors' intention. According to the principles of 'prosaic' cinema[27], the directors sought to 'bring the film closer to folk tale, or parable'[28], and this required a quite different kind of music. Its main role was to form a distinctive sound milieu for the characters of the film trilogy, based solely on song. As the musicologist Emilia Frid justly pointed out, 'the trade-mark of *Maxim* is the fact that all the songs there are original, borrowed from the real repertoire of the time: songs of revolution, songs popular among workers, the petty bourgeoisie, bar-files. They portray not only the face of the epoch but also the concrete peculiarities of this or that social milieu'[29].

The light-hearted, merry song 'Whirling and turning is a blue balloon' (based on the town romance 'A blue scarf' which was popular at the beginning of the century) is the pivot of the musical dramaturgy, and supports the construction of the whole trilogy; it also functions as the main leitmotiv and at the same time as a characterisation of the protagonist Maxim. In its unpretentious tune and melodic turns, so hackneyed as to be clichés, the directors perceived 'that very true and sincere lyricism of "the kopeck's worth" which determined the mood of the film'[30].

Initially, the tune of Maxim's song grew, from the atmosphere and the spirit of the workers district, Narvskaya Zastava, where Maxim was born and where he now lived, a dashing admirer, a mocker, and a true comrade, always ready to struggle against injustice (*Maxim's Youth*). Later, as the film showed the gradual spiritual regeneration of the hero caught in the whirlpool of the revolutionary movement, his re-appraisal of old values and finding of new ideals, the music of the trilogy was invaded by revolutionary and march-like melodies and rhythms, and by powerful and uplifting songs popular during the revolutions, such as 'Smelo, tovarishchi v nogu' (Courage, comrades, keep step...), 'Varshavyanka', 'La Marseillaise'. Through them, there arose a sense of the living pulse of the times, marked by an outburst of proletarian political activity, and by the spreading of socialist and communist ideologies.

The energy and purposeful, manly force of these songs were in sharp contrast to the melodramatic and somewhat trivial romance 'Charming

Eyes', which Maxim sang to the clerk Dymba, trying to win his favour, and worm himself into his confidence in order to learn what revenge his masters were going to take on the strikers. There was something in common between Maxim's romance and the couplets given to Dymba, 'I changed my women like my gloves', which were set to the tune of the then fashionable 'Hiawatha' dance, and revealed the utter moral squalor of the toady and informer. But irrespective of Maxim's stage transformations', and the qualitative transformation of his image within the three parts of the film, the leitmotiv song 'Whirling and turning is a blue balloon' preserved its original character, symbolizing the invariability of the hero's nature, and such features as his frankness, gayety, and joy in life, typical of a simple fellow from a Petersburg industrial suburb.

The symphonic type of dramaturgy became characteristic of the pre-war cinema. The composers who used it most frequently included Timofeyev (*Deputy for the Baltics*, 1936), Shcherbachev (*Peter the First*, 1937–1938, 2 parts), Kriukov (*Valery Chkalov*, 1941), and Popov, who wrote music for the legendary picture *Chapayev*, made by the Vasiliev brothers (1934) and acknowledged as a classic work of the Soviet cinema.

Among the films of the 1930s, *Chapayev* is distinguished by its thorough elaboration of all the elements of the sound realm: music is assigned a special role. There is hardly a 'passing' episode where it is merely auxiliary, neutral background. On the contrary, it plays an important role in the development of the action, sometimes entering into complicated relations with the subject, reminding the audience of past events, or anticipating those that were still to happen, and passing emotional judgment on what was shown on the screen. In other words, each time' its entrance into the frame had a clear, meaningful and dramatic function. In this sense, the episode with Beethoven's 'Moonlight Sonata' (No.14) is of great interest. The majestic beauty of the famous first part of the sonata, played with inspiration by the white-guard colonel, grows into a kind of moral torture for his batman, the change of mood being revealed through a dynamic montage counterpoint. At first the colonel's batman Mitrich, polishing the parquet, is simply listening to the music, moving about in time with its rhythm. But suddenly he is struck by the horrible memory of his brother flogged to death at the colonel's order. And now the expression of slave-like? submissiveness in Mitrich's face changes to one of anger, and he looks with hatred at the fat, clean-shaven nape of his master. The acceleration of montage rhythm in these two close-ups increases the emotional tension of the scene, foretelling the dreadful outcome. Music also plays a role in the action: the even flow of the piano passages, veiled, as it were, in the haze of the strings, is pierced more and more urgently with protesting cries from brass instruments, and the triplet movement rises in waves from the lower to the upper register and sinks down again, life the outbursts of sorrow and despair tormenting Mitrich. And when the general tension reaches a climax of unbearable suffering, the clatter of the broom which Mitrich lets fall interrupts both the colonel's performance and the soldier's mute suffering.

The emphatic realism of *Chapayev*, based upon historic events of the civil war which were still within living memory, had required a great diversity of folk-song genres to be introduced into the film. Songs appear one after another: the valiant, triumphal march 'En, the Red Army's moving along the road', and the sprightly *chastooshka* (a two-or four-line verse, humorous and often topical, sung in a lively manner), 'Come to me, my sweetie-boy'; a lyrical, long-drawn song about parting, 'A merry talk' and a sorrowful, severe 'Ermak' which the Chapayevites sang on the eve of their last battle, as if moved by a foreboding of death.

Almost all of these songs were subject-motivated and were used locally, in accordance with the frame contents. There was only one exception, 'The Black Raven', a well-known Russian song in the genre of rebellious peasant songs, which became a leitmotiv of the film. The fact that it had been selected as the leading theme and idea of the picture was logical enough. It was full of tremendous inner force, and permeated with sorrow, deep but manfully kept in check, and expressed man's eternal striving for freedom, and his will to retain it even at the price of his own life. Appearing first in the overture, it became closely associated with the leading character of the film, the legendary division commander Vasily Ivanovich Chapayev, a gifted military leader at the times of the civil war, a peasant by birth, coming from the lower sections of the people. In the further development of the plot, a certain parallel was drawn between his fate and the fate of Ermak, the song foretelling the tragic outcome, Chapayev's inevitable death, in which he found immortality.

The use of Russian folk-song, which was an integral part of the action, determined the peculiar, epic character of the film and also made it simple and democratic, intelligible to the broadest sections of the audience of the 1930s. At the same time, in *Chapayev* there was also symphonic music proper, such as the dreamy theme of love expressing Chapayev's aide-de-camp Pet'ka's feeling for Anka, the machine-gunner of the detachment; and the heroic funeral march which forecast the shattering advance of the Red Army in the finale of the film. But the best and easiest to remember, thanks to its music, noise, and visual arrangement, was without doubt the episode which dealt with the 'psychological attack' of select officer units of the White Army General Kappel on a handful of Red fighters who have dug themselves in.

The rapid interchange of close-ups, middle ground shots and pan-
oramas of marching White Guard columns is accompanied by an
uninterrupted roll on the side-drum. The mechanically monotonous, irritating banging and the White Guards, moving on in orderly rows without
pausing, as if on parade, fill the hearts of the Red fighters with terror and
despair. It seems to some of them already that there is no power in the world
that could stop these robot-like officers, marching in step so beautifully.
When kappel's officers approach the entrenched Reds, the drum roll ceases
and a dreadful, oppressive silence falls, which is suddenly broken by the
piercing cry: 'Shoot!' immediately followed by the rattle of Anka's machine-
gun. In answer to the signal, Chapayev's cavalry, which has been waiting
in ambush, darts like a whirlwind from the hills. On the sounds of the battle
are superimposed an exultant theme of victory which accompanies the
cavalry attack.

Of course, such a detailed working out and differentiation of the
sound component, making music a powerful means of artistic expressiveness which could model different emotional states, and control their development and time duration, were not very frequent in the cinema. It was only
in the 1960s that the problems of synthesis at different levels, and of dramatic
concordance of music, speech, and sound effects came to be an object of
immediate interest and attention. By then, the goals and problems the
cinema was facing were very different.

In discussing the process of developing the symphonic type of
musical dramaturgy in the Soviet cinema of the 1930s, one more film should
be mentioned. It wouldn't have left a trace in the history of native cinema art
had not Sergei Prokofiev taken part in its creation. *Lieutenant Kizhé* was his
debut in the cinema. It is curious that according to its outward characteristics, the picture belonged to the category of the so-called 'speechless' films:
in these music dominated the sound track. This gave the composer full scope
for his creative fantasy. However, at first Prokofiev refused point blank to
accept the offer of the Belgoskino studio (the state film studio of Belorussia)
about writing music for a film which was just being shot: it was *Lieutenant
Kizhé*, a picture by Alexander Feinzimmer (with Kozintsev as consulting
director). 'I've never written any film music, and I don't know what to make
of it', he replied to the producer, Rummel[31], in 1932. However, after he had
read the brilliant and witty script by Yury Tynianov, and after a six-hour
talk with the director, he changed his mind. Prokofiev decided to take the
opportunity offered to him 'as a test for the pen, if not on a Soviet subject
then in music for the Soviet audience, which is the broadest one, besides'[32]:
for the gifted musician, this film was the first Soviet offer made to him, even
before he finally returned to his country after a long (it started in 1918) tour
abroad.

The story and also the script, both written by Tynianov, were based on a historical anecdote about a clerk's blunder through which a non-existent, mythical Lieutenant Kizhé was brought to life, and made a dizzy career, rising to the rank of general. The subject seemed to have been specially invented for Prokofiev. Even in his early compositions one can detect a taste for the witty, the amusing, the comic (the piano cycle *Sarcasms*, the ballet *Chout: A Tale of a Fool who Out-fooled Seven Fools*), the opera *The Gambler*. No wonder, therefore, that the paradoxical, satirical plot of *Lieutenant Kizhé* seemed congenial to the young composer's creative strivings, which also told favourably on the character of the music for the film.

The composer unexpectedly rejected the interpretation suggested by the director, who considered low farce and caricature to be the plastic solution for the film: Prokofiev resorted, not to a castigating, merciless satire (as might have been expected) but to a graceful parody, reconstructing in music the Petersburg 'Early Empire' style. Such a device was not new to him, as he had already used it in his *Classical Symphony*.

As a whole, the orchestral score contained sixteen items. *Lieutenant Kizhé* opens with a roll of drums which at once introduces one to the atmosphere of barrack life in the Petersburg of Czar Paul's reign, where everything was arranged after the Prussian manner. The birth of Kizhé is also accompanied by military music which, however, impresses one as somewhat 'unnatural'. It is a cheerful, marionettish march, presented by a little bravado flute tune supported by *pizzicato* in the strings. It sounds somewhat unnatural and even false, thanks to its lydian mode and sudden modulation from F-major to B-major. Hence a feeling of absurdity in the fact that a fictitious, non-existent lieutenant is taken for a living person.

Ex. 2 The Leitmotiv of Kizhé, from the film *Lieutenant Kizhé*

Among the brilliant and impressive musical achievements in the film is also the song 'My little gray pigeon', which is a re-creation of the genre of an old urban romance. Proceeding from a very popular poem by Dmitriev, which had become a kind of symbol of Russian sentimentality, Prokofiev, however, would not adapt the well-known melody but composed a theme of his own. Like the original, it was true to the pattern of the classic sentimental romance of the 18th century, with its typical diatonic nature, passionate 'guitar fingering', and affected, drooping intonations at the conclusion of each stanza. In the film, the sweet voice of Princess Gagarina, who sang the romance, made Czar Paul I shed tears while he tried, almost unconsciously, to join her in the song. But in this strange duet the husky timbre of the Czar's voice was in obvious disharmony with Gagarina's luscious and languorous singing, bringing out the sham and affected amorous ardour of Paul and his female favourite.

A parody of old genres is also used in the episode 'Kizhé is getting married', built on the development of two themes. One of these is a pomp-ous, ponderous chant; the other is a light and very cheerful song emphasiz-ing the unnaturalness of the wedding ceremony. Unexpected accents and the sharp and loud timbre of the cornet make it sound mocking and overly free-and-easy in contrast to the official, 'buttoned up' chant. Thus the element of solemnity typical of such kind of ceremonies is mocked, and the wedding rite is turned into ordinary farce. It is only the music of the 'Troika' scene of all the other scenes, that was written by Prokofiev not 'playfully' but in earnest, though not completely without mischief. This fundamental, representative scene is based on a development theme of a good bold hussar song, which seems to be growing out of the sparkling brightness of a frosty winter day and the dashing progress of a Russian troika. To make the music more 'authentic', Prokofiev reinforces the percussion group with a *sonagli* — an unusual instrument which is a horse's collar with crotales, imitating the tinkling bells that are hung around horses' necks. A marvellous feeling of purity and freshness, of the purposeful energy of the 'Troika' music makes one forget for a time the phantasmagoric adventures of the unreal Kizhé, give oneself up to the element of motion, and become lost completely in the vast expanses of Russia.

The fact that Feinzimmer's film belonged to a transitional period was the main cause of the total dominance of music in the sound sphere, and the transformation of the action into a certain definite variety of musical and plastic performance which resembled pantomime[33]. At the same time, fol-lowing Shostakovich, Sergei Prokofiev contributed to the spreading of the symphonic type of musical dramaturgy in Soviet pre-war cinema. Although film music was looked upon as an applied sphere of the composer's creative work, he treated it quite seriously, for he saw it as a new and original aspect of the idea of artistic synthesis.

5

The role of music in creating a mythicised image of socialism. Song in the service of ideology: the musical film comedies of Alexandrov and Pyriev

The film which is traditionally considered to be the forefather of the 'song type' of musical dramaturgy was released in 1932. It was *The Counter Plan* by Ermler (in cooperation with Yutkevich), which, as Shostakovich admitted, proved to be a turning-point in his 'cinema-biography'. It was one of the first Soviet films which dealt not with the historical past, such as the time of revolution or of civil war, but turned to the peaceful present-day life of the people. In response to Stalin's demand that art should express the idea of building up a new socialist society; *The Counter Plan* opened the way to a torrent of optimistic, cheerful pictures glorifying the heroism of labour and mass enthusiasm. At the same time, assimilation of new themes and ideas resulted in a revaluation of all the components of cinematic means of expressiveness, including music, which had also to be in accord with the spirit and the rhythm of the '30s. It is of interest that Ermler, who perceived the ever growing popularity of the mass song, asked Shostakovich to write a cheerful, invigorating 'industrial' song. Composing it appears to have been something of a torture, for it involved long discussions. Yet the final version proved to be a classic example of the Soviet popular song of the pre-war years.

The melody of the 'Song of the Counter Plan', which is light, elastic' and permeated with a life-asserting feeling, became the main leitmotiv of the film, giving it the right finish and making it a whole. In contrast to the conventional practice of introducing a song into the frame, and incorporating it in the plot and the action, this song was associated with no particular image or character of the film, and played the role of a theme, or a 'thesis', which carried the general idea of the picture: the joy of the collective constructive labour of the people — the builders of the first five-year plans. A considerable role in making this song distinctive within the musical material of the film was played by its inclusion in the overture, where it rose against the background of documentary shots of Moscow waking up, people hurrying to work, a stream of cars moving up and down the street, and the general view of a busy, gigantic city.

From the moment _The Counter Plan_ was released and appeared on screen in Soviet cinemas, the song was sung by the whole country. The reason for such nation-wide popularity is easy to explain: in that song the golden mean had been found, it presented a symbiosis of the traditional, stable, melodic and stylistic stereotypes of the Russian peasant song, and the modern accentuated, march-like rhythm of the militant proletarian one. At the same time, the point was to make the tunes moving and 'responsive', laconic and will-inspiring; they summarized the most stereotyped properties of the popular genres of old (pre-revolutionary) and new (post-revolutionary) music. The structural symmetry of the motifs, and the simplicity of their melodies, the active and clear march-like rhythm, the emphasis on energetic anacrusial rising fourths and the keynotes of the major triad — all of these pointed to a continuing connection with the revolutionary song. At the same time, the type of the melodic structure and of its development resembled varied medley of tunes, characteristic of expansive lyric-epic song.

The birth of the 'Song of the Counter Plan' had far-reaching consequences not only for the fortunes of the Soviet cinema but also for those of Soviet music. Film music underwent a drastic change in its melodic sphere, and turned popular song into a spring feeding all genres without exception, including the opera and the symphony. However, the main contribution of this song to art was its, 'propagation of high spirits' (to cite Maxim Gorky) and optimism, which were to camouflage the monstrous crimes committed by the state, the arrest and detention of millions of people under the pretext of relentless struggle against 'class enemies' and 'enemies of the people', and to instil the idea of 'a happy future for each and all' into the masses' minds, a future for whose sake one could spare neither one's own nor anybody else's life. It was not by chance that academician Boris Asafiev, one of the initiators of Soviet musicology, thus defined the aims of the mass song which, owing to the genius of Shostakovich and also to many other outstanding composers, had proved to be extremely viable and fascinating: 'The cardinal way for the mass song is to be the way of cultivation of a rich melodic culture, as a second-speech addressed to and used by the people; it is also a way of drawing together, as closely as possible, the people's popular (but not simple!) musical speech and the artificial music of individual talents in a common purposeful striving for a happy and joyous life through labour and defence'[34].

Text by B. Kornilov
Allegro

Ex. 3 *The Song of the Counter Plan,* from the film *The Counter Plan*

1. The morning meets us with freshness,
The river meets us with a breeze.
My curly one, are you not happy
To hear the gay song of the whistle?
Don't sleep, get up, my curly one!
While ringing in the workshops,
The country rises gloriously
To meet the day.

2. And joy is continuously singing,
And its song reaches us,
And people are laughing when meeting,
And the sun rises to meet us, too, —
Being hot and brave
It cheers me up.
The country rises gloriously
To meet the day.

Ex. 3 (continued)

3. Our team will meet us at work,
And you'll give a smile to your friends
With whom you share your work and cares,
And the counter plan, and your life.
Beyond the Narva gate,
With thunder, with fire,
The country rises gloriously
To meet the day.

4. And together with it, to victorious end
You will be marching, our youth,

Until a new, younger generation
Appears and meets you,
And it will come in a crowd,
Replacing their fathers.
The country rises gloriously
To meet the day.

5. In such beautiful words
Proclaim your truth.
We are coming out to meet life.
Towards work and love.

The undoubted artistic merits of 'The Song of the Counter Plan', where commonly used, banal turns of melody are combined with unexpected fresh melodic turns, modern harmony and arrangements, explain why this song broke through the limits of film to live a life of its own. Moreover, it was an international success. It was sung by the soldiers of the International Brigades in Spain; in 1936 Shostakovich's song appeared, along with the 'Marseillaise' of Rouget de Lisle, in the film *Life Belongs to Us* by the French director Jean Renoir, who at that time was under the influence of Popular Front ideology. It was also popular with people who took part in the French Resistance during the Second World War and had the honour of being accepted as a hymn of the United Nations, while in Switzerland it served as a wedding song[35]. Later, such a multiple form of song-existence (i.e., on screen and on concert-platforms) came to be widely used, and the authors of songs exploited the cinema as a powerful and effective means of advertizing their songs, with a view to their 'off-screen' existence on stage, and in everyday life. In turn, cinema directors, having grasped the benefits of the high communicative potential, the democratic nature and the popularity of the song genre, deliberately introduced songs into their motion pictures where, interconnected with the plot, the song served as a generalized expression of the main idea of the film. Thus, favourable conditions were created in the cinema of the 1930s for a privileged development of the song-type of musical dramaturgy, which reached its climax in the musical film comedies of Grigory Alexandrov and Ivan Pyriev, with music by Isaak Dunayevsky.

Dunayevsky's debut in feature film took place in 1933, and within eight years he had written the music for seventeen films, which differed considerably in quality and professional mastery. He started his career in the 'Belorussian State Cinema' ('Belgoskino') studio, which was stationed in the 'Lenfilm' studio in Leningrad at that time. The film, by V. Korsh-Sablin, entitled *The First Platoon*, passed unnoticed both by the critics and the public. But his second picture, filmed by Grigory Alexandrov, a disciple and comrade-in-arms of S. Eisenstein, made the composer's (as well as the director's) name famous. This film, which evoked a storm of applause and a thunder of resentment, was *The Merry Fellows* (1934).

There was hardly a thing for which its authors were not reproached, e.g. for imitating second-rate Hollywood films; for a lack of dramatic integration, which resulted in twelve musical items existing as quite autonomous pieces, formally connected only by a primitive plot; finally, for the composer's borrowing of the Mexican rebel song 'Adelita', (from the American picture *Viva Viglia*) as the basic tune of the very popular 'March of the Merry Fellows'. Similar accusations were often addressed to the composer, supported by the examinations of biased experts who would discover now an affinity between 'The Song of my Motherland' *(The Circus)* and the folk song 'Sten'ka Razin', now a close resemblance between the song 'A golden smoke-like dust is whirling over the road' (in the film *Volga-Volga*) and 'The Song of a Free Wind' *(Captain Grant's Children)*; Between M. Glinka's 'Travel Song' on the one hand, and the 'Song of the Counter Plan', on the other. Indeed, there was good reason to suspect Dunayevsky of plagiarism, for he was prone to fall under other composers' influences — which can, in particular, be proved by the very immediate effect produced by the 'Song about the Counter Plan' upon the intonations and imagery of Dunayevsky's 'youth' songs. It is known, for example, that, fascinated by Shostakovich's music, Dunayevsky on his own initiative arranged the 'Song of the Counter Plan' for a mixed chorus.

The list of the (involuntary) musical borrowings of Isaak Dunayevsky (those to Brahms, Beethoven and some others included) was lengthy — which, however, is by no means to belittle his personal merits in the development and formation of the Soviet mass-song genre and the 'song' film of the '30s. In fact, the history of film music is literally overcrowded with examples of 'doubtful originals': one need mention only the great Charlie Chaplin, in whose films melodies of clearly 'Rossinian' origin are frequent. Besides, it may be that with Dunayevsky the case was much more complicated than his ill-wishers tried to suggest and one should not interprete his compositions as direct borrowings, but regard them as efficient constructive transformations of melodies that were in common use in everyday musical practice. He created on that basis a mainly new, *heroic-romantic style*, which contributed more than any mere words could to the strengthening of myth-creating socialist ideas in Soviet society. One of the chief merits of this style was that it helped Dunayevsky to destroy the ritual, cathedral sanctity of the folk and revolutionary songs canonized by the Bolsheviks. He did so through their 'modernization', i.e. by introducing variety and jazz elements in accordance with the musical fashion of the 1920–1930s. *The Merry Fellows* serves as a good example of this process. It had a long run, and was tremendous success both in the Soviet Union and abroad, where it was shown under the title *Moscow is Laughing*.

The film was based on the rather banal story of a shepherd who became a well-known jazzman. The subject gave the composer full range for the use of a great variety of musical material which could be 'embedded' into the action. The film opened with an 'entrance aria' for the leading character — Kostya's song 'One's heart is light with a merry song' ('The March of the Merry Fellows'), shot by the cameraman Vladimir Nilsen very ingeniously with one camera, panning in one sweeping movement. The absence of montage, and the very way of fixing on film the spectacularly plastic 'acting-out' of the song mimed to a recording (a method which was new in those days) were aimed at making the music dominate in relief-like fashion all the other elements of cinematic representation. Thus an emphatic and effective leitmotiv was created in the picture, which set the main tonality of perception and the elated, emotional tone characteristic of this sparkling jazz-comedy.

As compared to the musical dramaturgy of *The Counter Plan*, based on the recurrence of the central leitmotiv song, Dunayevsky employed a different formal principle. Possessing the characteristics of a hit, and supported by a varying recurrence of short, stringy fanfares and by tunes richly ornamented with chromatic alterations the marching song appeared only twice, when opening and closing the film. As a result, the comedy, which consisted of three parts unequal in their artistic merits and somewhat artificially adjusted to one another, was given a certain unity of content and conception.

A clear contrast to the energetic and high-spirited 'March of the Merry Fellows' which initiated the extremely popular genre of the youth parade march into the Soviet music of the 1930–1950s, was presented by two lyrical songs: the graceful and thrilling song of Anyuta 'I am aflame' and Kostya's song in tango rhythm, 'Oh, heart, you don't seek repose'. But it would be stretching a point to consider these songs as musical portrayals or character-sketches of these young people. Rather, they should be classed as 'situational' songs, which were usually part of the action, and were introduced as a check, a lyrical pause before a series of comic episodes. In the finale, which synthetized the basic musical material of the film while keeping up the dominance of the central leitmotiv in it, the melodies of Anyuta's and Kostya's songs and of 'The March of the Merry Fellows' are interlaced in a brilliant orchestral pot-pourri.

On the whole, in spite of Dunayevsky's expressive music and his hit songs, and the participation in shooting and recording of the then famous jazz-band conducted by Leonid Utesov (who also played the part, though he was not quite up to it, of the leading character, the shepherd Kostya); in spite of the brilliant debut of the actress Lubov' Orlova, and the tremendous success of the film with the audience, the picture met with a squall of violent criticism, justifiable in many respects. It was pointed out, in particular, that the director had been much too keen on eccentricity to the detriment of the development of the subject and the characters, too determined to make the audience laugh by all possible means, and had overloaded the film with tricks. Besides, reviewers attacked the producer's choice of the revue genre, which, in the ideologically-trained social consciousness of the '30s, was closely associated with alien Western bourgeois culture, antagonistic to Soviet art, deliberately indifferent to politics and incompatible with socialist ideals. Apprehensive of the danger which threatened them under the conditions of ever growing Stalinist mass repressions, Alexandrov and Dunayevsky abruptly changed the direction they had taken in their work, and in their next film openly adapted its theme and idea to the formal state-and-party policy, in accordance with the principles of socialist realism.

The musical comedy film *Circus* (1936) was certainly one of the best achievements of this creative partnership. It was based on the melodramatic love story of an American circus actress Marion Dixon and a Soviet inventor Martynov, masterfully interlaced with sharp dramatic motifs of political intrigue and comedy trick scenes, dealing with 'episodes of circus life'. Thus, the lyrical line of interrelations between the leading characters was set off by a *buffo* one, connected with the amusing adventures of another couple of lovers, Rayechka and Skameikin. This contrast between lyrical and comic duets, and the well-developed musical characterisations testified to an already more complicated structural organization, and to the composer's approach to a new genre, that of film operetta, which became the most important one in his artistic biography in the 1940–1950s. In principle, the

Figure 2 *Circus*

Text by V. Lebedev-Kumach
In a marching tempo, very energetically

Ex. 4 *Song of my Motherland.* From the film *The Circus*

Ex. 4 (continued)

Wide is my dear country,
Many are its forests, fields and rivers.
I know no other country
Where man could feel so free.
I know no other country
Where man could feel so free.

work on the music for *Circus* was for Dunayevsky nothing but a return to his native element, since before he entered the cinema he had already mastered what was required from the composer working in straight theatre, the circus and the music hall. At the same time, this film signified a decisive turn in the direction of creating an idealized, fairytale image of the Soviet way of life: a mythologem which was energetically propagated, though there was a wide gap between the myth and the reality. Outward attractiveness and authenticity to daily life were to be ensured by song, which being the most popular and democratic of all musical genres, was to become, according to Dunayevsky, *the ideological focus, the very essence* of the ideological conception of the film, stimulating and directing its dramatic development. Further, in revealing the mechanism of his work on the film song, the composer pointed to its potential for symphonic enrichment, elaboration and variety[36].

The idea of symphonized-song, which permitted various genre transformation of the initial theme material, with a 'montage' pliability of form, was tested for the first time by Dunayevsky in the film comedy *Circus*, where the 'Song of My Motherland' ('Wide and vast is my native country') functioned as the leitmotiv. As distinct from 'The March of the Merry Fellows' written in the style of a sports song, 'The Song of My Motherland' synthesized the characteristics of the Russian lyric-epic song and the heroic revolutionary hymn. It is curious that it began, not with an introduction, but with a majestic refrain, which resembled the celebrated 'Volga' songs in its flowing, measured melodic movement, it emphasized, steady steps in a major mode, and its specific inward linking of short tunes. In the introduction, which was written in a parallel minor mode (a device of mode alternation typical of Russian song) there was a certain enlivening of the general development. The extending of the anacrusial movement to the octave, the penetration of the elements of emotional recitation and oratory into the melody, a frequent emphasis on the dominant — all of this made the introduction sound incomplete as compared to the confident, determined refrain. Thus, introduction and refrain were presented as two elements which were closely connected with each other, one of them being individual and personal and the other social and popular. The presence of related melodic turns, and the uninterrupted dotted rhythm passing through both, combine them in one integral image.

The leitmotiv was first introduced in a voiceless instrumental version in the overture, under the credits, being so far in no direct contact with the visual representation. Its ideological meaning, its turning into a song and 'growing' into the plot of the film, occurred much later, when the audience became acquainted with the hardships of Marion's life, her flight with her black baby from racist America, and her arrival in Soviet Russia. Here, in an atmosphere of kind attention and care, among well-wishing, open-hearted people, the scared and persecuted woman relaxed, relieved from her fear of 'exposure'. A deep mutual feeling arose between her and Martynov, the producer of a new circus. According to the authors, such a feeling, inspiring and elevating, could be born and flourish only in a country like the USSR, where there was no class inequality, no racism, and no other vices typical of capitalist society. It is significant that Martynov, while making his declaration of love to the woman he adores, expresses it in the form and words of 'The Song of My Motherland', which assumes a particular softness and lyricism in his rendition. But in the next moment, taking his place at the piano, Marion Dixon demonstrates her own 'version' of the leitmotiv, trying to drown the baby's crying in the adjacent room with the sounds of a brilliant improvisation in Lisztian style.

For the last time 'The Song of My Motherland' rises in the apotheosis of the film, symbolizing not only the love and happiness of the hero and the heroine of *The Circus*: breaking forth beyond the frame limits, this leitmotiv song grows into a generalized image of the Soviet people, and it resounds with symphonic power. Solo singing gives way to choral and flowing lyrical melodies are replaced by the even stride of the many-thousand-strong marching rows of the May day parade in Red Square. In this way, the formation of the civic and patriotic pathos of the central leitmotiv is abetted by the visual elements of the picture.

Thus, to see the general in particular, to elevate the personal to the national, this was the goal the directors and the composer strove to achieve, and they did achieve it with the help of a song: the song proved to be a powerful means of ideological and political propaganda, which instilled into the masses' minds the idealized notion of the new social order.

Emphasizing and heightening the functional significance of the leitmotiv was to a great extent achieved by the presence of two subsidiary dramatic plots, one lyrical, one comic. But if the comedy plot, built in the best traditions of operetta, played on the whole a secondary part, the lyrical one, connected with the character of the American circus-actress, was more independent and revealed the individual features of the heroine's personality.

A mother full of tender love for her child, and a woman capable of a deep and ardent feeling, Marion's character is reflected in her songs: the lullaby 'Sleep, my Baby', with its spicy, blues-like intonations, and 'The Moonshine Waltz' reminiscent of the famous waltzes by Johann Strauss. The wonderful plasticity and expressiveness of 'The Moonshine Waltz', which were achieved by combining an ascending sequential development with an exultant exclamatory figure at the end of the phrases, the reiteration of the most flowing melodic turns, and the smartness and richness of the orchestration, filled the music with a joyful sense of life's beauty and infinite happiness.

The charm and dreaminess of 'The Moonshine Waltz', in which an obvious influence of the Russian classical school, and of Glinka's 'Fantasia Waltz' in particular, could also be clearly traced, made it one of the most fascinating specimens of the waltz-song composed in the '30s. Some years later it served as model for another celebrated waltz, 'The Song of Moscow' by Tikhon Khrennikov, which also became known thanks to the cinema, in the film by the director Ivan Pyriev *Swineherd and Shepherd* (1941).

The phrase 'Every day makes living still more joyful' in 'The Song of My Motherland', which was in fact a slightly altered copy of the notorious dictum of Joseph Stalin: 'Life has become better, life has become more joyful', might have been used as an epigraph to the next comedy of Alexandrov and

Text by V. Lebedev-Kumach
In a slow-waltz tempo

Ex. 5 The Moonshine Waltz from the film *The Circus*

Ex. 5 (continued)

Solo:
All is floating in the rhythm of the waltz, / all the huge vault of heaven. / Together with the sun and the moon / the globe is going round / - all is dancing to this music of the night. / All is floating in the rhythm of the waltz, / all the huge vault of heaven. / All is going round, gliding, / one can't get out of it. / All is floating in the rhythm of the waltz.

Dunayevsky, *Volga-Volga*. Formally classified as a musical film comedy, this film, however, was made according to a different genre structure, that of the musical film-revue. Nevertheless, by 1938 (i.e. by the time *Volga-Volga* was released) Isaak Dunayevsky had already worked out his creative method, and developed the main techniques of 'song' dramaturgy — which were later adopted and repeatedly employed by many composers, both contemporaries and successors. As Dunayevsky himself explained it, his method of writing music for a 'song' film was as follows: 'Proceeding from the need to create music and song for the powerful educative medium of cinema. I first set myself the task of creating the central song in the motion picture and, proceeding from there, I compose the rest of the music for the film. Further, I am for an ample use of illustrative music, which brings home to the spectator, in an intelligible way, all the basic peripeteias of the plot; and thirdly, I use a method of musical association closely related to the theme content. I don't like things which don't grip the spectator and don't elevate the given motion picture; and, on the contrary, I like things which do so more effectively. These are the three principles I keep to'[37].

All of Dunayevsky's work in the cinema of those years gives proof of his practical realization of these principles. Besides the above films, there are such motion pictures as *Three Comrades* (1935) and *The Goalkeeper* (1936) filmed by Vainshtok, *A Rich Bride* (1938) filmed by Pyriev, and *The Radiant Way* (1940) filmed by Alexandrov. As for the film *Volga-Volga*, it should be noted that, compared to *The Merry Fellows* and *The Circus*, it included quite a 'bunch' of songs: lyrical, comic, dance songs, as well as romances and sprightly village chastooshki. But the leading role was still played by the march-song, which was the dominant musical theme of the film, helping to overcome the thin and fragmentary development of the subject matter and the action. Thus, the composer's use of the rondo form had to some extent been programmed by the very subject of the film, in which the story of how the song had been created was shown.

The action in *Volga-Volga* was based on the amazing metamorphoses undergone by a simple chastooshka composed by one Dunya, the letter carrier[38] of the small Siberian town of Melkovodsk ("Shallow-Water"), whom nobody had known or heard of before. As the action unfolded, the melody of the chastooshka was transformed, now into a dashing Russian dance song, now into a composition for brass-band, until in the finale it turned into a majestic and solemn hymn (extremely pompous and high-flown), in which all the nations of the Soviet Union, joined, infusing the audience with the idea of the boundless genius of a people who lived in a country following the road of socialism.

On the whole, the structural scheme of the musical dramaturgy in *Volga-Volga* coincided in its main points with that of *The Circus*, although when compared with the latter, the former seemed somewhat simplified. It manifested itself in sticking strictly to the main plot with no additional story lines or characters in the dramatic construction. The ideological bias underlying its leading theme was revealed even more clearly in the last pre-war film by Alexandrov and Dunayevsky, *The Radiant Way*, which glorified labour for the welfare of society, inspiring a man, enabling him to make a dazzling career and — above all — to gain his own happiness as a reward for his valiant work. It is no surprise that, as in the preceding films, here too the realization of this idea was entrusted to a march-song, 'The March of the Enthusiasts', another addition to the series of 'production' songs which owed their appearance to Shostakovich. In contrast to the free and easy mood of 'The Song of the Counter Plan', however, 'The March of the Enthusiasts' sounded official; there were clear indications of the canonisation of genre and the turning of the song into a hymn. However, the undoubted artistic merits and the melodic attractiveness of the central leitmotiv remained 'in shadow' because of the poor and frankly declarative propagandist subject, which was overcrowded with scenes of sterile beauty, and which had nothing in common with the reality the authors were trying to shape. Of course, the fairytales of Cinderella, as well as different versions of the story about the 'ugly duckling', which attracted Alexandrov and Dunayevsky like magnets, had become a characteristic sign of their creative partnership. But in *The Radiant Way* they surpassed themselves in showing the miraculous transformation of a half-literate peasant girl, a poor char, into a progressive weaver, a shock-worker of communist labour. This kind of story gave full play to the composer's fantasy in the creation of numerous 'versions' of the leitmotiv themes, each varied in intonation and melody, rhythm, orchestral timbre, genre, etc., as well as in the composition of grandiose crowd scenes.

Dunayevsky's experience was taken into account by other composers who worked in this 'singing' cinema; they considerably enriched the thematic content of songs and extended their genre sphere. The music by the Pokrass brothers for Dzigan's news-reel *If a War Breaks Out Tomorrow* (1938) may serve as an example. It was in this film that the march song 'If a War Breaks Out Tomorrow' was first presented: a song born under the influence of the alarming situation in Europe, and illuminated by glimpses of recent events in the Far East[39]; a song of courage, connected with the theme of defending one's country. But real triumph and all-Union recognition came to the composers after the comedy *The Tractor Drivers* filmed by

Pyriev had been released (1939). Here the comic plot was set off by the heroic theme of the defence of one's Fatherland. The energetic song 'Three Tankmen', and the victoriously optimistic, belligerent 'March of the Tankmen', brought into the peaceful and cheerful atmosphere of the action a presentiment of the severe and tragic ordeals by which the country would soon be faced.

6

The formation of other genres in musical cinema

The musical comedy was without doubt the leading genre in the Soviet pre-war cinema, yet the 'song film' was not its only representative. In the early '40s, film director Ivanovsky, in cooperation with Rappaport and composer Kabalevsky, made an attempt to widen the limits of the 'song' film and to extend the range of its musical application. Their first film, entitled *A Musical Story* (1940), was noteworthy for the fact that the leading man was Sergei Lemeshev, a young but already well-known opera singer. *A Musical Story* belonged to the number of pictures in which 'stars' of the variety and opera stage were engaged, and it was a favourite not only with cinema-goers but also with cinema workers. True, the rather late development of this genre in the USSR often resulted in its being second-rate also in its artistic material, and in its elaboration, casting and means of expression, differed but little from its Hollywood prototypes. Of course, there was a lot of music in it. A considerable part of it was connected with Lemeshev's performance of arias from the classical opera repertoire, selected for the film by Astradantsev. As a result, the original music composed by Kabalevsky played rather a humble, shadow role, appearing practically only in the scene of the hero's explanation scene with his fiancée.

Quite a different situation was presented in the film comedy *Ivan Antonovich Is Angry* (1941), where a rather trivial conflict between the adherents of 'serious' music and those of 'light' music was the motive power of the plot. According to a standard scheme, the conflicting parties were represented by an old conservatoire, professor who believed that only classical art was of real value, and a young composer who was in love with operetta. But their conflict was not uncompromising, and therefore the music which accompanied the controversy and 'collisions' of these characters was not sharp or shrill: it was imbued with an element of soft humour, which could be summed up in the simple, unsophisticated statement: any kind of music is good except bad music. The authors did not make any declarations: they clearly demonstrated their idea by showing the 'creations' of the formalist composer Kerosinov.

It should be remembered that in the Soviet Union reproaching an art worker with formalism was until the late '70s tantamount to a most dreadful sentence, classifying his activities as being hostile to the people, deserting the cause of socialism and using his art for propagating' depraved, vicious and unprincipled' Western culture. No wonder that the character of Kerosinov and the musical 'opuses' composed by him sounded like parody, caricature, or sharp grotesque.

In one of the scenes, for example, Kabalevsky represents satirically the work-process of the new-fangled composer, which result in a senseless, chaotic conglomeration of sounds. The acme of Kerosinov's 'creation' is a 'work of genius', which in an absurd and affected manner reproduces the melody of the popular comic children's song, 'for a long while a large green mother-crocodile walked the streets'. Seemingly innocent, it assumes both an aggressively impudent and poor profile, mercilessly emphasizing the spiritual wretchedness of the 'pure' art apologists and the social evil which, according to the authors of the film, such people embody.

Attention should also be paid to Kabalevsky's earlier film compositions, of which his dramatic music for *A Petersburg Night* (1934) filmed by the directors Roshal' and Stroyeva after Dostoevsky is of special interest. As the authors had focused on the tragic fate of a serf musician, Egor Efimov, Kabalevsky chose a monothematic principle of building the musical drama, its material being correlative, in one way or another, with one theme — a folk song 'The Song of a Pogorélets': 'Do give a copeck to a poor pogorelets!' (The Russian pogorélets, a person who has lost all his or her property in fire). It is sung in the film three times, and each time it is dynamically connected with the preceding one. At first it rises as a wailing lamentation, which grips the heart of Egor Efimov: he hears the voice of the suffering people in it. 'The Song of a Pogorelets' inspires him into writing a brilliant violin 'Improvisation'[40], imbued with a sincere, agitatedly-pathetic emotion. But the cold-hearted and prim Petersburg audience receives the music of the serf violinist with undisguised hostility. Thus, this second man's fate is sealed; but, contrary to all expectations, the melody of the song continues to live, and is infused with a new spirit. In the final scene of the film the lonely man, degraded to the state of a drunkard, suddenly recognizes his own music in a stern, heroic revolutionary song of oath-taking sung by the convicts who are being deported to a far-off place of exile.

This dramatic story of the broken life of Egor Efimov, a gifted violinist and composer, is offset by some subsidiary musical and dramaturgic themes which are in a contrapuntal relation to the former. One of these is associated with the subject-motivated music of everyday life. It is rather varied, and includes a merry tarantella played by the serf orchestra in which

Efimov 'serves'; a dance episode in a tavern; the music of a vaudeville performed on a provincial stage; and a folk song in a 'white nights' episode. This mosaic of musical items represents kaleidoscopic impressions of a composer who has to encounter all the different kinds of social groups and individuals in Russian society as it was in the middle of the past century.

Another musical strand personified the world of fashionable and official music, which was alien to the composer. It was represented by a military march; the hack-work performance of a touring virtuoso, who was favourably received by the 'music lovers' of metropolitan drawing-rooms; the efforts of the untalented yet extremely enterprising violinist Schulz, who would stop at nothing (plagiarism included) in order to gain success and public acknowledgement.

On the whole, the integrity and the harmony of the composer's musical concept, typical of this film, were to a great extent due to Kabalevsky's creative interpretation of the traditions developed by the Russian classical school of the 19th century. It is no coincidence that the dramatic principles of musical construction in *A Petersburg Night* clearly show the influence of Glinka's opera-theatre, of Mussorgsky's popular musical dramas, and of Tchaikovsky's symphonism. Afterwards, this type of musical dramaturgy became widely spread, and was even canonized in the historico-biographical films of the '40s and the early part of the '50s.

7

The development of film music
in the cinema of the Soviet Republics

In the 1930s, the Ukraine was second only to the RSFSR in its level of professional mastery and the intensity of development of the cinematographic process. The Ukrainian cinema owed much of its efflorescence to the creative activities of Alexander Dovzhenko, the leading representative of the poetical-romantic trend in the cinema. In 1935 he released his film *Aerograd*, which was later defined by the critics as a lyric-epic poem about his contemporaries, about their work and struggle, and love for their native land. The director asked Dmitry Kabalevsky to write music for this film. The composer was faced with a number of serious problems, part of which remained unsolved because of his own stereotyped approach to the film material.

Replete with musical poetic metaphors, the most impressive of which were its unhurried, meditative 'landscape openings', the *Aerograd* required the solution of certain specific problems. Besides characterizing the scene of the action, creating the emotional atmosphere and commenting upon the representation, the music had to, by all possible means, reveal close affinity between the characters and Nature. Moreover, according to Dovzhenko's conception, the music needed to become part of the sound and visual image of the film and exist in an unbreakable relationship with other elements of the screen synthesis. However, taking up the director's lead slavishly, Kabalevsky lapsed into banal illustration. As a result, the music of *Aerograd* — including its leitmotiv, the song 'Good-bye, Mama, I'm flying to far-off lands', written as an almost faultless imitation of a cheerful popular song — lacked that depth of philosophic and imaginative generalization of events in real life which characterized the visual solution of the film's content.

Four years later Dovzhenko turned to Kabalevsky again, in connection with a historical revolutionary film dealing with a hero of the civil war, Shchors (1939). But as before, the composer did not break the bonds of tradition, and followed the ways of the Russian classical school in reflecting the national Ukrainian theme, which presupposed an extensive use of quotation and the incorporation into the original music of stylized melodic and pitch characteristics from southern Slav folklore and some specific devices of folk musical culture. However, such a detached relationalist view prevented the composer from penetrating into, and perceiving the spirit and the foundations of, Ukrainian national musical culture (although that was just what Dovzhenko was dreaming of). True, Kabalevsky was not alone in failing to cope with the task set to him. More or less similar problems confronted cinema crews from Moscow and Leningrad, who came to shoot films in Central Asia and the Trans-Caucasian republics, and who largely contributed to the formation of local national cinema. But, as a rule, they could not go beyond representation of some well-known ethnic features of life, character, customs, folk music. Hence the only solution that suggested itself was as follows: each republic should train film workers of its own, nourish its own directors, actors, dramatists, composers and people of other creative professions. This problem was most acutely felt in the East.

In the thirties, the cinema schools of Georgia, Armenia, Azerbaijan, Kazakhstan and Central Asia still were either in embryo, or taking the first steps, learning the ABC of the new art. No wonder that most of their works bore the stamp of immaturity; yet it is interesting that, with respect to music, each of them often felt most emancipated and most natural in displaying national peculiarities, temperament, language, world outlook and artistic, imaginative thinking. The use of folklore, of the ancient layers of popular art; introducing instruments and techniques of execution peculiar to oriental music into the traditional European orchestras; the amazing and fascinatingly unusual blend of the oriental and the western styles — all of these could be found in the film music of the thirties. This can be shown by one of the early Armenian sound films, *Pepo*, released by the Erevan cinema studio in 1935.

The strong script, the mastery of director Amo Bek-Nazarov, the talented cast, and — the adornment of the film — the rich and high-spirited music by Aram Khachaturian, who was making his debut in the cinema, attracted general attention. The film was a great success with the audience, and was even acknowledged as the most outstanding work of Soviet cinema in the pre-war decade.

As concerns its music, *Pepo* is first of all interesting for the composer's resolute rejection of any superficial illustration and exotic ornamentation. He searched for a method which could adequately reflect the picturesque popular scenes that represented the everyday life and the customs of the inhabitants of old Tiflis, the most distinctive among them being *Karachogeli*, the town craftsmen and pedlars. It was just to these people that the poor man Pepo belonged. The film opened with the musical exposition of the leading character. The pastoral overture was followed by the hero's song, one of the most expressive musical items of the film. The refined ornamentation

Verses by E. Charents

Russian text by A. Globa

Ex. 6 *Pepo's Song* from the film *Pepo*

Ex. 6 (continued)

Solo:
Out of the fog a wet wind is blowing. / The weary day is like evening. / A tsotskhal fish has started playing like sparkling ripples in the loops of the fishing-net. / A tsotskhal fish has started playing like sparkling ripples in the loops of the fishing-net.

of its melodic pattern, the capriciousness and whimsicality of its rhythm suggested the deep national sources of this song, and their roots dating back to the most ancient art of the ashugs — folk poets and singers.

The music score of the film contained nine developed symphonic items. They were very varied stylistically; they included genre sketches, ritual scenes, songs and instrumental music characterizing the protagonists. The general image of *Karachogeli* was highly colourful: besides citing well-known Armenian folk dance and song melodies, Khachaturian had turned to earlier examples — to the works of the great ashug of the 18th century, Saiat-Nova, as well as old tunes played on national Caucasian instruments; they breathed life into the small narrow streets of the ancient city, and brought to the fore its peculiarity and beauty. In particular, all the lyrical episodes in the film were accompanied by the sustained sound of the *duduk*, infused both with sadness and sensual passion.

In the film, the world of the common people is opposed to that of the petty bourgeois, and the merchants and Philistines. With their appearance, the style of the picture undergoes a sharp change. The tuneful gracefulness of Armenian melodies, and the dynamics of the picturesque folk-genre scenes, give way to angular 'oriental' themes in pointedly European inter-pretation which are intended to portray the negative characters. First and foremost among them is Zimzimov, a rich Armenian merchant, who is receiving high-ranking guests in his house on the occasion of his having been awarded a medal 'For developing Russian trade'. Of course, the czar's generals and state officials would prefer listening to the military band they are used to, rather than to folk instruments. But even the awkward attempt of a merchant (who is already drunk) to dance the celebrated *lezginka* turns into clowning, to a rough imitation of 'oriental music'. No less disgusting is the ugly and pitiful grimacing of Zimzimov and his wife, who are trying in a strained manner to pose as 'people of the world'.

According to the strict ideological directions of those days, the film director should implicitly sympathize and side with the poor, who have come to help Pepo when he has been put into prison for his uncompromising struggle against the rich. Therefore, following the communist canons, the film ends with a great folk scene by the prison walls. The basis of its musical solution was the heroic song 'Ker-Ogly', which was held as a symbol of freedom and courage by the peoples of the Trans-Caucasian republics on the fringes of the Russian Empire.

Khachaturian's cooperation with the director Bek-Nazarov was resumed in the film *Zangezur* (1938, co-director Dukor). However, unlike *Pepo*, where the composer used the principle of dynamic juxtaposition of contrasting musical items, in *Zangezur* he for the first time turned his attention to monothematicism, to through-development of material, and to the leitmotiv.

The leitmotiv first emerges as the song of an old man, and it expresses sorrow and wrath. These are just the sort of feelings that could be evoked by a treacherous attack of armed *dashnaks* on a defenceless village, an event shown in the opening scene of the film. The song, performed to the accompaniment of the folk instrument *tar*, assumes an ever more dramatic character and turns into funeral march at the moment when the peasants are taking their last leave of their dead comrades. But there is neither submissiveness nor humility in it. A craving for vengeance breaks out in the people's hearts, and the music, sensitive to emotional changes, traces this shift of feeling: heroic and hortatory intonations appear in the leitmotiv, growing more and more persistent. They become especially urgent and expressive in the episode 'Before the battle', transforming the song into a march full of will-power and masculine energy. In the final scene of *Zangezur*, which represents the plight of the peasants against the dashnaks, and a smashing defeat of the dashnaks and the invaders with the help of the Red Army, the main theme reappears, rising up as a solemn hymn, the melody driven along by tough, marching rhythms.

Thus, as the screen action is developed, the musical leitmotiv image undergoes essential changes. They embrace not only its melodic and rhythmical structure, but also its instrumental timbre. The dynamic movement from the folk instrument *tar* to the symphony orchestra gives the composer the chance to stimulate the spectator's perception, and give the film coherence and emotional intensity.

Some attention should also be paid to the debut of Azerbaijan film directors. Released in 1938 by the director Samed Mardjanov, the picture *Kendilyar* ('Peasants'), dealing with the struggle of the Azerbaijan peasants against the bourgeois nationalist government, was an event of importance in the Azerbaijan cinema of the 1930s. Of special interest was the musical material, since the leading character was the young ashug Gaidamir. This enabled the composer and conductor, Taghi-zade Niyazi, to fill the picture with spirited, colourful national melodies which enhanced the expressiveness and drama of the story. However, he failed to achieve more than illustration and commentary. Azerbaijan film music had still to travel a long way before it could create a coherent musical conception for a film.

8

Elaboration of the idea of sound-visual counterpoint in the film
Alexander Nevsky

The second half of the 1930s was marked by two outstanding events in the history of Soviet film music. One of them was the appearance of film opera, the other was the creation of *Alexander Nevsky*.

In 1936, the Ukrainian film director Ivan Kavaleridze released the first film-opera in the Soviet cinema. It was a screen version of the classical Ukrainian opera written by Lysenko, *Natalka Poltavka*. Two years later this was followed by the opera of Gulak-Artemovsky, The *Zaporozhets beyond the Danube*, filmed by the same director. It is interesting that, although both the operas were then in the repertoire of the Kiev Opera and Ballet Theatre, the film director rejected the simple method of recording the already staged performances, for he did not wish to act as 'a technical go-between' for the opera and the audience. On the contrary, Kavaleridze wanted to make his own *cinematographic* interpretation of a musical work. The presence of spoken dialogues in both operas made their adaptation to the screen easier, and helped him achieve a smooth modulation from an ordinary feature film with characteristic everyday reality to the rather conventional imaginative world of the opera.

Among the undoubted merits of Kavaleridze's film operas is his firm rejection of theatre props and machinery, and his shooting on location instead of placing the action within the limited space of a stage. Panned landscapes play a great role in his opera-pictures, emphasizing the peculiar beauty and the poetic qualities of Ukranian music, with its emotionally inspired romantic sound world. Besides, considering the contemporary level of cinematographic development, in *Natalka Poltavka* and *The Zaporozhets beyond the Danube* the director managed convincingly enough to solve one of the 'eternal' problems of opera: that of the correspondence — or rather the lack of it — between singers' exteriors and the images of the characters they impersonate. It is well-known that many a singer who possesses an excellent voice may lack dramatic talent, the absence of which is notorious for turning an opera performance into a 'concert in costume'. In addition, when acting in front of the camera, 'vocal technique' is highlighted, and any physical strain and any distortion of the face are relentlessly recorded on the film, to say nothing of possible defects of appearance, figure etc.

But since in the sound cinema the shooting and the sound recording were done separately, it occurred to Kavaleridze that he could employ dramatic actors who could dub the singers on the screen. Thus the idea of the 'double cast' materialized, which has been practiced to this day when operas are filmed.

Early film operas did not yet possess high artistic merit; nor did their producers have that as their object. They saw their principal mission as enlightenment and popularization, bringing the classical musical heritage within the reach of millions of cinema-goers. No wonder that the way they chose was the *adaptation* of opera to the techniques and voice of the cinema. It took years and much experience before film makers ventured to create the original genre of *film opera* — although as early as 1938 a unique film was released in the Soviet Union: *Alexander Nevsky* by director Sergei Eisenstein and composer Sergei Prokofiev. The film broke down all established stereotypes and notions of the ways in which music and representation should interact, and it was built as a complex polyphonic composition.

True, the authors of *Alexander Nevsky* did not set themselves the task of making a film-opera, and strictly speaking it cannot be termed that as in any 'pure' sense. Nevertheless, it was exactly in *Alexander Nevsky* that the basic principles and technology of the composer's and the director's work on film-opera were discovered.

The building of the frame as a many-voiced complex embracing a number of strands,'in which every line has compositional movement of its own, yet closely allied at the same time with the general compositional movement of the whole'[41]: this was the purpose the makers of the film strove to achieve in the process of its creation. Its cinematic realisation led the director to the idea of *polyphonic montage* (a term introduced by Eisenstein) on the basis of the harmonic image synchronisation of representation and sound. Two years later (1940) Eisenstein's empirical findings were developed theoretically in his fundamental analytical article *Vertical Montage*, where, using one of the central scenes of the film ('The battle on the ice'), various kinds of correspondence between music and representation were analyzed. Besides, Eisenstein found that there was a likeness between the structural principles of *Alexander Nevsky* and the form of a fugue. This definition, however, should be treated with some caution, since only one dramatic strand connected with the theme of patriotism was elaborated polyphonically. In fact, the structural composition of *Alexander Nevsky* sug-

gested definite associations with sonata form. The reason for such an assertion was the fact that there were four parts, or sections, typical of sonata
form: introduction, exposition, development and recapitulation, correlating
with one another.

The film opened with a short prologue ('Rus' under the Mongol
yoke'), which was followed by an expanded presentation of two antagonistic imaginative spheres: the Russian and the Teutonic. Their gradual drawing together resulted in an open conflict (the central section, the battle on
Chudskoye Lake). Then came a lyric-dramatic intermezzo (mourning for
the warriors who had perished in the battle). The film ended with a majestic
finale, i.e. a recapitulation, which synthesized the main thematic material
(both musical and visual-plastic) of the 'Russian' theme of *Alexander Nevsky*.

Among the undoubted merits of a picture distinguished for its
architectonic harmony and well thought-out dramaturgy is its wide and
varied use of the form-building possibilities of rhythm, which is unhurried
in an epic fashion in the opening and the concluding part, and accelerates
in the middle of the film. A change in rhythmic pulsation within the film
helps emphasize the borderliness and proportions of the parts, gives integrity to the whole structure and, just as importantly, electrifies the spectators'
perception, especially in dramatic episodes.

As mentioned above, the dramatic structure of *Alexander Nevsky* was
based on the antagonism of two imaginative spheres, each of them possessing its own system of visual-plastic and rhythmic — melodic expressiveness.
Grotesqueness prevailed in the portrayal of the German crusaders and the
Russian traitors who took their side; grotesque devices emphasized their
malice, perfidy and cruelty by showing their sharp profiles, which suggested some likeness to beasts of prey. The music supported the verbal and
visual imagery, intensifying the impression produced by the characters of
the invaders. The driving and aggressive and at the same time mechanically
monotonous rhythms, the harsh polytonal harmony, the forced and piercing
'shrieks' of the wind instruments all created a repellent image of the enemy
treading on Russian soil. The negative emotional effect of the Teutons' music
was, to a great extent, enhanced by bizarre timbres and changes in the sound
intensity of some individual instruments, due to various manipulations of
the sound-recording equipment and of the sound-track of the film.

The latter device was prompted by chance during the recording of
one of the musical fragments. It so happened that one of the orchestral
players was placed too close to the microphone: this caused a distortion of
instrumental timbre, and the appearance of crackling and other noises on
the film. This seemed to be a technical defect. However, Prokofiev,
prompted by the paradoxical cast of thought typical of him, considered this

an excellent new possibility for creating disagreeable sounds, such as should, in his opinion, be the aggressive fanfares of the German trumpets as heard by the Russians. This device, which was found empirically, gave impetus to a long series of similar experiments. Perhaps this daring handling of the sound-recording equipment could be explained not only by the composer's bent for invention, but also by the fact that in the spring of 1938 (i.e. just before starting work on the music to *Alexander Nevsky*) Prokofiev had visited Hollywood, and was greatly interested in the musical techniques of American sound film and particularly in the technology of sound recording. Thus, when sitting in the sound recording studio of 'Mosfilm' ('Moscow Film') he did not feel a novice in a field in which most composers were largely ignorant.

Prokofiev's experiments in the removing from, or bringing nearer to the microphone, of individual instruments or whole orchestral groups were aimed at getting necessary expressive sound effects. They permitted him to make the trombone 'weak' and 'helpless', the trumpet 'small', the bassoon 'fearful' and 'formidable'. Eventually these experiments brought him to the discovery of a *law of inverted orchestration*. This was valuable because it led directly to the idea of multichannel stereophonic sound-recording.

A specific quality of the music recording of *Alexander Nevsky* was its use of a complex variety superimposed sound layers. In particular, in the celebrated 'Gallop of the Boar' (the Russian for the crusaders' battle array known in Europe as 'The Boar's Head') in the scene 'The Battle on the ice', Prokofiev and sound engineer Volsky together made the first separate recording of orchestral and choral groups: it permitted them to manipulate freely their volume and, when necessary, to isolate the sonority of one of them in a 'close-up'.

The group portrayal, devoid of any individual features, of the Teutonic knights (the episode 'The Crusaders in Pskov') consisted of three interconnected leitmotiv themes. The first of them, a terrorizing, brutal roar of trombones and trumpet, rose from a sharply dissonant harmony (the major seventh breaking into the triad of sharp mirror). The second leitmotiv was a Catholic Plainchant, stern, ascetic and soulless. The third was the above-mentioned menacing signal, or call, of four French horns ('the Teutonic trumpets'). It is interesting that, in creating the musical image of the crusaders, the composer rejected all attempts to restore authentic music of the Middle Ages. He explained his decision as follows: 'There was, naturally, a temptation to make use of the original music of those days. But my acquaintance with the Catholic canticles of the 13th century was enough to show that, during the past seven centuries, that music had become so alien to us, that it could not have nourished the spectators' imagination. It seemed, therefore, more reasonable not to follow the style of the time of the Battle on the ice, but to offer it in a style in which we can imagine it today. The same concerns the Russian song: it had to be given after a modern fashion, which is quite different from the way it was sung 700 years ago'[42].

Prokofiev's approach to the musical expression of Russian images was, on the whole, in accordance with the best traditions of art in the past century. The clear diatonicism and the vocal flexibility of melodic lines, the flowing rhythm, the transparent orchestration where precedence was given to choral singing, and the warm timbres of strings: all of this pointed to the close connection of Prokofiev's music with national roots, which were for the first time clearly shown in his creative work. This tendency towards a closer relationship with folklore, which showed in the 'Russian music' of the film, was later developed in the 'Bogatyrskaya' Fifth Symphony, then appeared in the music to the film *Ivan the Terrible*, and reached its climax in the opera *War and Peace*.

The 'Russian' themes in *Alexander Nevsky* included a heroic soldier song ('Rise up, Russian people!') and a long-drawn lyrical song (the middle part of the same chorus, 'No enemy shall ever stay in our dear Rus', our great Rus''); an ancient epic poem ('A song about Alexander Nevsky') and dashing chastooshki tunes ('The Battle on the ice'). Sometimes the composer himself was surprised at what he had written: 'How strange it sounds! The music is quite unlike Prokofiev'.[43] This humorous remark was made after the music of 'The Field of the Dead' had been recorded, an episode that followed the extensive battle scene 'The Battle on the ice' and functioned as a tragic climax in the film.

On the whole, the episode 'The Field of the Dead' produced a very contradictory impression because its deliberately operatic character did not quite fit he general stylistic of the picture. It was based on an expressive and beautiful solo, an aria stylized as a Russian lament, which was associated with the image of Olga on the field of battle, looking for the dead bodies of heroic bridegrooms, on the other hand, executed off frame, it assumed the generalized meaning of the people's mourning for the Russian warriors who perished in the battle. At the same time, the illustrative character of the Russian narrative which accompanied the song, and consisted of a sequence of long, static plane-shot, produced the impression of a complete cessation of action, especially noticeable and hard to bear when compared with the expressive and dynamic 'Battle on the ice' which had preceded it.

'The Battle on the ice' which formed a considerable part of the film (35 minutes of screen time), brought together in confrontation all the leitmotivs of the film which had been introduced at its beginning. It is amazing that the music of this grand scene, replete with dramatic collisions, was written for a completely finished plastic montage with the help only of a stop-watch. Moreover, by means of the poor technology of those days, Prokofiev managed to obtain striking results which cannot today be achieved without the use of a computer: he contrived to reproduce exactly in his music the march of the swiftly developing events of the screen action. To avoid any fragmentariness in the scenic material, the composer used methods of musical symphonism and through-composition. Making music subservient to the montage rhythm of representation helped combine them both in an integral visual-sound complex based on a synthesis of a higher order.

The scene of 'The Battle on the ice' opens with a marvellous and colourful introduction, a shot of sunrise on Chudskoye Lake. On the ice, the Russian army is standing, motionless and strained, listening to silence, waiting for the enemy to appear. And then, from afar, the iron rhythm of a drum-beat is heard; and with it the hoarse cries of trombones and trumpets, frenzied and fanatic passages on the organ, and phrases of the Latin *Tonus Peregrinus* rise in the sound-track. A mighty crescendo, rolling like a snow ball, reaches fortississimo at its climax, working up the tempo of the montage movement. But when the knights' square gets close to the Russian army, bristling with pikes,the crusaders' music, having reached its climax, suddenly collapses; there is a pause of suspense, then a fierce fight to the death. And then, after an oppressive stillness, the viewer is drowned in a chaos of sounds: the clanging of weapons, yells of the soldiers, groans of the wounded.

Alexander Nevsky, watching the progress of the battle and seeing the weakening resistance of the Russians, orders the cavalry to attack. At his call, 'For Rus'!' the theme of the patriotic chorus, 'Rise up, Russian people!' is developed in the sparkling timbre of the trumpets. A little later they are joined by piercing pipe-tunes intertwining with them.

The episode of the Russian cavalry attack, which brings about a crucial change in the fight, is accompanied by a heroic, luminous theme, inspiring in its energy and joy. It suppresses the crusaders' fanfares, creating complex polytonal contrapuntal combinations with the leitmotiv of the 'Teutonic horns', and moving in parallel with representation frames. True, Prokofiev sometimes fails to cope with Eisenstein's tempo and slips into mere illustration, but these slips are rare, and they do not weaken the highly emotional effect produced by the music of 'The Battle on the ice' as a whole.

The impetuous pressure of the 'Russian attack' gradually breaks the resistance of the fanfare theme: the latter is deformed, droops and looses its former grandeur and self-assurance. When the Teutons, having lost courage, are seized with panic and take to flight, the crusader themes begin falling away. The organ melody breaks off in the middle of the phrase as soon as

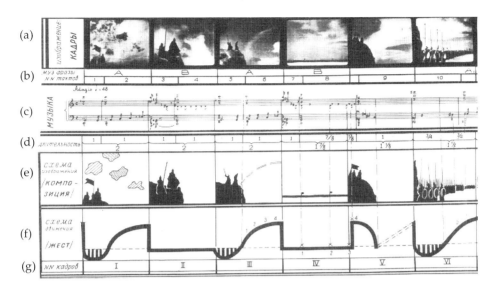

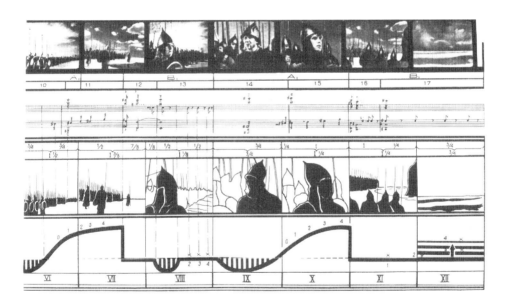

Figure 3 Table of the musical-visual montage of the scene of the battle on the ice from the film *Alexander Nevsky.*

Key: (a) representation: sequences; (b) musical phrases and bar no.;
(c) music; (d) duration; (e) scheme of representation/composition/;
(f) scheme of movement/gesture/ (g) sequence no.

Vasilisa, dressed in a warrior's array, knocks a black monk off his feet. The sound of the knight's horn drops to a tragic note when the last of the enemies are swallowed by the icy waters of Chudskoye Lake. And again, as at the beginning of the battle, silence sets in, emphasizing the sublime beauty of the Russian winter landscape. This is the end of a scene, celebrated in the history of world cinema, which puts one in mind of no less famous battle interludes in Russian classical operas, such as 'The Poltava Battle' (in the opera *Mazepa* by Piotr Tchaikovsky), and 'The Battle of Kerzhenets' (in the opera *A Tale of the Invisible City of Kitezh*), by Nikolai Rimsky-Korsakov). But the uniqueness of 'The Battle on the ice' and its significance for the development of further contacts between music and cinema, have been in the elaboration and putting into practice of the ideal of 'vertical montage', based on the polyphonic synchronisation of music and representation. Their coordination was so perfect that afterwards Eisenstein was able to draw up a scheme which proved graphically the absolute matching of the 12 frames of the 'sunrise' with the 17 bars of music as regards rhythm, tempo, the direction of movement of the melodic line with the trajectory of the eye's movement within the frame, and register (the musical and visual low-dark, high-light, juxtaposition which anticipated sound-colour cinematography).

Since then, the idea of 'vertical montage' which was first tested by Eisenstein and Prokofiev in the film *Alexander Nevsky* has found its peculiar realization in so-called 'visual music', a creation of modern television and video tape-recording.

One more essential detail is worth mentioning. Eisenstein's theoretical works and personal utterances permit one to deduce that he always thought highly of music. Moreover, he had an acute sense of the deep kinship of music and cinema, and strove to transfer to cinema the principles of musical thematic development, the devices of musical expressiveness, and even the laws of musical form building. Thus, Yurenev, a film critic of repute and a researcher into Eisenstein's creative work, pointed out emphatically that 'Eisenstein defied the traditional forms of dramaturgy, as well as the passion for psychologism, for the drama of characters, which were predominant in the '30s. He carried on the tradition of the epic, montage cinema of the twenties, in spite of the new conditions created by the appearance of synthetic sound-visual film'[44]. In Yurenev's opinion, this explained the elevated and passionate tone of *Alexander Nevsky* and the highly important role of music. Given the 'operatic' quality of this first joint work of Eisenstein and Prokofiev, its roots, according to the critic, should be looked for in films of the 'intellectual' cinema, innovatory in their language, such as *Battleship 'Potemkin'*, *October*, and *The Old and the New*, which rely upon the emotional support of music. This statement, though perhaps far-fetched, is rather interesting, for it suggests the existence of possible connections between *Alexander Nevsky* and the above-mentioned films. In addition, Sergei Prokofiev can be quoted. He wrote that 'the director's respect for music was so great that in some cases he was ready to "pull" the visual representation of the film forward or backward, if it would help preserve the integrity of the musical fragment'[45].

This approach to the problem of the interaction between music and representation, which presupposed a 'supreme unity' (Eisenstein) at the level of everyday, metrical, rhythmic, melodic, and key synchronism[46], was certainly accompanied by a deformation of some characteristics of the feature film, which can be illustrated by the frankly 'operatic' structure of the scenes 'The Field of Death' and 'Alexander Nevsky's entrance into Pskov'. Unambiguous associations with the epic opera of the Russian classic tradition proceeding from Glinka, Borodin, Mussorgsky, and Rimsky-Korsakov were also prompted by some other episodes of the film, such as 'The ruined Rus', 'Pskov', 'Vetche'. It was they that determined the un-hurried tempo of the unfolding of the imaginative material of *Alexander Nevsky*, as well as the principle (selected as the main one) of the contrasting juxtaposition of static scenes and positions, in whose *fermate* the characters' remarks were heard, (sing-song, in rhythm, with elements of recitation to music).

The close connections which existed between the music of the film and autonomous academic genres created prerequisites for the subsequent 'transformation' of 'applied' music into one of the outstanding compositions of the 20th century — the cantata *Alexander Nevsky*. Moreover, the artistic merits of Prokofiev's music for the first sound film made by Eisenstein, which was inferior to none of the best specimens of operatic and oratorio art of the time, shook the conventional opinions of some musicians and critics, who considered that film music was second-rate. At least, Sergei Prokofiev's work was convincing proof of the fact that aesthetic-philosophic notions of artistic value could, and even should, be applied to film music as well.

The further development of forms of music and representation synthesis on the basis of their image synchronisation, or counterpoint, was continued in the new work of Eisenstein and Prokofiev, a film made in collaboration and dealing with an outstanding personality in Russian history, Czar Ivan the Terrible. This film, recognized as a classical work of world cinema, was shot in the hardest days of the war.

Thus, within a decade of the existence of sound film in the USSR, film music had become a particular, specific kind of compositional activity. On the one hand, its formation was greatly influenced by operatic and symphonic genres, which conditioned the appearance of a 'symphonic' type of musical film dramaturgy; on the other hand, the music which had to deal with one of the most communicative arts of those days tended towards mass democratic genres. The latter tendency naturally raised an interest in, and a bias for, the Soviet mass song which was just coming into being, and led to the development of a dramaturgy of the 'song' type, which became prevalent in the comedy film and in pictures dealing with modern subjects. However, the supremacy of song in the 'song' film by no means precluded the use of the symphonic method of thought, or the principle of through development: this resulted in the creation of an integral musical concept which was concordant in its main parameters with an ideological and artistic conception of film. At the same time, the '30s were marked by an expansion of the genre limits of the musical film, and the appearance of the opera-film. Also cinema-goers' were acquaintanced with the national peculiarities of music in the pictures of Armenian, Ukrainian and Georgian film masters.

In the late thirties, the first experiments in sound-recording were made, the result of which was Prokofiev's development of his original idea of 'inverted orchestration'. This attracted composers' attention to the possibility of various manipulations of both the film and the sound-recording equipment.

But the most important achievement of the Soviet cinema of that period was, perhaps, winning the co-operationof the best composers of the country, young people who were starting their artistic careers, and who saw in film music a unique laboratory where they might try out and put into practice their own plans and conceptions. Many of the discoveries made by them were later put to use in works of autonomous music. On the other hand, the collaboration of film directors with gifted young musicians stimulated the quest for new means of expressiveness, and contributed to making music closely allied with screen representation and imagery. All of this put together makes it possible to consider the music of the Soviet pre-war cinema as a remarkable and significant phenomenon in the art of the given period.

Part 2

1941–1958

9

The fortunes of film music in the hard times of the War

When the war broke out the cinema, which was considered the most important means of mass the ideological influence upon the people, was reorganized in accordance with war conditions. Hundreds of cinema teams went out to the front, and as early as the summer of 1941 their war reports were run in the Soviet cinemas. At the same time, the issue of operative *Battle Film Collections (BFC)* was begun by the central film studios. As a rule, the *Battle Film Collections (Boyevoi Kinosbornik)* consisted of several short films, including newsreels and also features such as cartoons, sketches, dramatic short stories; their task was to glorify the greatness and moral superiority of the defenders of the country, and to expose the brutal cruelty, perfidy and moral worthlessness of the fascists. The characters in the *Battle Film Collections* were often those of such popular pre-war films as *Volga-Volga* (the letter-carrier Strelka, acted by Lubov' Orlova), the film trilogy about Maxim (the never-say-die young worker Maxim, played by Boris Chirkov). They appeared on the screen, together with their songs which Soviet cinema-goers loved so much ('The March of the Merry Fellows' and the song 'Whirling and turning is a blue balloon'); however, these songs now had a new text infused with passionate patriotic pathos.

The composers who wrote music for *BFC* were Dunayevsky, Muradeli, Shvarts, Kriukov, Miliutin, Meitus, Pototsky, and others. Unfortunately, the music in the *BFC* subjects functioned merely as background and, being limited to sound illustration of film action, was soon forgotten, except for the song 'Night over Belgrade', composed in a ballad style by Nikita Bogoslovsky for a short-story film of the same name. It had been shot by director Leonid Lukov and was published in *Battle Film Collections* No. 8 (1942). The heavy, regular step of its march-like rhythm, and a melody immersed in the dense and dark key of C minor, in the development of which a descending movement prevailed, and a caesura at the elusive second step of the minor mode, all made the theme sound stern and tragic. At the same time, a flowing melody twining about the rhythmically supporting texture, and an unexpected triplet 'fault' in the seventh measure of a period, which

disturbed the symmetrical alternation of strong and weak beats characteristic of a march, both made the song sound warm, with a lively human
feeling.

Ex. 7 *Night over Belgrade*

Verses by B. Laskin

A still night over Belgrade has come to replace the day.
Remember how brightly the furious thunder of fire would burst out.

'Night over Belgrade' added a new page to Bogoslovsky's creative biography. It was associated with the genre of battle-front song: thanks to the cinema it became widely known among the soldiers and officers of the army in the field.

The minimum time periods allowed for issuing the monthly numbers of the *Battle Film Collections (BFC)*, the banning of the shooting teams from the theatre of operations, and hence their somewhat primitive understanding of what was going on at the front, could not but affect the quality and artistic value of their work. Besides, the difficult situation they found themselves in, unfavourable as it was for the editing and release of new films, was aggravated by the evacuation of the creative staff and technical bases of the Moscow, Leningrad, Kiev and Belorussian studios to remote southern regions of the USSR (to Alma-Ata, Tashkent, Stalinabad, Ashkhabad). Nevertheless, the main problem of those set to *BFC* work was solved: these elementary propaganda films had paved the way for full-length feature films about the war. In August 1942, having exhausted all their possibilities, the *Battle Film Collections* ceased.

During the war, a peculiar and makeshift genre of film-concert became popular. In fact, its formal structure presented a number of theatrical and recital items shot in studios and linked together in an arbitrary order. They were executed by professional and amateur actors and musicians, by ensembles and companies from one of the Soviet republic (or a group of republics of near nationalities). Within the four-year period of the war, nine films of this kind were released, demonstrating in panoramic review the musical culture of Russia, Belorussia, Kazakhstan, Tajikistan, Georgia, Turkmenia, Uzbekistan, Kirghizia, and the Ukraine. The Showing of such films both at the battle front and in the interior to some extent replaced the performances of concert groups at the front, infused spirit into the troops,and united peoples of all nationalities. The filming of concerts was also carried on after the war, but the static character of the genre, which gave no impetus to any creative development, soon turned film concerts into grandiose gala-accounts of Soviet republics 'exhibiting the achievements' of their national art. Thus one more stone was laid in the foundation of the tendentious, massive and uniform official state-culture, which reached its climax in the late seventies.

The first feature films devoted to the tragic days of the Great Patriotic War were *The Secretary of the District Committee* by Ivan Pyriev and *Mashen'ka* by Yuli Raizman, both dated 1942. Due to the conditions caused by the evacuation, the lack of studios specially equipped for sound-recording, and the incomplete orchestral staff, sound engineer Volsky was forced to turn to the almost forgotten principle of music compilation. Later, however, film workers were joined by composers.

On the whole, the film music of the war years was of minor importance in composers' creative work (as compared to the pre-war decade).
Moreover, all experiments, both in the sphere of expressive means and in
that of sound-recording were effectively stopped, and composers did not
see anything reprehensible in including the material of their earlier compositions in new films. Thus, Prokofiev reproduced some developed fragments
from his symphonic suite *The 1941st* in Savchenko's film *Partizans in the
Steppes of the Ukraine* (1943). Much of the music of the opera *Semeon Kotko*
was contained in Prokofiev's score for the film *Kotovsky* directed in the same
year Feinzimmer. This was especially obvious in the dramatic scenes where
the German occupants were characterized, in the portrayal of in whom in
both operas similar devices of satire and grotesque were used.

However, it would be wrong to think that, being temporarily shifted
to the fringe of the composer's sphere of interest, film music completely lost
one of its chief attractions, i.e. the possibility of serving as laboratory for the
working-out of conceptual ideas and themes for future great works in
autonomous genres. The music written by Popov for the well-known film,
Ermler's *She Is Defending Her Country* (1943) may serve as an example. It is
a passionately told story about the tragic fate of a simple Russian woman.
The war has deprived her of everything: of a quiet and happy life; a husband
who was lost in action; a child whom she saw perish under a fascist tank.
The horrors she went through made her join the formidable people's avengers, in order to kill the enemies who had invaded her country. The character
of the heroine, Praskovya Lukyanova, gripped the composer's imagination
and inspired him to write one of his most outstanding compositions, the
symphony *Motherland,* which included, practically unchanged, the whole of
the music he had composed for the film.

A direct response to the actual events of the Great Patriotic War was
Arnshtam's *Zoya* (1944), devoted to the heroic deed of a partisan girl, Zoya
Kosmodemyanskaya (1944). Many years have passed since the time when
the film was released, and its shortcomings, which were then considered to
be its merits, can now be seen in their true light. Thus, there is an idealized,
iconic image of the heroine, whom the authors wanted to represent as a
typical Soviet girl, pure and whole-hearted, sharing in the joys and troubles
of her country, and in no ways differing from the other Soviet young people
of the '30–40s. Hence came the rather moralizing and didactic tone of the
sentimental narration, which showed Soviet life's realities. Fortunately,
some failings of the film were redressed by the music of Shostakovich, who
once again proved his mastery as a film composer.

The film *Zoya* opened with an extensive exposition taking the audience back to the heroine's childhood and adolescence. Preceding the action,

the introductory nocturne, with its expressive melody and flowing barcarole rhythm, drew a gentle, romantic, girlish character. It was only after this 'musical meeting' with her that Zoya appeared on the screen. It is interesting that, two decades later, Shostakovich reverted to this wonderfully flexible theme with its leisurely, gliding movement of consecutive thirds and sixths, but with modal alterations characteristic of the Russian melos: he made out of it the song 'Motherland hears', which celebrated Yuri Gagarin's flight into space.

The character of this heroine attracted the composer's attention not only by her personality: in the partizan scout he detected the perpetuation of a centuries-old Russian tradition of patriotism, of readiness to sacrifice one's life for one's country. It is not accidental that an episode was introduced (a history lesson at school) where Zoya told the class about the heri_oc_ deeds of the Russian peasant, Ivan Susanin, who saved Moscow at the cost of his life, having misled a detachment of Poles into a thick forest. And, like an echo of the events which had taken place centuries earlier, the melodic phrases from the celebrated chorus 'Glory!' from Glinka's opera *Ivan Susanin* began to penetrate the music of the scene. Again the melody of the same chorus arose in the scene in Red Square, in Moscow, where Zoya and her school friend came after wandering in the empty streets at night. This episode crowned the development of the plot of the heroine's peaceful life before the war, linking together the pure and luminous theme of Zoya's 'seventeenth spring' and the theme of Glinka's chorus, a symbol of the great state and its capital, Moscow. And finally, the chorus 'Glory!', arising once more in the finale of the film, exalts the martyrdom of Zoya Kosmodemyanskaya, murdered by fascists, and to glorifies the country which could bring up such heri_oc_ young people. Today, after a long lapse of time, such a 'quotation' of a well-known theme might, perhaps, seem naive and even too straightforward and didactic; but in those days it was perceived as something quite natural, since it answered the propagandist purposes which Soviet art had to serve, and assisted in enhancing patriotic feelings in Soviet society. Besides, because of Shostakovich's skill, Glinka's music in the film did not seem to be an alien element: it was naturally 'written into' the authentic musical material, and made an integral part of it.

However, in spite of the important dramatic role played the chorus 'Glory!', all the key episodes of the film were inseparable from the music of Shostakovich. This helped the authors elevate the scene of Zoya's death, with its staggering tragedy and harsh naturalism, well beyond a mere description of the brutal violence of the fascist sadists in killing a defenceless girl, and show her not as a victim but as a victor. Based on the Zoya leitmotiv, the music of this scene sounded liked a hymn, the driving force of which supported the young partisan and helped her withstand the torture and die unbroken and with dignity.

Thus, the symphonic type of musical dramaturgy, which had assumed a definite form in the thirties, proved to be usefully adaptable to war themes. The dramatic antagonism and conflict between hostile forces, characteristic of the contents of most patriotic, historico-revolutionary and historical films during the war period, fed the creative imagination and gave an impetus to developing in music such aesthetic categories as the beautiful and the ugly or the horrible. Their antagonism stimulated the quest for new devices and means of expressiveness, though the hard working conditions and the pressures of the time were hardly favourable to experimental work. In spite of good intentions, and the enthusiasm and sincerity of composer's aspirations, Soviet film music in the years 1941–1945 failed to rise to the high level which was achieved by the music of the opera and the symphonic, chamber-instrumental and song genres of the war period. Yet even in film music certain discoveries, however small, were made, certain happy and original solutions were found, which were later worth recording in the history of Soviet film music. In this connection, besides the above mentioned film *Zoya*, with music written by Shostakovich, the picture *Girl No. 217* (1945) should be mentioned. It was the first collaborator of director Mikhail Romm and composer Aram Khachaturian.

Unlike many other films of those days, *Girl No. 217* was almost devoid of music. Moreover, there was in it hardly any so-called 'background music', for the composer's attention was focused on one theme, that of the suffering, sorrow, hatred, felt by the Soviet people transported as slaves to Nazi Germany. Its extraordinary utmost concentration of expressive possibilities charges Khachaturian's music with maximum energy, turns it into the tragic nerve of the picture, and makes the development of the action especially dynamic, bringing it to its climax in the finale.

The rejection of melodiously unfolding structures; the use of harsh, angular melodies, shot through with 'creeping' chromatisms, and of pointed, stabbing chords (*pizzicato*), sharply dissonant combinations, polyrhythm, ostinato patterns within a limited compass — all help create an atmosphere of growing emotional and psychological tension. Only one episode, for a moment, breaks the feeling of overwhelming despair and terror: it happens when the young girl Tanya, confined in a punishment cell, recalls her childhood, and her country. On the screen, half-forgotten scenes of peace-time life are superimposed. The transition from the dreadful reality to these visions is brought about by a quivering tremolo in the strings, with a flute intertwining with it, and then a waltz streams into the auditorium like a sparkling waterfall (a reminiscence of the school-leaving ball). Its melody bears a resemblance the popular waltz from Khachaturian's music for Lermontov's drama *Masquerade*. But this alienation from reality appears short-lived; it emphasizes the inevitability of the impending tragic outcome: Tanya kills some Nazi officers. This is shown against the background of an air-raid, and the bombardment of a German town by the Soviet air-force.

10

Problems of 'song' film

During the period described, the fate of the 'song' film, which had been a stunning success in the pre-war decade, was far from easy. By 1944 it had practically disappeared from the cinema, and returned to the screen only when the victory of the countries of the anti-Hitlerite coalition over fascist Germany was already sure. But the song as such had never ceased sounding in Soviet film, though its tone was now somewhat different. It was no longer the steady, energetic march that had prevailed in the genre of the thirties: the cinema of the war years, the forties, turned to a gentle lyrical song, imbued with a feeling of homesickness, and expressing devotion to one's beloved. It was just what distinguished one of the most popular, evergreen songs by Bogoslovsky, 'Dark is the night', which was first sung in Lukov's film *Two Soldiers* (1943). But if in earlier films the song, as a rule, characterized a particular person or conveyed a certain conceptual idea or a slogan, now it served a different purpose: film makers used an alienation device, which helped them reveal the personal side of army life, indiscernible in the roar of warfare.

Sung with an extraordinary warmth and sincerity of emotion by the outstanding film actor and singer, Mark Bernes, the song 'Dark is the night' won the sympathy of millions of people both at the front and at home. At the same time, it was treated with great irritation and anger by critics: they accused the composer of propagating music which they considered sentimental, trivial and Philistine, and of unnerving a people which did everything in its power in the struggle against the enemy. Indeed, unpretentious and restrained as it was in the expression of simple, inner thoughts and feelings, Bogoslovsky's song strikingly differed from the war song of the time, which was meant to be either a field marching-song or a civil patriotic one. No wonder that the lyrical song 'Dark is the night', built on the variation of a limited melodic 'germ' motive, was ostracized by the official experts. But in spite of all the attacks, it remained in people's memories and eventually became a kind of trademark of the war years, the forties — a symbol which was widely used by directors of Soviet as well as foreign films (for example, the Polish director A. Wajda used it on the sound-track of his film *Ashes and Diamonds*, 1958).

Verses by V. Agatov

Ex. 8 *Dark Is the Night*
A song from the film *Two Soldiers*

Ex. 8 (continued)

Dark is the night, only bullets are whistling over the steppe, / only the wind is zooming in
the conductors, / the stars are glimmering dimly. /
At a dark night you, my love, are awake, I know, / and, sitting by the child's cot, / secretly
wipe off a tear. / How much I love the depth of your kind eyes, / . . . /

Thus, until 1944, the film song played the role of an auxiliary and incidental element in the action. But with the release of the lyrical musical picture by Ivan Pyriev (the director) and Tikhon Khrennikov (the composer), *At 6 p.m. after the War*, the film song recovered its rights and became one of the leading dramatic components of the film, directing the movement of the plot.

If judged by its genre indications, the film would hardly do for the elaboration of a war subject. Nevertheless it not only dealt with the hardest period in Soviet as well as in world history, but also was the first openly to mention the name of the victorious country, almost a year before the red flag was hoisted on the dome of the Reichstag.

The film possessed some individual artistic peculiarities which distinguished it from a number of pictures in the same genre, and offered favourable conditions for its enrichment with songs. The alternation of lyrical and comic episodes, where a personal, intimate feeling was inseparable from the patriotic duty of a citizen, might put one in mind of the traditional comedy film of the thirties, if it were not for the high style and the verses which helped the characters express themselves, and permitted a smooth modulation into song.

The main points which cemented the framework both of the musical . and the whole dramatic structure of the film were three marching songs: 'The March of the Artillerymen', which was at the same time the main leitmotiv and appeared first in the overture during the captions; 'The Bold Cavalrymen's Dance', written in the manner of a dashing Russian soldier song; and a march-hymn 'Long live our Motherland'. Thus, the genre of the musical comedy, with an energetic marching song in the centre, returned to the Soviet cinema, and the line along which the 'song' film of the thirties had been developing, until interrupted by the war, was now restored: it demonstrated that the people's general feeling was changing, and that they were growing confident that the war would soon be over.

The leitmotiv, the theme of patriotism, was interpreted by the composer in various hypostases which included practically all the song types of the war years. Besides the energetic collective marching songs, there was also the lyrical waltz song 'That is not the point, my friends'; the poetic duet 'Moscow', imbued with nostalgic recollections of the native city, dear to one's heart, and perceived as a reminiscence of the well-known 'Song about Moscow' from the pre-war film *Swineherd and Shepherd;* and finally, the sprightly and cheerful song which was sung by Varya: 'All of us girls dream in the evening'. Put together, these songs seem to make up a 'group portrait' of the people who had ensured victory in the most dreadful of wars in the recent history of mankind.

The theme of love for one's country is revealed not through heroism alone. There is also a personal aspect: the thrilling love of the young girl Varya for the young artilleryman Vasya Kudryashov. However, the musical interpretation of their love is not limited to expressing the inner emotions of these particular characters, for through musical generalization their firm belief in their own long-awaited happiness is connected with the emotions and expectations of all those driven asunder by the war. It is in this context that the song 'Parting' ('Rise up to a hard-fought battle') should be 'read' — stern and restrained, full of deep, tragic pathos. One can hear in it both a bitterness of parting, anxiety, and the blessings of lovers and of mothers seeing the defenders of the country off to the front. The emotional expressiveness of the song is enhanced by a long view of an endless column of soldiers passing.

But if in the 'Parting' the heroic and the lyrical principles were united on an equal footing and even with a slight shift towards heroism, in Varya's song 'The Cossack was going to War' the lyrical theme was clearly dominant. The beauty and the vocal plasticity of the melody, developing in undulatory movement, imparted a feeling of pure and quiet joy to the music, as if anticipating a happy issue — the joining of the lovers, their future reunion 'at six in the evening after the war'.

Distinctive additions to the lyrical theme, which enriched the film with new shades and colours, were Varya's arioso and Kudryashov's lullaby.

On the whole, the musical structure of the film resembled a complex three-part form with a contrasting middle part, in the centre of which was the song 'The Cossack was going to War', setting off extremes of the heroic pathos. The concluding frames of the picture (the reunion of Varya and Kudryashov after the war) functioned as a dynamic recapitulation: the heroic and patriotic themes developed at the beginning of the film appeared again, paving the way for the optimistic finale-apotheosis. This coda was accompanied by a majestic march 'Long live our Motherland' a device which had been widely used in pre-war films and was now restored by Pyriev and Khrennikov, taking account of the new 'war' material. Later many songs of the film *At 6 p.m. after the War* became popular throughout the country, and 'The March of the Artillerymen' was given the status of the official hymn of the Soviet rocket and artillery forces, adding one more item to the long list of cheerful, life asserting Soviet mass march songs engendered by the myth-creative ideology of socialist realism.

The success of the comedy film of Pyriev and Khrennikov was a signal for the reappearance of 'song' film. It was closely followed by its 'double', *A Celestial Slowcoach* (1945), shot by the director Timoshenko in collaboration with the popular song-composer Solovyov-Sedoy. However, it could not equal its prototype because of its expressive emphasis on purely

Ex. 9 *The Cossack was going to War.*
(for soprano or tenor)

Over the free, quiet Don, / a marching song resounded. /
A Cossack was going to a great war, / his bride was seeing him off.

amusing and comic situations, and its simple substitution of artillerymen with pilots. Even the brilliant songs written by Solovyov-Sedoy could not make up for the schematic and imitative collisions of the plot. These songs, stirring and cheerful, were somewhat unusual in Soviet music of those days, for in their informational and imaginative sphere they tended towards a

Text by V. Gusev

Ex. 10 The Song of the Artillerymen
(for a male chorus)

Ex. 10 (continued)

1. Our hearts are burning with love for our native land.
We are fighting to the death to defend the honour of our country
Towns are ablaze, enveloped in smoke, the severe god of war is thundering in grey woods.
Know, oh my mother, know, my devoted wife,
know, my far-off home and all my family, that our storm of steel is crushing and burning up the enemy,

that we are bringing liberty to all parts of our land.
The hour of victory shall come and our campaign will be over.
but before we turn homewards, we shall fire a salute of joy at midnight in honour of our dear party, in honour of our people
Refrain
Artillerists, a strict order is given.
Artillerists, our Fatherland calls upon us.
/ . . . . /

'variety' style which was then regarded as not only lightminded but also inappropriate. Nevertheless, two of these songs ('Because we are pilots' and 'It's time to take off') became the first post-war hits. Imitation of the already formed standard was also characteristic of the film *A Troublesome Household* (1946) by the director M. Zharov and composer Miliutin, which had been shot in the victory year of 1945.

Sings of the deep crisis which had for the first time been evident in the films *A Celestial Slowcoach* and *A Troublesome Household*, due to editing of the same or similar subjects and song clichés and stereotypes, became more and more distinct in the 'song' film of the post-war period. And the cause of its gradual death is to be sought not in individual creative failures, or in self repetition by script writers, directors, composers or actors, but, above all, in the altered life conditions of the Soviet people, the ruin of their hopes for radical changes in the post-war world, and the impossibility of returning to the idyllic and beautiful, but false, fairytales about a happy and carefree 'tomorrow' in the land of socialism (although there were some attempts of this kind which will be discussed below). People who had undergone severe trials, many of those who had crossed half of Europe while fighting, who had undergone the ordeals of occupation, captivity, concentration camps, or hard labour and famine at home — such people could not believe in the sweet dreams of an invented reality, like that which had been shown in the films of Alexandrov and Dunayevsky in the thirties. And these new circumstances had to be taken in to account, both by the Stalinist regime which had started a new, even more murderous series of persecutions and repressions and by Soviet artists submitting to and following all the directions of the 'guiding and leading force', the communist party.

11

Extending the bounds of the musical film: initial steps towards mastering the genres of film-opera and film-operetta

The year 1944 was interesting as a year of renewed work not only on the 'song' film, but also on two kinds of film belonging to musical genres, i. e. the opera film and the operetta film. Within one year an opera and an operetta were filmed: *Tchaikovsky's Cherevichki** (director Shapiro) in Alma-Ata and Kalman's *Silva* (director Ivanovsky) in the Sverdlovsk film studio[1]. In the Victory year, 1945, a film was released by two directors, Takhmasib and Leshchenko in Baku. This film was based on the musical comedy of Uzeir Gadjibekov *Arshin Mal Alan*. It was the third screen-version of this classic of Azerbaijani music, but unlike the two preceding it, which had been released before the revolution of 1917 in spite of the composer's protest, this version, was approved by the now sixty-year-old artist. He called it the best version, which was not surprising, for only sound cinema was able to show millions of cinema-goers of all nationalities the beauty, the refinement and the melodic wealth of his music. It was music which directed the development of the plot, characterized the protagonists and led the comic action, especially in the crowd scenes, which were distinguished by a detailed portrayal of everyday life, dynamic montage rhythm and spectacular performance. This was largely achieved through very careful handling of Gadjibekov's original score by the composer and conductor of the film *Arshin Mal Alan*, Niyazi[2], who, from a professional point of view, had prepared its filming almost irreproachably and, proceeding from the comic leitmotivs, had written some additional fragments to link the items. The picture was a great success, due not only to good direction and the brilliant, spirited music. It became polular also thanks to the film debut of the well-known singer, Rashid Beibutov, who played the leading part of the merchant Asker.

Three years later a similar attempt was made by Georgian film makers, who undertook a screen version of the first Georgian comic opera by Dolidze, *Keto and Koté* , based on the subject of the famous comedy of

---

* Cherevichki (*The Little Shoes*), 1887.

Tsagareli *Khanuma*. The directors, Tabliashvili and Gedevanishvili, strove to make music the central character of the picture, which should then dictate the inner rhythm, the dynamics, the compositional structure of the episodes, and the dramaturgy of the film in general. Accordingly, the composer Kereselidze wrote a number of additional musical fragments, building them on modified Georgian folk song melodies. Unfortunately, an exaggerated decorativeness and prettiness of orchestration, a disbalance of sound volume, an inaccurate connection between the components of the soundtrack, which sometimes resulted in its being too noisy and incoherent, and finally a certain naiveté in coordinating the music and the action, affected the artistic merits of this screen version, making it shallow and illustrative.

12

A breakthrough in sound-visual cinema:
Ivan the Terrible by
Eisenstein and Prokofiev

The idea of the grandiose film epic *Ivan the Terrible* occurred to Sergei Eisenstein before the Second World War, but it was not until 1942 that Sergei Prokofiev started writing music for the first part of the picture. It is interesting that his working methods in the cinema had by that time assumed the form of a harmonious, well-adjusted system which included certain stages:

(1) a survey, stop-watch in hand, of roughly assembled episodes and the determination of the exact time of the necessary music fragments;
(2) writing a piano version of the scenic music and recording it on tape;
(3) coordination of music and representation and, if the result is satisfactory, the beginning of work on the orchestration.

Today nobody would be surprised at this approach to writing film music, but at that time it was a novelty which demonstrated not only Prokofiev's ingenuity but also his pragmatism, his search for maximum effect in his work. For his part, the director took every opportunity to stimulate the composer's imagination, in accordance with his own conception of the film. Thus, aware of Prokofiev's striking ability to reproduce living images in music, Eisenstein made a series of drawings and graphic sketches of the most important scenes, which the composer wittily termed, 'squibs'. He turned to such, 'squibs', especially often when he had to write music before the image had been fully assembled, and the director was seeking a key to the melodic, rhythmic or dramatic organization of a particular scene. Besides, Prokofiev was given a detailed list of supposed musical themes, which he jokingly called 'themelet'. This list included a description of each particular theme as well as the director's commentary on the episodes in which the themes were to be used.

The work on this epic took some years and remained practically unfinished because of the gross interference of the authorities who imposed a ban upon its continuation: for it was the tragic year 1946 which marked the beginning of the totalitarian Stalinist Crusade against art.

Cinema was among the first victims of the Moloch of Stalinist censorship and Zhdanov's cultural policy. On the 4th of September, 1946, all central newspapers, followed later by magazines, published a *Resolution of the Central Committee of the Communist Party of the Soviet Union (Bolsheviks), On the film "The Great Life"*, which plunged Soviet cinema art into a deep crisis, creative and spiritual, and from which it could never fully recover. Many outstanding masters of the director's art, the 'golden fund' of Soviet cinema, Pudovkin, Eisenstein, Kozintsev, Trauberg, and others, were persecuted and tested 'for loyalty'. Many films were banned and shelved in archives for years, and one of them was the second part of the monumental *Ivan the Terrible* by Eisenstein and Prokofiev[3]. Moreover, the anonymous authors of the *Resolution* paid it special attention, and their conclusion was worded like a bill of indictment: 'In the second part of his film *Ivan the Terrible*, director Eisenstein showed himself ignorant of historic facts, in representing the progressive force of the opritchniks of Ivan the Terrible as a band of degenerates, like the American Ku Klux Klan, and Ivan the Terrible himself, a man of will and strong character, as weak-willed and characterless, something like Hamlet'[4].

The Resolution of the Central Committee of the Communist Party of the Soviet Union (Bolsheviks) ended in a rather menacing, sinister phrase: 'Workers of art should understand that those who persist in being lightminded and irresponsible in their work may easily find themselves thrown overboard, outside the sphere of progressive Soviet art...'[5].

This was just what happened to Sergei Eisenstein: he was forbidden to work on the third (concluding) part of the film, and all the material that had been shot disappeared without trace. A year and a half later he died a premature death from a major heart attack[6]. After Eisenstein's demise Prokofiev left off work in the cinema, considering his 'cinema activities finished for good'[7]. Some fragments of the opera *Ivan the Terrible* which he had intended to write and stage with Eisenstein's help, remained in sketches... However, in the Stalinist USSR there was hardly a person who would be surprised by this story.

Today it would make no sense to discuss or try to comment upon the text of that monstrous *Resolution*, since it was absurd and preposterous. Nevertheless, its 'authors' had correctly noticed a 'dangerous tendency' in the director's interpretation of Czar Ivan IV's character, which showed the deeds of that czar in a new light, and set one to thinking on the consequences of unlimited and uncontrolled power. When starting work on this epic, Eisenstein had dreamed of making a film about a czar as an outstanding political man who was supported by the people, and at the cost of great sacrifice strove for nothing but the flowering and strengthening of Russia. However, closer investigation of this most contradictory and complicated personality of Russian history, whose reign plunged the country into seas of blood, made the director turn from the outer, illustrative and eventful story to the world of the secret emotional experience and perturbation of mind of a man who was ready to go any length in order to keep his autocracy. And if in the first, panegyric, part of *Ivan the Terrible* the leitmotiv of a 'Monarch's heavy crown' was only slightly touched upon, in the second part it was so pointed as to become dominant. Thus, in spite of the initial intention, the central theme became the tragedy of a czar, betrayed by his friends, suffering from loneliness, unable to tear himself from the clutches of his own crimes and having no mercy for his victims. One may doubt whether Eisenstein thought it possible to draw direct historical parallels with contemporary life. Yet 'impermissible' associations could be discerned, and they evoked immediate response from the party oligarchs, headed by Stalin, who put the second part under ban and demanded a 'correction of errors that had been made'. For thirteen years (i.e. till 1958) the second part of *Ivan the Terrible* remained under the ban, as well as the music of Sergei Prokofiev, which contained many excellent pages and was the greatest achievement of his cinematic heritage.

As mentioned above, the film epic *Ivan the Terrible* was conceived as a work in three parts, i.e. three films linked in a dynamic unity. The first film showed Ivan's childhood, his youth, his ascending the throne, the capture of Kazan and the strengthening of his autocracy. Its epigraph might have been a quotation of the czar's own words: 'For the sake of the great Russian realm'. The second part, 'The Boyars' Plot', showed Ivan the Terrible as a grown-up man; the opritchnik force, or oprichnina established by him (as an instrument of reprisal against recalcitrant opponents); his irreconcilable and bitter struggle with the boyars. 'Allied but alone' — such was the idea of the second part. And, finally, the third was to deal with the routing of Novgorod by the opritchniks, and with the victory in the Livonian war.

Such a wide time-scale of dramatic events from Russian history, presented in a polyphonic interlacing of human fortunes, required the singling out of a dominant, constructive element which would hold together the whole structure. This role was played by musical leitmotivs. In the director's archives a note addressed to Prokofiev was found, in which Eisenstein stated his general idea and his wish that it should be reflected in the musical conception of the film. According to the director's intention, the dramaturgy of his film cycle should be supported by the development of two musical themes: 'One is sunny, sparkling with an ideal, we see its highest flight in the finale of Kazan, it is pure and serene'.

The second component is the *oprichnina*, the theme of the dark side of autocracy, properly terrible, tragic, in certain places sombre. Sometimes it dominates, and then also in two aspects: militant, buoyant, two "Romes" over a coffin[8], and heartrending when the oprichniks begin taking their oath'[9].

The antithesis of good and evil in the film was to be the song 'Ocean-sea' and the music for the 'Oprichniks' Oath', which were both starting points for the work on the film in November 1942. However, the radical change in the director's attitude towards his initial concept in the process of its realization made him reconsider the key knots of the whole structure. As a result, the 'Oath' episode, conceived as a ceremony of initiation into the oprichnina (the second part) was not included in the film, whereas the music written for it was used in the cruel and even sadistic scene of the sham coronation of Vladimir Staritsky, the imbecile son of Efrosinia Staritskaya, aunt of Ivan the Terrible. The incongruous little figure of Vladimir attired in magnificent czar's robes is sharply contrasted with the black featureless mass of the oprichniks moving in on him under the guidance of Ivan. Vladimir does not suspect that his death is approaching. The tragic mood in the scene of the impending murder is enhanced by a ritualised, prayerful male-voice chorus. The singing of this chorus, in the opinion of the critic Leonid Kozlov, gives rise to 'associations with the Greek tragic', for, when accompanying the procession, it expressed in its meaning-ful singing 'something higher: both sorrow and judgement, mourning, and the grim knowledge of what, after all, so-called fate means'[10].

A certain lifelessness and cold aloofness can be felt in the theme, moving in parallel octaves, broken by chromaticisms in the tenor and bass parts. The subsequent addition of the altos to the main melodic line, as well as the polyphonic splitting of chorus parts (the device of choral *divisi*), emphasized by dense, sharply dissonant harmonies, enhances the depress-ing atmosphere of the fatal predestination of events and the feeling of growing terror. Imperceptibly, the inarticulate 'mooning' of the chorus acquires a verbal concreteness: 'I swear to god a terrible oath that I will serve the Sovereign of Rus' like a dog'. A blind, fanatic faith pervades these lines, which are interrupted by the sharp whistling strokes of a prison-warder's lash — an instrument of reprisal and torture. But in the second couplet the chorus begins a patter-song, which forcefully conveys the hypnotically benumbed state of mind both of the victim and his persecutors when they become aware of the inevitability of a bloody outcome. The growing density of tragic emotions is also supported by the visual and plastic shaping of the scene. Gigantic iconographic images of saints in the cathedral frescoes, and quaint, frighteningly fantastic shadows of people and objects in the semi-dark cathedral — all of these details put together create the almost tangible, tense, sound-visual situation in which the intended crime is to take place.

If 'The Opritchniks' Oath' was used in the film epic in a different place and in a different context from that initially planned, the song 'Ocean-sea' was not used in the film at all. The reason why one of the most brilliant and original musical items of the film score disappeared from *Ivan the Terrible* can be easily explained: it possessed a stern, ascetic beauty and resembled ancient Russian epic songs (*bylinas*) in its character and melodic pitch. This song was to become the dramatic focus, and at the same time the meaningful climax, of the third part of the picture. Its main role was in giving a generalized expression of Czar Ivan's dream of making his way to the Baltic Sea: this was the completion of the long and painful process of building a powerful, centralized monarchical state. Besides, this song was also intended to sum up the development of the heroic plot, and formed a peculiarly meaningful arch with the music of the great battle scene 'The Capture of Kazan' in the first part of the epic film.

The episode of the Kazan battle gave more than one occasion for drawing image parallels with the celebrated 'Battle on the Ice' in *Alexander Nevsky*. First, in both cases there is the idea of the honour of Russian arms, of the defence of the native land from foreign invaders, and of freeing Russian people who had been taken prisoner. Just as in *Alexander Nevsky*, the preparation for the battle, for the storming of the town of Kazan, was shown in slow motion, the action developed in a slowed-down tempo, and staged on an epic scale. Static frames, shot mainly in a long view, were commented upon by music, which sounded practically without interruption through the entire episode and was characterized by a programme representativeness and picturesqueness.

The scene of 'The Capture of Kazan' opens with a shot of the Russian forces approaching the town: along a dusty road the gunners are drawing a heavy cast-iron gun uphill. The fatigue of the warriors exhausted by the long march, and their superhuman efforts to cope with the cumbersome gun, are expressed in music by a heavy, slow-moving theme against the background of a hollow rumble of kettledrums — portents of war.

The episode with the gunners is followed by a lyrical 'arioso' — 'Ivan's Tent'. It is perhaps the only scene in the film where the director succeeded in showing with convincing sincerity the czar's feelings of compassion for the sufferings of common people; implying by this what a great responsibility a czar has to take upon himself, on behalf and for the sake of his people. Watching a long line of warriors who are dropping money into a common bowl before the fight, the czar reveals the meaning of this ritual in one sorrowful remark: 'As many coins will remain in the bowl after the fight as warriors will have fallen in the field of battle.' And as if an answer to his words, comes their musical counterpart, a superimposed capella chorus suffused with a piercing sadness, tragic and yet surprisingly radiant, the song 'Oh you, my bitter sorrow, the Tartar steppe'. Soviet musicologists were unanimous in calling it a pearl of patriotic people's song. Later, the theme of the chorus 'Bitter Sorrow', in which the musicologist V. Vasina-Grossman detected a connection with the peasants' chorus from the opera by Alexander Borodin *Prince Igor*[11], was without any modifications repeated by Prokofiev in his monumental opera *War and Peace* (Kutuzov's aria in scene 10).

As a contrast to the philosophically meditative music of 'Ivan's Tent' is a juicy genre sketch, a masterful translation of the dashing song 'The Gunners' into visual images. Its folk sources are old songs of war and songs of toil. From the former come the sweep and drive of rushing melodic movement based on energetic invocatory phrases: from the latter, the obstinate persistence of repeated rhythmic formulas and recurrence of short, lapidary tunes, which seem to reflect great bodily strain, and which often occur in the songs of Russian barge haulers.

As for the music to the scene of the storming of Kazan, Prokofiev put to use his experience acquired when working on *Alexander Nevsky* connected with the technique of 'cinematic montage'. The extensive fragment of 'The Attack', reminiscent of his early spirited, explosive and brutal scherzos, abounds in sharp rhythmic shifts and rushing, kaleidoscopic changes of thematic material, the logic of thematic appearance being fully determined by the unfolding screen events. The polyphonic interlacing of visual images and subject motives induced the composer to bring together in contrapuntal conflict the varied musical leitmotivs. True, such cases were not frequent: by contrast with the preceding film, where the conflicting forces were the Russian warriors and the crusaders, in *Ivan the Terrible* the enemies of the Russian host, the Tartars, were a minor element, having no developed musical characteristics. The Tartars' characters are schematic, barely outlined, in order to off set the daring boldness, the might, the valour, and the exhausting, burdensome daily military effort of the Russian fighters. Therefore in the 'musical action' of the scene 'The Capture of Kazan', the priority was given to Russian themes, whereas the Tartar theme, devoid of any dramatic significance, played a subsidiary role.

On the whole, this extensive war episode, the only one in the entire film epic, had a complex mosaic structure and contained a series of contrasting mini-parts, united by music into a peculiar instrumental and choral suite. The framework keeping the structure together was the song 'The Gunners', which made it possible to single out the lyrical and the dramatic culmination points of the scene, i.e. 'Ivan's Tent' and 'The Attack'.

Besides the battle episode, 'The Capture of Kazan', which raised some associations with 'The Battle by Kerzhenents' by Rimsky-Korsakov, there are in the first part of *Ivan the Terrible* some other scenes in whose structure some features of musical genre forms can be discerned. Thus, in the ritual magnificence of the scene where Ivan is crowned it is not difficult to detect the outlines of religious ritual. To make the scene more historically authentic, Prokofiev even introduces the canticle 'Many Years', framed by the merry, festive chiming of the bells of the Uspensky Cathedral.

The coronation is followed by a scene of a wedding feast, which also has many a prototype in the Russian classical opera and carries on the traditions of *Ivan Susanin* and *Ruslan and Ludmila* by Glinka, *The Mermaid* by Dargomyzhsky. *The Snow-Maiden* and *The Czar's Bride* by Rimsky-Korsakov. In accordance with conventional canons, in this scene there is an alternation of the ceremonial song of praise ('On a small hill little oak trees grow') and a lyrical round-dance song traditionally sung by girls ('A white swan is swimming'). However, apart from the scene of coronation, Prokofiev confined himself to stylization, and succeeded in reconstructing the oldest folk-song layers in their primordial purity and archaism.

Formally, the scene of the wedding feast was quite a self-contained concert or theatre item, which again illustrated the deep penetration of operatic aesthetic principles into the musical dramaturgy of *Ivan the Terrible*, as well as Prokofiev's continued quest for the symbiosis of music and representation, which he had tried to achieve in *Alexander Nevsky*. But if in that first film the narration was partitioned into close blocks, and the epic statuesque style of action sometimes turned the latter into a collection of 'tableaux vivants', whose 'subject' was dictated by music, in *Ivan the Terrible* the way chosen was somewhat different. Although the director said afterwards that 'in some places, the first part of *Ivan the Terrible* narrowly escapes slipping into a train of slowly flowing dreamy visions, moving past the spectator's perception, according to laws of their own, following their moods, almost for their own sake,' he concluded his self-critical confession by stating with a feeling of relief that 'fortunately, they are not so numerous; fortunately, the nerve of tension breaks through in the proper places. And, fortunately, the audience does not fall asleep'.[12]

In spite of such a severe self-appraisal, this work of Eisenstein's as compared with *Alexander Nevsky*, was a great step towards mastering new potentials of sound-visual cinema. Firstly, the rationalism and constructivism of thought which characterized the director's first film gave way to expressive emotionality, while the schematism and poster-like characteristics of the personages were replaced by a striving to penetrate into the mystery of the human soul, and to understand the secret motivations of human conduct. Secondly, while in *Alexander Nevsky* music and representation were to act in unison, in *Ivan the Terrible* their relationship became more complex. According to Eisenstein, in *Ivan the Terrible* he continued elaborating his theory of contrapuntal montage, the practical testing of which he had started in the *Battleship 'Potemkin'*, one of the greatest achievements of the world cinema before the arrival of sound film. He wrote, pointing to the continuity of the two films: 'Polyphonic writing, the principle of fugue and counterpoint, growing from the principles of composition of *Potemkin* . . . determine in the main the stylistics of *Ivan the Terrible*'[13].

Fugal structure is based on a subject. In the film the subject's function is performed by the central figure of the epic, czar Ivan the Terrible. The psychological complexity and contradictions of the czar's personality make his musical characterisation grow into a set of leitmotivs, which in different ways modify the pivotal conception of the film, the theme of the integrity of Muscovy. The key role among, these leading themes is played by the 'demiurge' theme, which combines the stateliness of the *bylina* (the Russian epic tale) and the elevated stern simplicity of the *znamenny* chant. The heavy, resolute stride of trumpets and French horns, set off by whirling passages of the strings, creates the impression of destructive might which is concealed in the depths, and is capable of quenching any resistance from the recalcitrant, 'for the sake of the great Russian land.' Besides, in the outline of the main leitmotiv of Ivan the Terrible, a close relation with Borodin's 'heroic' themes can be detected. This is corroborated by Prokofiev's choice of the key *B flat major*, which is typical of the epic imagery of his compositions (cf. the main theme in the first part of his Fifth Symphony, 'A song about Alexander Nevsky' in the film *Alexander Nevsky*, the finale of the Seventh sonata for the piano).

The use of the leitmotiv of Ivan the Terrible as a characteristic epigraph preceding the development of the action emphasizes its dramatic significance and its importance in revealing the conception of the film. At the same time, this musical theme, which is actually the idea or thesis given in the overture, is followed by the male chorus 'A Black Cloud', based on a harsh, prickly melody supported by short, dry chords of the woodwinds. The combination of recitative and march-like structures within one theme makes it possible to point up in relief the text of Vladimir Lugovskoy's poem, recited by the chorus:

> *A black cloud is rising,*
> *In scarlet blood the dawn is bathing.*
> *It is the evil treason of the boyars*
> *That's advancing to attack the czar's force.*

These words and their imagery give a generalized and concentrated expression to the central conflict of *Ivan the Terrible*, which took the form of a deadly fight between the czar and the boyars, and resulted in the building of an autocratic state 'on the bones of the enemies'. The reappearance of the

Ex. 11 The leitmotiv of Ivan the Terrible from the overture to the *Ivan the Terrible* Oratorio

Ex. 11 (continued)

Ex. 11 (continued)

Ex. 11 (continued)

Ex. 11 (continued)

leitmotiv of Ivan the Terrible in the final theme of the three-part overture foretells Ivan's victory, though there is not a hint as to how it was won, or what sacrifice was laid on its altar, in order to suppress civil strife and to bring together the scattered state of Russia. But it was exactly the 'mountains of dead bodies' on the path the czar had taken that probably struck the composer: and in the second part of the epic this motif gradually ceases to be an active element in the development of the subject, loses its human and spiritual potential, and turns into a dreadful force, punishing both the righteous and the guilty.

One of the episodes where the leitmotiv of Ivan the Terrible acquires a great emotional force is the final scene of the first part, entitled 'Alexandrovskaya Sloboda' (Alexandrovsky settlement). Submitting to the czar's will that all the people should entreat him to give up his self-seclusion and resume his power, thousands of common people make for Alexandrovskaya Sloboda. Strains of a great multitude chanting, 'Save Thy people, O Lord...' resound over the boundless expanse of snow. As if in answer to the humble prayer, a gigantic sharply outlined profile of the czar appears (in close up), inclined towards the featureless human mass streaming over the horizon line, and his leitmotiv takes over the entire sound track and drowns the doleful chanting. But instead of its former confidence and pride, menace, which warns the people of terrible disasters and sufferings. These themes will be developed in the second part of the film.

The leitmotiv of Ivan the Terrible sounds for the last time in the conclusion of 'The Boyars' Plot' (the second part), superimposed on the czar's announcement of his victory over the refractory boyars. However, after the cruel and cynical scene of the murder of Ivan's cousin, prince Vladimir Staritsky, this appearance may be perceived as having a purely formal function. It may be supposed that the director and the composer treated it as a link between the second and the third part, and wished to put it to use in focussing the narrative on the czar's military deeds and reforms, aimed at strengthening the State of Russia; but since the concept of the third part never materialized, this is no more than a supposition.

The other (second) leitmotiv of Ivan the Terrible is to some extent a contrasting supplement to the first one, serving as a lyrical variation: this melody reveals the czar's idealized notion of the future state he is striving to create. Based on a lucid, tranquil tune, it first emerges in the scene of the wedding feast and rises to a climax in the episode 'Ivan's Tent'. Its contemplative character and emotional restraint, its nobility in the expression of feeling favourably affect the leitmotiv, the theme of Ivan the Terrible, which, in contrapuntal combination with this lyrical theme of Ivan's dream, is 'softened', loses its aggressive drive and, in spite of its low key scoring, sounds balanced and reserved. Ivan's lyrical motive appears once more in the second part of the epic, in a scene which is extremely important for understanding the tragic moral metamorphosis of Ivan's personality: the scene of the czar's reminiscences of his childhood. At a moment of grave doubt and meditation, when the czar's soul is writhing with pain at the thought of the growing number of bloody victims at his feet, his memory unfolds a picture of the greedy and shameless partition of both sovereignty and Russian lands among the boyars in the presence of the small boy, the czarevich; of their unconcealed neglect and even betrayal of the country's interests for the sake of their own profit. The use of the polyphonic device of superimposing lyrical motive of Ivan the Terrible and frames from the first part ('Ivan's Childhood') help to convey the belief of the grown-up Ivan IV in the righteousness of his course of action which is inseparable from his patriotic idea of Russia's integration.

A lively, anxious, humane feeling pervades the theme which characterizes Ivan's wife Anastasia and also, in a sense, supplements the lyric side of the czar's image. The smooth, unhurried flow and the soft winding of its melody suggest an affinity with long-drawn out peasant songs which go back to the roots of Russian folk music. Following this line, Prokofiev introduces the oldest archaic intonations into the tragic scene of the poisoning and death of Anastasia. These intonations, dating back to pagan times, sound like funeral wailing and lamentation, and give the scene its ritual, ceremonial character.

As distinct from the screen image of Ivan the Terrible, a prey to doubt and moral suffering (a retribution of sorts for his acting on the Machiavellian principle 'the end justifies the means'), the czar's image created by the music possesses a wonderful integrity. There is nothing of duality in his nature, of moral torment and degradation of his personality bringing him to the verge of a bloody abyss. It can hardly be considered as a chance artistic error on the part of the composer and consequently as one of the drawbacks of the film. On the contrary, such a confrontation of the two images, apart from a direct, almost 'physical' contact — Ivan the Terrible interpreted only in a positive light, and Ivan the Terrible as Sergei Eisenstein saw him, full of contradictions, capable both of evil and of good deeds and finally falling victim to his own uncontrolled power — this confrontation permitted them to obtain a striking artistic effect. As a result, the viewer can see how a man who has violated the laws of God and, without giving a thought to his own doings, has repaid evil with evil, gradually estranges himself from the noble ideal of serving his people and his country to which he was going to devote his life.

The second part of the epic, under the descriptive subtitle 'The Boyars' Plot', was based on a complex counterpoint conveying the ever widening gap between ideal intentions and real deeds, as well as on emphasis of the dark and gloomy sides of the czar's personality. As R. Yurenev pointed out, it differed from the first part in showing that 'the image of Ivan the Terrible was not opposed to, but stylistically unified with, the image of Efrosinia and the boyars. The hero and his enemies employed the same methods of struggle such as spying, whispering, eavesdropping, poisoning, using the dagger or the noose'[14]. These sinister metamorphoses in the image of Ivan the Terrible also found expression in music, in the dramatic principles of the second part.

As compared to the first part, the musical drama of 'The Boyars' Plot' is distinguished by greater cohesion of its parts and a wider use of the through development principle, though some episodes of discrete structure can also be found. However, the shift of accent from a historical chronicle to a psychological drama characteristic of this part made Prokofiev think of new solutions and, in particular, apply the principle of symphonic development here throughout. Indeed, the embodiment in music of the dense atmosphere of hatred, suspicion, cruelty and ambitious claims which surrounded Ivan the Terrible required special musical means for the characterisation of the personalities who were the czar's enemies.

The czar's aunt, Efrosinia Staritskaya, is without doubt the most colourful and striking figure among the boyars. She attracts the attention of the audience and is remembered from her first appearance: her flowing black clothes, her hopping, 'crows's' gait. The expressiveness of these details is enhanced by the music: by the pointed 'crowing' sounds of the strings *sul ponticello* and piercing trills, which turn into light, meandering movements which sometimes subside into rustling.

According to Eisenstein, Prokofiev possessed an amazing gift of translating visual representation into music and perceiving the film image as a sound-visual complex[15]. In portraying Staritskaya's character, he created musical illustration which rose almost to the level of visual materialization of the individual features of her personality. Her boundless ambition, her frenzied wish to see her weak-minded son Vladimir on the throne, the crowned sovereign of Russia, drives her to crime, making her offer the fatal cup of poison to Anastasia, and instil in her son the idea of the necessity of killing Ivan the Terrible. While lulling him she in fact explains to him in detail how to do away with the lawful czar and seize the throne. Her lullaby 'A Song about a Beaver' is not an introduced musical item: it proves to be the last decisive stimulus, which starts a horrible mechanism of evil deeds and serves as a signal for the czar to deal with the upper circle of the boyar nobility, beginning with the annihilation of Efrosinia's family.

Every line of her lullaby, for all its innocent text, has a covert 'secondary' meaning which is decoded by the orchestra's music. Prokofiev followed Eisenstein's directions: he 'wanted the thoughts of a singing person to be expressed in music: in the orchestra first and then also in the voice'[16], and was sure that music must 'finish saying emotionally that which could not be expressed in words'[17]. Prokofiev wrote an extensive composition, something like a dramatic ballad, which carried the idea of hypnotic suggestion paralyzing man's will, and an element of predestination. Besides, 'A Song about a Beaver' resembles a folk-song. But gradually Efrosinia forgets about her son, who has fallen asleep, and becomes fully engrossed in her own fantasies and secret dreams; then an entirely different meaning begins to 'grow' into her song about the beaver, distorting and breaking up its melody, while her singing is now and then interrupted by ominous muttering.

The mother's tender lullaby gives way to words poisoned by hatred, which betray her plan of killing Ivan. His image drives her almost to madness. It is not surprising that at the phrase: 'After bathing the beaver walked up a mountain, up a high regal mountain', Ivan the Terrible appears in her imagination, and the theme of Ivan's coronation rises in the orchestra. The old woman is furious. 'He dried himself, and shook water off, he looked back and looked round': she no longer sings but hisses; and in answer to her, the motive of Ivan the Terrible in the orchestra resounds in all its beauty and grandeur, severe and powerful. The juxtaposition of Staritskaya's half-recitative and the czar's leitmotiv produces an ominous and eery impression, fills one with horror and a presentiment of evil.

Although the basic musical 'subject' is developed in the orchestral part, its echoes sometimes break through into the vocal part like great pools of emotion: Efrosinia, engrossed in her visions, interrupts her melodic singing in favour of a nervous rhythmic recitation. At the end of her song she seems to come to; she resumes the lullaby only to stop suddenly and shout ecstatically about a plot she has been hatching, to elevate 'czar Vladimir' to the throne. Vladimir, waking up and grasping the true meaning of his mother's words, is seized with fear and utters loud wail which together with a chain of dissonant chords and a male choral shout, breaks off the lullaby. But the fanatic Efrosinia, beside herself with passion, entreats her son to stand his ground.

The distinctive feature and the dramatic significance of this monologue is that, in spite of the seeming poverty of action and event in the 'Lullaby' scene, the composer's music produces an impression on never-ceasing, dynamic development, which is accompanied by a growing

Ex. 12 *A Song about a Beaver* (Efrosinia's Lullaby) from the film *Ivan the Terrible*

. . . In the river, the cold little river, in the Moskva-river, a beaver was bathing, a
black one was bathing.
He failed to wash himself clean, but got dirty all over. / After bathing the beaver walked
up a mountain, up a high regal mountain.

Ex. 12 (continued)

Ex. 12 (continued)

emotional tension, making the audience closely follow the text of the song and try to decode its symbolic meaning.

Such is the prologue to the tragedy, whose main events take place at the feast of the opritchniks.

The feast of the opritchniks is the climax of the whole film, where the tension and the heat of passion rise to their highest and lead to the bloody outcome of the central drama of *Ivan the Terrible*, entitled by Eisenstein '*Ivan the Terrible and the Boyars*'. To emphasize the special role which the scene plays in the context of the film, the director resolved to do something unprecedented in those days: he used colour in a black-and-white film, considering it the most effective means of expressing the very essence of the dramatic collisions unfolding on the screen. The result was a complex polyphonic composition based on a synthesis of music, colour, speech and choreography, with fragments of action inserted in it. The supporting structure of the opritchniks' feast scene are the song of Feodor Basmanov with the chorus, and the dance of the opritchniks. It is of interest that both are characterised by that resilient dynamism which was not infrequent in the works of the young Prokofiev, and also by rhythmic ostinato, and closely resemble the 'Scythian' images of his early period (in the Scythian Suite 'Ala and Lolliy').

In character, Feodor Basmanov's song differs little from a dashing, spirited folk song. In particular, its rollicking, 'robberish' refrain 'Goi da, goi da, speak, speak' and ecstatic yells, 'Oi, burn, burn, burn', make strong allusions to Toropka's song in *Askold's Grave*, an opera by Alexei Verstovsky, a Russian predecessor of Glinka. However, Feodor Basmanov's song is not as inoffensive as it might seem: just as Feodor, dressed in a woman's sarafan and with his face concealed behind a young girl's mask, can at any moment throw off his masquerade, so his song may lose its sham joyfulness and transform what has seemed like banter into cruel, humiliating mockery. The rough, almost primitive opening tune sounds at first unwilling, or 'lazy', though it does not quite disguise the opritchniks' scoffing at Vladimir who, half-drunk, dressed in the czar's robes, is sitting on the throne. At the same time, the persistent reiteration of the same archaic tune, without further development, offers a strong suggestion of dull, obtuse force, the czar's opritchnina, utterly devoted to Ivan the Terrible.

The fading phrases of the opening tune, taken up by the chorus, and the following glissando upward octave (a device frequently used in old long-drawn out peasant songs) were reinterpreted by Prokofiev so that, the effect was that of audacious challenge instead of the submissive humility expected by folklore tradition. In the refrain, irony is dispensed with altogether (like a bothering mask) and the melodic line is distorted by awkward leaps, unexpected harmonic and tonal alterations and chromaticism. The impression of a wild elemental revel is intensified by the orchestration, which is noisy, flashy, pierced by shrill woodwind glissando. A short theme appears now and then in the whirlpool and interlacing of musical strands: in its outline it is reminiscent of the celebrated *Dies irae* sequence, which emphasises the sinister atmosphere of the opritchniks' feast scene.

The passionate revelling continues in the opritchniks' dance. There, the visual element becomes subservient to the musical bacchanale which dictated its montage development (the sequence was filmed to the pre-recorded sound track). In undulating movements, linked by non-stop 'play' with remote tonalities and by the juxtaposition of different types of texture and dynamics, sarcastic chastooshka motifs are especially noticeable and seem to infect the visual images with their seething energy. Suddenly an assertive fanfare motif rises up for a moment in the midst of this musical thematic kaleidoscope, betraying the unseen presence of the organizer and 'director' of this eery farce, which represents the ceremony of Vladimir Staritsky's sham coronation. In the opritchniks' revelling dance, in the combination of red, gold and black colours, each of which have a certain symbolic meaning[18], all the successive stages of the drama can be traced, and the tragic issue is prepared.

Gradually the black cassocks of the opritchniks overshadow and dominate the gold of the czar's kaftans. Evil is triumphant and celebrates its victory. Only the tolling of the bell which calls people to matins breaks off the dreadful, mad orgy. The colour disappears, and the picture sinks back into black and grey shades. Thus the climax of 'The Boyars' Plot' — the scene of Vladimir Staritsky's murder — is prepared.

The sharp rhythmic transition from the wild dance to a sombre, sorrowful vocal prayer, with the, god-like voice of the trumpets (the scene in the Cathedral) makes one forget about the subject-matter for a time, and think of philosophical categories like good and evil, and understand how a criminal may acquire uncontrolled, superhuman power. Vladimir Staritsky's death, by the hand of the hireling who was to have killed Ivan the Terrible, comes down upon Efrosinia like a horrible, unbearable burden, when she perceives that the dead man lying on the tiled floor is not the one she expected to see. A terrible wail of anguish soars up and is lost in the vault of the cathedral. There is a moment of stillness, which is broken by the monotonous moaning of the mother who has lost her senses through grief. Placing her dead son's head in her lap, she sings her lullaby. Without its orchestral accompaniment, distorted so as to be almost unrecognizable, 'A Song about a Beaver' produces an awful impression of revealed evil, which can generate nothing but evil. Later, a similar device, borrowed originally from Rimsky-Korsakov (the scene of Marfa's madness in his opera *The Czar's Bridge*), was used again by Shostakovich in the scene of Ophelia's madness in Kozintsev's *Hamlet*.

On the whole, the music of *Ivan the Terrible* demonstrated the deeply national sources of Prokofiev's art (though he was more than once criticised, groundlessly, for their absence from his art). It also showed his connection with the traditions of the Russian classical school. *Ivan the Terrible* paved the way for his monumental operatic epic *War and Peace*, which incorporated much of the musical material of the film. Finally the immortal value and importance of the score of *Ivan the Terrible*, original and innovatory in its language, was that the music of that last great joint creative effort by Eisenstein and Prokofiev broke the established, stereotyped notions of the functional role of film music, enabling it to approach the nature of a sound-visual image based on a synthesis of a higher order. Thus, the music of *Ivan the Terrible* may be considered as an isolated and to a large extent experimental phenomenon in the history of world cinema, having no analogue as far as the artistic results achieved by its creators are concerned.

13

Music in the post-war cinema of the late forties and early fifties. The period of imposed compromise and conformism

The victory in the Great Patriotic War inspired many Soviet people with hopes for radical changes for the better in their lives, and the belief that the pressure of the totalitarian regime upon the individual would be eased. But those expectations were wiped away by a new and more horrible wave of repressions and arrests. An oppressive atmosphere of fear, of informing, enveloped the country, growing ever denser against a background of the patriotic struggle against subversion, executions, mass exile of those condemned without trial to concentration camps. The beginning of the 'cold' war and the enclosing of 'the first socialist state in history' within an 'iron curtain' required the consolidation of all possible forces which could foresee and suppress any resistance in society to the dictate of the reigning party oligarchy, headed by Stalin.

As usual, art was allotted one of the most important roles in the ideological training of the people in the spirit of the established dogmas of Leninism-Stalinism. No wonder that under such conditions, the Central Committee of the Communist Party needed a sure guarantee that the greatest workers of Soviet art should be loyal and uncompromisingly devoted to the political course maintained by the Soviet Union. Thus, soon after the war, the first victims of the regular 'purges' which were designed to expose elements alien to socialist ideology proved to be writers, theatre workers and film makers: see 'The Resolution of the Central Committee of the All-Union Communist Party (Bolsheviks), 14 August 1946, *On the Magazines "Zvezda" and "Leningrad"*'; 'The Resolution of the Central Committee of the All-Union Communist Party (Bolsheviks), 26 August 1946, *On the Repertoire of Drama Theaters and on the Means of its Improvement*'; and 'The Resolution of the Central Committee of the All-Union Communist Party (Bolsheviks), 4 September 1946, *On the Film "The Great Life"*'. A year and a half later came the turn of composers ('The Resolution of the Central Committee of the

All-Union Communist Party (Bolsheviks), 10 February 1948, *On the Opera "The Great Friendship" by V. Muradeli'*). The losses which the arts suffered were catastrophic, especially in literature and in the cinema. As for the latter, the publication and implementation of the main postulates and 'recommendations' of the party bosses led to a sharp restraint of creative processes and a rapid cut back in the film industry. As early as 1948, the Ministry of Cinematography stopped all work on 143 cinema scripts by special order, leaving only 60 in studio schedules. By 1951 the rapid cutting down of the film industry had reached a crucial point, where the number of motion pictures in as large a country as the USSR was limited to nine per year. Moreover, work on every film in all its stages (from the writing of the script to the montage and re-recording) was kept under the strictest control by higher powers instances supervising cinema art, and by 'comrade Stalin in person'. This led to many alterations, and changes which sometimes brought a picture to naught.

　　To defend themselves from groundless accusations of un-scrupulousness, professional incompetence, and political unreliability, but at the same time to secure their jobs, directors resorted to all kind of tricks and cunning: they filmed classical stage performances, shot biographical 'sagas' about great people, 'safe' from the standpoint of official critics. There were few orders for war films, and those which did materialize were made under pressure and directly depended upon personal ambitions, biased views on history and, finally, far-reaching plans of the upper reaches of the party and State powers. As for pictures on subjects from modern life, they were generally banished to the fringes of Soviet cinema. This, however, was natural after the severe criticism of the second part of the film *Great Life*[19], by the director Leonid Lukov, who had been accused of creating a false, distorted representation of the Soviet people[20]. Harsh words were said concerning the songs of the composer Nikita Bogoslovsky, written to poems by A. Fatianov and V. Agatov and, according to the authors of the 'Resolution', suffused with a 'pub melancholy' alien to Soviet people[21]. Only the 'rehabilitation' of the second part of *The Great Life* in 1958 made it possible for cinema-goers to hear one of the most sincere lyrics of Bogoslovsky, 'Three years I saw you in my dreams', which was an immediate hit, and remained popular for many years, together with the ingenuous and sincere romance 'The dark burial mounds are sleeping' from the first part of the film, released before the war.

14

Crisis in the genre of musical comedy film

The end of the second world war and the restoration of peace in the country not only inspired film makers in their quest for new themes and subjects, but also raised some hopes for the revival of a genre which had been a tremendous success in pre-war years: the musical comedy film, buoyant, full of life-giving optimism and good-natured humor. However, no efforts to resurrect it, in its old form, proved successful. The very first of them, the comedy by Alexandrov (director) and Dunayevsky (composer), *Spring* (1947), showed no potential for the development of this genre. Moreover, the failure of *Spring* was to a great extent the result of its authors' intention to revert to the scheme they had once tested in the film *Volga-Volga*. The copy appeared to be poorer than the original, and less successful artistically. As for its genre characteristics, it was a film-revue in which heterogeneous song episodes were 'tied up' with variable success in a simple narrative by means of short intermediate episodes. Unfortunately, Dunayevsky, who had kept in the background during the four years of the war, could not, even in his habitual genre of musical comedy film win back his lost reputation as the leading song composer of the country. True, his leitmotiv song 'Brooks are babbling' ('A Song of Spring') written for the film *Spring,* does not lack fascination, yet persistent reiteration makes it somewhat monotonous, in spite of the heroic efforts of the director, who had used all his inventiveness and imagination in the scene where a chorus of the 'men of science' are learning the song, under the direction of a young actress. At the same time, in *Spring* Dunayevsky made a great advance towards 'enlivening' the musical language of Soviet comedy film by using jazz intonations and rhythmic formulas from the Soviet variety stage: this gave an additional stimulus to the revival of the genre, and opened up new vistas in its development. However, *Spring* was the last picture made in cooperation by Grigori Alexandrov and Isaak Dunayevsky; they never collaborated again.

Another attempt at reviving the musical comedy film is associated with the name of Ivan Pyriev. It is of interest that both of his films, *A Siberian Story* (1948) and *The Kuban Cossacks* (1950), which gravitated toward the genre of film operetta, met with directly opposed responses from the critics.

Figure 4 *The Kuban Cossacks*

At different times they were praised as highly artistic, classical specimens of the Soviet comedy film, which ought to be imitated and held up as models; or they were declared to be carefully varnished, myth-creating pieces which led people away from reality, into a world of make-believe and sweet dreams. The severest contrasting judgements fell on *The Kuban Cossacks*, although it was of higher quality in its musical and professional skill than *Siberian Story*, in spite of the greater opportunity for compositional skill the latter offered.

The leading character of the film *Siberian Story* was a former conservatoire student, Andrei Balashov, who was possessed by the idea of writing an oratorio and dedicating it to Siberia and its people. The performance of this oratorio should have been the corner-stone, the apotheosis of the film. However, the sluggish, inexpressive music by N. Kriukov disappointed both the director and the audience. As a result, the finale of the picture was muffed. Besides, the overwhelming number of quotes from the works of Liszt, Rakhmaninov, Tchaikovsky, Skryabin in the score, as well as numerous Siberian folk melodies, made the musical dramaturgy eclectic and loose. The choice of the well-known song, 'In the wild steppes of Zabaikalye' as the central leitmotiv was rather surprising. This song had a definite semantic and historical meaning underlying it, which was neither elucidated nor supported. Its appearance in the film may probably be explained only as an attempt to create an image of Siberia by means of a Siberian song: a device both obvious and naive, dictated evidently by a low opinion of the perception of the unsophisticated and simple-hearted cinema-goer.

In *The Kuban Cossacks* the experienced Dunayevsky did not permit himself any such blunders, and created a sort of a holiday-film, a kind of a fair-ground merry-making[22]. There is everything here — sports competitions and dances, love and suffering, misunderstandings and quarrels which were happily made up at the end of the film. But, even at that time, the picture of a fabulous abundance of goods and foodstuffs on crowded shelves, of the joyful and merry life of collective farmers burdened only by love affairs, seemed unreal when compared with the post-war life of the ruined, suffering country; later the film was perceived as a cynical falsehood. The characters were all good people striving to become still better. This was to a great extent connected with the forced inculcation of 'scientifically grounded' artistic method into socialist art: afterwards this method was termed the non-conflict theory. Applying it to art, the ideological leaders of the socialist system wanted to emphasize the idea of the unquestionable advantages of the political order, and to do away with all doubts concerning the superiority of socialism over capitalism. Therefore the film *The Kuban Cossacks* did contribute to the introduction of that artificial non-conflict theory into the cinema.

The rich and colourful screening of *The Kuban Cossacks*, reminiscent of the paintings of Malyavin and Kustodiev, led Dunayevsky, always sensitive to visual and plastic film stylistics, to intensify the expressiveness of the screen action with rich, sparkling, cheerful music. However, he failed to create a true synthesis of music and representation, and to escape making the music merely illustrative. As a result, M.Hanisch, a German critic and an admirer of the composer, had sadly to admit that 'not as in the works of Alexandrov, here Dunayevsky's music is only an accompaniment to the action'[23]. This is really a pity, since in Pyriev's comedy film there is indeed plenty of excellent music. The soulful song, or romance, 'You have remained your former self', written in the style of peasant folklore, and the women's round-dance song, 'Oh, the guelder rose is blossoming', can serve as examples. They have stayed popular even today and are regarded as folk songs by many Russians.

The dominance of lyrical song in the musical dramaturgy of comedy films, unthought of in the pre-war cinema, was an immediate reflection of a gradual social re-orientation from the cheerful 'sports' marches of the thirties and the manly and austere hymns of the early forties toward the intimate lyric song of the fifties. At the same time it should be noted that, in the post-war period, Dunayevsky's music had lost much of its natural and spontaneous charm, becoming ever more pompous and ponderous. Youthful romanticism and sincerity in the expression of feeling had decayed into the artificial working up of emotions, which did not pass unnoticed. Tormented by the decline of his popularity with the wide audience, Dunayevsky once with striking precision pointed out the main cause of his fame ebbing away: "I am a singer of Soviet *success*"[24].

The Kuban Cossacks was not the final comedy film: it was followed by others which had much in common with it. But these imitations could not infuse a fresh spirit into the decrepit organism of the Soviet musical comedy film. Even the fascinating and graceful picture *The Carnival Night* (1956), the debut of Eldar Ryazanov as a film director, with the first screen appearance of the gifted actress Ludmila Gurchenko, could not save the situation. Nor was the composer Lepin able to cope with the conditional character and schematic plan of the script: he was caught in the sterile clichés of film-revue, where the plot was reduced to the level of an interlude which linked independent concert items. Earlier, a similar principle had been used in the film-revue *Merry Stars* (1954), directed by Stroyeva, with music written by Dunayevsky and Tsfasman. Later it was taken up again in the film-concert *Our Dear Doctor* (1958, directed by Karpov, composer Zatsepin), where the plot played a subsidiary role and moved, as it were, in fits and starts.

The lowering of professional requirements as to the quality of film scripts and, hence, of film direction finally led the musical comedy film up a blind alley. Besides, in those days it was faced by a strong rival and competitor, the lyric comedy, interspersed with songs, simpler in execution, more democratic and easier to understand (*The First Boxing-Glove*, 1947, directed by Frolov, music by Solovyov Sedoy; *True Friends*, 1954, directed by Kalatozov, music by Khrennikov). Its success for a long time ousted the 'pure' musical comedy film off the screen.

15

Music in the role of step-daughter.
Multiple music clichés in the genre of
biographical film

Musical films were, perhaps, the least numerous group in post-war film production. That period (1946–1952), known in the history of Soviet cinema by the sad term 'film-famine' ('malokartinye') was marked by an extraordinary flowering in the genre of biographical film. Suffice it to say that within a six-year period only about twenty pictures were released, dealing with outstanding scientists of the past, war generals, writers, travellers, musicians. The choice of historic persons to be 'immortalized' on the screen was arbitrary enough. It was difficult to see the reason for it, except for one rather obvious detail: the hero of the picture was to be identified with the nation and all the progressive people of his time, on the one hand, and to undergo all kinds of oppression and persecution, to be in active or passive opposition to the czar and his retinue, and to suffer injustice at the hands of those in power, on the other. Moreover, all their actions, as well as their numerous monologues, had to be absolutely sinless and prophetic and carry 'the light of truth'. Considered from the standpoint of the present, it can be seen how tendentious such an approach was, distorting historic truth in order to serve the ideological dogmas of Stalinist policy.

The dramatic scheme of the biographical film was elementary, presenting a collection of scenes and episodes illustrating the life of an outstanding scientist, or a general, an artist, a composer, etc., and the spectators were expected to gaze at him with great respect, as at a monument cut in granite. The obvious varnish and idealization of the personality, the diffuse, dim outlines of individual features, made the composers's work so difficult that sometimes their task was reduced to the writing of extensive musical fragments, or blocks, of *general dramatic content*, and the choice of some suitable folk material: the latter was used to embellish the action, and to show the unity between the hero and the people. The abundance of crowd scenes, in turn, stimulated the use of music as a means of commentary and illustration. This practically led to a revival of the technique of piano accompaniment, typical of the days of silent cinema, i. e. to a setting aside of the best traditions of Soviet film music.

This process was offset by the fact that by the early fifties a number of the best composers had come to work in the cinema. True, they were attracted by other than creative opportunities. To a certain extent, the collaboration of directors with Khachaturian, Shebalin, Popov and especially with Shostakovich, as well with Sviridov (1952), was accounted for by the need to collect a highly professional and distinguished group of film makers, and thus to prevent the unfounded attacks of the party and state officials who supervised the arts. But the main reason was the precarious situation in which all outstanding Soviet composers found themselves after the Resolution *On the opera by V. Muradeli "The Great Friendship"* (1948). The 'proper conclusions' made by the Union of Composers of the USSR, which followed the Resolution, resulted in the banning of performances of the works of Shostakovich, Prokofiev, Khachaturian, Shebalin, Popov, and Myaskovsky, and in the deliberate isolation of these composers from musical and cultural life, from their audiences in all spheres, *except cinema*.

Between 1947–1953, for example, Shostakovich wrote music for seven films, Shebalin for five, Khachaturian for four. Of course, the artistic value both of the films and of their music was different: they had lost much of their merit and significance, but it was not this that really mattered. What did matter was the fact that enlisting the services of composers of such a high rank (whatever their personal views of the condition and the role of Soviet cinema might be) saved Soviet film music from sinking to the level of mechanical hack work, and supported its status as an integral and sovereign component of the screen synthesis.

The numerous appeals of Zhdanov (appointed by the party oligarchy to supervise the arts), calling upon composers to pay attention to programme music and to 'democratic', as distinct from 'abstract' symphonic, genres associated with verbal material (i. e. oratorial, choral, vocal and song music), found a peculiar reflection in a number of historico-biographical films. Such was, in particular, *Michurin* (1949), directed by Dovzhenko, with music by Shostakovich. The characteristic thematic development of the film was originally given out by the composer in a condensed form in the overture: he broke up this condensation gradually in the further development of the leitmotivs.

A specific feature of *Michurin*, which directly influenced the principles of the structure of its musical dramaturgy, was the oratorial character, the epic measured rhythm of the narrative. It is significant that, impressed as he was by the idea of the film, world-wide as it seemed in those days (the theme of the reformation of nature), the composer tried to re-create it, this time in a great autonomous work, the oratorio 'Song of the Forests' (not at all one of his best works), including in it some extensive fragments from the music of *Michurin*.

One of this score's peculiar characteristics, hardly typical of his film music, was the quotation of a great number of authentic folk songs. Though functioning somewhat differently from the original music, these quotes were nevertheless harmoniously integrated into its intonational and imaginative structure. Later Shostakovich put to use this device (or rather a variant of it) in a tendentious historico-revolutionary film by Mikhail Chiaureli *The Unforgettable Year 1919* (1952) and then in a number of large symphonic compositions, including The Eleventh Symphony, *The Year 1905*.

As for *Michurin*, Shostakovich's singling-out of a folklore layer in the music score was probably prompted by his wish to escape repeating the 'mistakes' made by Gavriil Popov, the composer who had started working on *Michurin* before him, but who had been dismissed[25]. Besides, trying to prevent any possibility of being accused of formalism, Shostakovich resorted to a simplified style of musical composition — for which he was praised by Tikhon Khrennikov, the General Secretary of the Union of Soviet Composers. Khrennikov pointed out with satisfaction the simplicity, the expressiveness and the democratic spirit of Shostakovich's music in *Michurin* as compared to his other film scores (from the *Mountains of Gold* to *Pirogov*). It is worth mentioning that Khrennikov had no doubt as to the close connection between the composer's turning back to popular genres and the published Resolution of the Central Committee of the Communist Party of the Soviet Union on the opera by Muradeli *The Great Friendship*[26]. Shostakovich gave in to powerful pressure from the state and communist policy, just as he had been forced to do earlier, in 1936, when *Pravda* printed its notorious anonymous editorial *Chaos instead of Music*[27], severely criticising him, while his opera *Lady Macbeth of the Mtsensk District* was declared unpatriotic and formalistic. Now, in 1947, he was again compelled to reform in the required manner, that is, to begin writing *'music which could be understood by the masses'*. It was not only the party leaders who liked such music. Prompted by his interest in the music of *Michurin*, Kozintsev later asked Shostakovich to compose a choral suite to popular texts and the poems of Nekrasov for his film *Belinsky* (1953). Shostakovich tried to fulfil the commission. As a result, the film contained a number of choruses 'in Mussorgsky style'. However, the 'copy' appeared poorer than the original, though it was a stimulus to composing *Ten Choral Poems*.

A rare exception in this sequence of dull, highflown and ostentatious pictures was the film by the Ukrainian director Igor Savchenko, *Taras Shevchenko* (1951). The image of a folk poet, the portrayal of the moral strength and beauty of a man capable of resisting violence and arbitrary power — these were the attractive qualities of the film. They required that the composer, Boris Lyatoshinsky, should go further than the use of the method of musical illustration and quotation which was widely used in historico-biographical films. There was a peculiar plasticity of visual imagery in the landscape episodes, in order to reveal adequately by music the folk sources of the talented poet's work. Unfortunately, the fragmentary dramatic conception of Savchenko's film led him to divide the narrative into three self contained autonomous parts. In turn, the composer decided to write music only for several landscape scenes (e. g. 'The Steppe', 'The Sea') and to work up some songs for chorus and instruments to Shevchenko's poems, which were considered to be Ukrainian folk songs. Such a limiting of the sphere of action turned the music into a passive commentary on this or that scene. Moreover, being strictly tied to representation, it lost its emotional potential and turned into a tedious background accompaniment. The absence of leitmotivs and characterisation of the leading personalities[28], the mosaic character of the material, and the amorphous musical dramaturgy of *Taras Shevchenko* resulted in irreparable failings in the film, aggravated by the director's errors.

A peculiar group among historico-biographical pictures was represented by films about composers: two of them were devoted to Mikhail Glinka (*Glinka*, 1947, directed by Arnshtam, musical composition by Shebalin; *Composer Glinka*, 1952, directed by Alexandrov, music by Shcherbachev and Shebalin)[29]. There were also films about Mussorgsky (1950, directed by Roshal, music by Kabalevsky)[30], as well as about Rimsky-Korsakov (1953, directed by Roshal' and Kazansky, music by Sviridov). However, it is difficult to speak of their artistic merits or even of their significance as means of enlightenment. Many factual and biographical errors, deliberate misrepresentation, and persistent attempts to associate the creative works of a given composer with events of his personal life affected the value of these films. In addition, their interpretation of well-known works of Russian classical music was often too arbitrary, and the material quoted by the creators of the films sometimes disagreed with the authentic material. Nevertheless it would be unjust to disregard completely the contribution of the musical biographical film to the history of Soviet cinema and Soviet film music. It was this particular genre which excited film makers's and cinema-goers' interest in such specific areas of cinematic art as the film-opera and the film-ballet.

16

Russian classical opera and ballet in the cinema of the '50s: new attempts at relationships

In 1953, in the Lenfilm Studio, director Sidelev completed the film-opera *Aleko* to music by Rakhmaninov, and soon after that Lapoknysh in the Kiev studio released his screen version of the opera by Gulak-Artemovsky *The Zaporozhets beyond the Danube*. Another screen adaptation was the film-opera *Boris Godunov* after Mussorgsky (1955, directed by V. Stroyeva). Parallel to the film-opera, screen versions of ballets already staged were created, *Swan Lake* by Tchaikovsky (1958, directed by Tulubayeva) and *Romeo and Juliet* by Prokofiev (1955, directed by Arnshtam and Lavrovsky). As mentioned above, their appearance was connected with the interest excited by films about composers. Particularly impressive had been the celebrated scene 'By Kromy', excellently directed and brilliantly screened by Roshal' in his film *Mussorgsky*. The thoroughly worked action of the groups playing the participants in the spontaneous popular revolt, and a dynamic montage rhythm of visual representation made up for the seemingly static character of the scene. This opened up promising vistas for the creation of good and original films, if the artistic principles offered were developed. However, in her variant of *Boris Godunov*, Vera Stroyeva did not carry on Roshal's experiment but preferred to film the performance by the Bolshoi Theatre. As for the screen version of *Swan Lake*, the director Z. Tulubayeva's 'innovation' did not go farther than introducing an off-screen announcer's text, without cinematic interpretation of the stage performance.

Roman Tikhomirov was the only one who attempted to get free from the stage clichés which restricted the director's imagination. In filming Tchaikovsky's *Eugene Onegin* (1958) he ventured to combine the opera and Pushkin's 'novel in verse' and to introduce fragments of poetic text as links between episodes separated in time. Besides, there was a wide use of expressive cinematic devices such as location and pavilion shots, a detailed reconstruction of period objects, close-ups which made it possible to imprint the finest nuances of thought and emotion, and to reveal covert longing. At the same time, faced with the insoluble problem of economy and the

necessity to 'place' the opera within the short length of a film, Tikhomirov
had to make numerous music cuts, which damaged the live organism of the
opera. Added to this was his failure to cope with a schoolboyish, rather
tendentious approach to the subject matter of *Eugene Onegin*, in which he
saw only the drama of Tatiana Larina and Vladimir Lensky, whose dispo-
sition was similar to hers, for both of them suffered from loneliness and the
futility of their existence. Opposed to Tatiana and Lensky, with their impetuous, romantic natures, were Onegin, a cool and haughty dandy from
the metropolis, and the provincial gentry, vain and shallow, wallowing in
squabbles and gossip. The emphasis on the ideological, class subtext in the
film *Eugene Onegin* had a negative effect on its artistic qualities and
shortened its screen life. Thus, in spite of an enthusiastic response from the
critics, Tikhomirov's film was soon forgotten.

17

The ideological function of music in the war film

The wounds inflicted by the war made artists again and again revert to the events of the recent past. However, the time-lapse was probably too short; and so hypnotic was the worship of Stalin, and so loud the praise of his role in the victory, that none of the war films of those days could escape being biased and pseudohistorical in representing the events of the Great Patriotic War. Neither should one ignore the pressure from party critics which mercilessly banned anything that interfered with the loud toasts in honour of 'the great leader of nations'. But especially depressing was the fact that, in the representation of gigantic battles, attacks, and operations which filled the motion pictures of the forties and early fifties, the authentic man was lost, the soldier, whose courage, heroism, fanatical persistence, and patriotism had actually won the war. Instead, there were caricatures, divided up into 'ours' and 'not ours', moving on the screen.

Three films were distinguished for their abundance of developed battle scenes, the shooting of which had required much technology, crowds of people and even some army units. Soviet cinema specialists referred to them conventionally as documentary-genre features. These were *The Third Blow*, directed by Savchenko (1948, music from the works of Tchaikovsky), *The Battle of Stalingrad* directed by V. Petrov (1949, 2 parts, music by Khachaturian), and *The Fall of Berlin*, directed by Chiaureli (1950, 2 parts, music by Shostakovich). In the first of these the director did not find it necessary to employ a composer: resounding with the thunder of battles and the rumble of shelling, the film did not, in fact, need any music. But keeping up the tradition, Savchenko literally drowned the picture in Tchaikovsky's music. Anachronism, and in places even the absurdity of combining fragments from the well-known symphonies and ballets using the compilation technique typical of silent cinema, betrayed the tendentiousness and the mechanical direction of the film, its simple and schematic ideological undercurrent.

The other two films were no better. The noisiness of the sound-track, the thunderous, superfluous density of the enlarged orchestra which some-

Ex. 13 The theme of Glorification from the film *The Fall of Berlin*

Glory to Stalin! Soviet banners / and our Leninist party be praised!
We are marching to / ... /

Ex. 13 (continued)

times accompanied the rumble of the artillery cannonade, the shouts of the soldiers rising to attack, etc., provoked emotional and auditory fatigue and irritated the audience, who associated the noise with the music. In *The Battle of Stalingrad*, Khachaturian gave free rein to his Oriental temperament, and embellished the episode of the Soviet advance at Stalingrad with whimsical Armenian rhythms and melodies. But the leitmotiv of the film was the widely known Russian folk song 'There is a cliff on the Volga bank'. Appearing at the climax of the symphonic development, it served as a symbol of the indestructible and unconquerable spirit of the Russian people. But it was not felt to be an integral part of the action, and therefore did not sound very convincing.

Still more distressing was *The Fall of Berlin*, a grandiose film epic, the climax of the Stalin cult in the cinema. True, it should be admitted that the music of this monster film contained quite a few items of high value. However, the chilly, majestic tone of the narrative, the endless attempts at monumentality, the pompous manner of representing events from the peaceful pre-war days to the victorious spring of 1945, — all these were reflected in the music as a whole.

The musical scheme of *The Fall of Berlin* was based on the gradual emergence of a central leitmotiv, a theme of glorification, and its further spatial development. It appeared first in the overture. Then some of its melodic phrases penetrated the idyllic children's song 'A fine day' which opened the first part of the epic. But soon it became obvious that the possibilities for development of the glorification theme were limited. In spite of some elements of folk-tale and of solemn panegyric chant, it sounded stiff and monotonous. This was partly due to the obtrusive emphasis placed on conjunct motion in the major-minor mode (*B flat major — G minor*), the repetition of rhythmic and melodic formulas, very simple harmony, but above all, to the tediously prolonged exclamatory choral greetings in honour of Stalin.

These characteristics of the leitmotiv became particularly clear in the apotheosis of the finale where, besides a crowd of many thousands of people, there was a large mixed chorus and two symphony orchestras.

Among the badly arranged and directed scenes in *The Fall of Berlin*, perhaps only one episode, that of the storming of Zielona Gora, stands out as being natural and emotionally expressive in its visual, plastic, and musical solutions. For it, Shostakovich wrote an extended symphonic fragment. It was based on the montage device of linking a number of discrete sections by repeated rhythmic *ostinati* and short, energetic, aggressive motifs which gave the impression of constant dynamic growth. At the same time, the composer's quotation from his own Seventh ('Leningrad') symphony seemed inadequate. It had become both in Russian and world music a generalized symbolic image both of fascist aggression and the tragedy of the second world war. Thus, when correlated with the particular content of the scene, the theme of the invasion-march from the first part of the symphony unduly elevated and hypertrophied the episode of the war's beginning, which did not call for deep philosophic interpretation. This irrelevance distorted the dramatic structure of the film as a whole. It is certainly not difficult to see the reason for the quotation's appearance: like many other things in this picture, it was placed there to imprint the idea of the greatness of Stalin, who had liberated Europe from the brown Nazi plague at the cost of millions of devoted Soviet lives. Thus, even Shostakovich's genius had to serve ideology, and was made to contribute to the unification of mass consciousness, in the spirit of the main postulates of socialist realist doctrine.

Among other compositions written by Shostakovich for the cinema in the late forties and early fifties, his music for the film *The Young Guard* by Gerasimov (1948) is of interest. If in the picture *Meeting on the Elbe Banks* (1949, directed by Alexandrov) the composer reverted to the song type of musical dramaturgy and to Soviet folk music, focusing upon the key number 'A Song of Peace' ('The wind of peace is swaying the banners of victory')[31], in *The Young Guard* he was still true to the symphonism congenial to him.

The film score of *The Young Guard* contains several easily-discovered associations with the Seventh Symphony, although there are no exact quotations like the one in *The Fall of Berlin*. But the central leitmotiv, the theme of resistance, is reminiscent of the beautiful theme of Motherland. Moreover, the theme of resistance is presented in two hypostases: as a heroic call-theme (in the overture) and as a flowing lyric song (in the episode 'By the River'). The unity and the struggle of opposites, initially given out by the leitmotiv, when combined with scenes of different meaning and content, both intensify the state of inner tension and prepare the film's climax. This is the scene of the Young Guards' death, a sort of 'progress to execution' by quite young boys and girls, where the theme of resistance sounds like a requiem, mourning for them, and imprinting in the hearts of the living the heroism of those who ventured to rise against the occupation. The capacity of the leitmotiv to allow various intonational and imaginative transformations contributed to the integrity of the film's conception, and to the highly, emotional expressiveness of the film as a whole, which gripped the audience with its spirit of heroism.

18

A wind of change:
film music of the post-Stalinist period

The critical condition of the Soviet cinema which, thanks to the 'paternal care' of the dictator, had concentrated almost entirely on filming stage performances, made the 19th Party Congress, even in Stalin's life-time, pass a resolution requiring a sharp increase in film production. The pressure of censorship was also somewhat slackened: film directors were now, to some extent, at liberty to choose their themes and subjects. The genre range widened, and the names of new, gifted young composers appeared more frequently on the film captions. They were Shchedrin, Molchanov, Vainberg, Karavaichuk, Shamo, Oganesyan, Simonyan, Zatsepin, Pakhmutova, amongst others. Their arrival in the cinema brought about important changes, which affected the expressive means and the very language of film music. It was now less dependent on opera, oratorio, and symphonic genres; the manner of expression and the style of composition became more individualized and free, enriched by all the questing diversity and striving characteristic of the development of contemporary music in the second half of the 20th century.

In the Soviet republics, national film industries were gradually gaining confidence and experience. But in spite of the obvious 'warm spell' in the political, social and spiritual climate of the country, and the beginning of Soviet cinematic revival, the time for change in film music was yet to come. True, certain principal differences in the functional treatment and in the typical musical devices of the pictures released by film schools in the republics were already clearly marked. Most of the studios preferred introducing folklore material in its original shape, with careful preservation and reconstruction of the forms of folk music styles. Thus, the rich national culture of the Moldavian people, the uniqueness and originality of ceremonial rites, and fiery temperamental dance melodies, created a vivid musical background to the action in one of the early feature films of the 'Moldova-Film' studio, *Lyana* (1955, directed by Barnet, music by Aranov). This carried on the traditions of the musical comedy films of Pyriev — Dunayevsky. Of interest also was the Kazakh film *His Time Will Come* (1958, directed by

Begalin, music by Brusilovsky), built on symphonic development of Kazakh folk songs. It brought to an end the genre of the historic-revolutionary biographical film, on the Stalinist model. In Georgia and Armenia, film music was feeling its way, searching for an organic synthesis of authentic music and the ancient melos of the people.

If the national schools of Soviet film music in most republics of the USSR took their cue from the school of Russian film music, the film music of the Baltic countries found its orientation-point in the experience of the pre-war and wartime Western European cinema. As a result, the song type of dramaturgy was hardly ever used in the films released by Latvian, Lithuanian and Estonian studios. Symphonism prevailed there.

Most frequently the symphonic type was used in films where the music was written by Dvarionas. His cinema debut took place in 1947 in the picture *Marité*, directed by Stroyeva. It was the first film shot entirely by Lithuanian actors, camera man, composer, etc. It was a story of the heroic deed of a Lithuanian partisan girl, Maria Melnikaite. Dvarionas' music spoke a melodious and lucid language; its close relation to the roots of folk song; its tendency towards a romantic rhapsodic style which never grew into sham pathos; its rich orchestration: all of these attracted directors' attention, and Dvarionas soon became one of the most popular film musicians in Lithuania. But his most significant works in the cinema were created in the fifties. Among them was the music for *The Sunrise over the Neman* (1953, directed by Feinzimmer) and *Before It Is Too Late* (1958, directed by Fogelman and Žalakiavičius). A contribution to the development of the Lithuanian film industry was also made by Edwardas Balsys (*The Bridge*, 1957, directed by B. Shreiber).

At the same time, a feasible role in the formation of Estonian national cinema was played by the composers Eugen Kapp (*Life in a Citadel*, 1948, directed by Rappaport; *Light in Koordi*, 1951, and *Andrus's Luck*, 1955, also directed by Rappaport); Gustav Ernesax (*The Yachts Sail Out to Sea*, directed by Egorov); Boris Körver (*In the Days of June*, 1958, directed by Nevezhin and K. Kijsk). In the Riga film studio, the most outstanding composer was Skulte (*Rainis*, 1949, directed by Raizman; *Rita*, 1958, directed by Neretniek). A characteristic feature of his creative method was his striving for the symphonization of the score by the establishment of an intonational affinity between various leitmotivs. At the same time, Skulte often enriched his own music with quotations from folklore, or from the works of other composers. Thus in *Rainis*, devoted to the well-known Latvian poet and revolutionary J. Rainis, there was an authentic Latvian song 'Who sang it here', which described the hard labour and bitter lot of the serf. The melody of a folk dance served as the basis for one of the most vivid scenes in the film, that of a village holiday: the rich national colouring of the dance was emphasized not only by the accentuation of diatonic phrases and the precise trochaic metres typical of Latvian music, but also by instrumentation (a clarinet solo set against a background of a two-part drone accompaniment in violins). The appearance in the film of the popular song 'How loudly our Daugava is moaning', by Karl Baumanys[32], became symbolic, for in Latvia it was associated with the patriotic idea of liberating the country, and was perceived as a call for the solidarity of the Latvian people in their struggle for independence. However, this device was far from new to cinema-goers, having often been used in the historic-revolutionary films of the '30s.

19

Music in screen versions of works from world literature

Although some interesting things were achieved in the post-war period in all parts of the country, none of these films were important in the history of Soviet film music between 1940–1950. Only three films proved able to rise above the general level and attract public attention to the artistic merits of their music. It is worth mentioning that all of them belonged to a genre which had been affected less than others by the persecution of Stalinist criticism. These films were: *The Gadfly*, a screen version of the novel by Voynich, directed by Feinzimmer, with music by Shostakovich (1955), *Othello* after Shakespeare's tragedy, directed by Yutkevich, music by Khachaturian (1956), and *Don Quixote* after the novel by Cervantes, directed by Kozintsev, music by Karayev (1957). It may seem almost fantastic that these three musical interpretations of well-known literary subjects had features in common, while differing in other ways. There was a certain musical affinity, permitting the three films to stand side by side: a romantic pathos in sound a theatrical vividness, a 'visual quality' in the leading themes-the leitmotivs, an inclination to use an episode structure of a wide employment of musical stylization for the recreation of the correct atmosphere of the epoch recon-structed in the film and, finally, a concrete characterisation of the leading personages in the manner of the given genre. At the same time, the music of each film bore the unique stamp of the individual character of its creator. As for the differences, they depended on varying degrees of complexity in the structure of the musical dramaturgy, correlated with each director's conception of the film.

The Gadfly was perhaps the simplest and most traditional of the three pictures, both in form and directional practice. This was probably why Shostakovich's music for the film surprises and fills with admiration even today's audience: it still seems so communicative, easy to understand, open and fervent in the expression of feeling, reaching from heart to heart. Its stylistic roots lie in the beautiful and immortal melodies of Bellini and in the Italian compositions of the young Glinka: this can be proved by the cele-brated *Romance* by Shostakovich which has for many decades held sway at recitals, and holds a high rank among the most popular classical hits, alongside with 'The Dance of the Cygnets' by Tchaikovsky and 'The Turkish March' by Mozart.

Ex. 14 *Youth.* Romance from the film *The Gadfly*

Ex. 14 (continued)

The musical dramaturgy of *Othello* differs from that of *The Gadfly* in its greater complexity and wider scope of intention. Here, development is built on the intertwining of musical and visual leitmotivs (i.e., the theme of the ship, the theme of Desdemona's handkerchief, etc.). However, this does not in any way contradict the existence of spectacular, theatrical scenes such as that of the popular holiday set to the music of the fiery 'Tarantella' by Khachaturian.

The music score of *Othello* contains a number of quotations. One of them, the celebrated medieval sequence *Dies irae*, has been inserted (somewhat too obviously) into the scene of the murder of Desdemona. Two others-one from *Et incarnatus* from the mass *Pange lingua* by Josquin des Pres and a fragment from a canzonet by Caccini from the collection *Nuove Musiche*, form a meaningful arch, which combines the scene of Othello's and Desdemona's wedding (the prologue of the film) and the episode where Othello, mad with grief, carries the dead Desdemona in his arms.

On the whole, the use of the folk genre and the quotation of given material permitted the composer to put into relief the key idea of the film, i.e. the tragedy of man's faith, but to some extent obscured the central conflict of Shakespeare's drama, that between Othello and Iago. The latter has no musical characterisation. Khachaturian's attention is focused on the leading personage, Othello. His image is revealed in three aspects; as man, as lover, as general. These are reflected in his leitmotivs, which are already revealed in the prologue. Further, they take an active part in the drama, irrevocably driving towards the tragic end. Critics have more than once pointed out involuntary allusions the ballet *Spartakus*, the staging of which was almost concurrent with the work on *Othello*. Of course, there may be a certain affinity between the ballet and the film, but there are no coincidences or borrowings, since each of them was quite independent and original, both in conception and in artistic realization.

Compared to the mosaic musical dramaturgy of *The Gadfly* and *Othello*, which combined separate fragments, or parts, in an integrated whole with the help of a ramified system of leitmotivs, the musical dramaturgy of *Don Quixote* was based on the monothematic principle. All the musical thematic material of the film revolved around the main leitmotiv of Don Quixote's wanderings. It assumed various aspects, and underwent unexpected imaginative metamorphoses. These transformations in the leitmotiv of the 'Knight of the Rueful Countenance' took place against a background of short folk-genre scenes marked by sharp and picturesque orchestration, fiery passion, and majestic, austere melodies of a pointedly national character. It should be emphasized that Kara Karayev, with a boldness rather unusual in a beginner, chose the unusual device of stylistic mimicry to represent Spanish everyday musical life and, without resorting to quotation, offered his own notion of the uniqueness and the folkloric roots of Spanish-Mauritanian culture. His method proved successful, saved the film from boring clichés, and made it more impressive and emotionally expressive.

In any summing up of this review of film-music development during the 1940–1950s, it should be stated that this sphere of musical creation remained on the periphery of composers's interests. There were a number of reasons for this, all connected with the hardships of the war and post-war times, as well as with 'ideological considerations' imposed by the leaders of the party oligarchy which had brought Soviet art to into long-drawn out crisis. Not only did film music fail to make progress toward a deeper understanding of the basic principles and nature of cinema: it even lost some of the important things it had achieved during the pre-war period. Experiments with sound-recording equipment were largely stopped, as were the search for non-traditional devices for the synchronic and asynchronic synthesis of music and representation, and the modelling of sound-visual counterpoints on different levels. The brilliant results obtained by Eisenstein and Prokofiev in their sound films had been forgotten by their contemporaries, and remained in oblivion for years. Narrowness and monotony in subject matter, illustrative and tendentious treatment of themes and images, ostentation and unconcealed varnish in representing daily reality, -all of these became typical features of many films of the period; they paralyzed and emasculated the imagination both of film directors and composers. This process resulted in an excessive use of musical cliché (the heroic leitmotiv, the lyrical theme, the song, 'dramatic music', etc.), and in making music a neutral, tiresome symphonic background. This affected the artistic value of film music and its stature in the world of professional musicians; composers lost interest in writing for the cinema. A neglectful attitude towards such work was growing, as if it were 'hack-work' which did not require any particular talent, or high professional mastery, or any great effort. The shaking and destruction of such a stereotype proved to be more difficult than its creation, as became clear later. This was achieved only in the next decade.

Part 3

1959–1969

20

Change of fortune.
New means of expression in the
language of film music.
Evolution from sound-musical illustration
towards the creation of an integral
film sound-world

The appearance of a new leader in the Soviet Union, who was the first to dare to condemn publicly the personality cult of Stalin, and who somewhat softened the rigid pressure of the state censorship on art (at least at the beginning of his rule), evoked hope in the progressive part of society for democratic reform. It was during that period which later was poetically and tenderly referred to as 'Khruschev's thaw', that a peculiar burst of intellectual and creative activity took place. It was accompanied by the powerful spiritual and moral liberation of the artistic intelligentsia from the dead dogmas of the Stalin–Zhdanov cultural ideology.

The 'thaw' period proved short-lived. But even during those few years Soviet art experienced a tremendous breakthrough, being able to extend the genre range of themes and subjects, and to renovate the language and enrich the world with a veritable constellation of talented artists. This creative impetus was so strong that even the close and gloomy atmosphere of the Brezhnev stagnation period which replaced 'the thaw', could not suppress the flight of ideas and fantasy in the best representatives of 'the men of the sixties'. Some of them had to leave their country, branded as dissidents. Others however had the courage to share the burden of the communist regime with their public: the names of the writers Vasily Aksenov, Viktor Nekrasov, Veniamin Erofeyev, Alexander Solzhenitsyn, the poets and singers Bulat Okudjava and Vladimir Vysotsky, the sculptor Ernest Neizvestny, the artists Elian Belov and Vladimir Sholtz, the composers Alfred Schnittke, Sofia Gubaidulina, Edison Denisov all entered the annals of national culture.

Considerable progress was made by the Soviet cinema. Its activity was encouraged by a special resolution of the Council of Ministers of the

USSR in July 1959 'On the measures to be taken for further development of the film industry and the introduction of new technical equipment in the cinema'. The reason for its appearance was the extremely low technical level of most of the twenty film studios working in the country. Their equipment was out-of-date, sometimes thirty years old. This directive of the Council of Ministers gave impetus the beginning of a cardinal reformation in the system of film production. New buildings were quickly erected for the film studios, such as 'Uzbekfilm' in Tashkent (1959), 'Belarusfilm' in Minsk (1961) and 'Azerbaijanfilm' in Baku (1965), while all the other studios underwent reconstruction. This made it possible to increase film production. This in turn demanded an inflow of young talent. There were several brilliant debuts of new directors and actors, and a lot of original and innovative films.

The liberation of directors' creative imagination, the departure from the traditional canons of film plot, the destruction of the Stalinist film clichés, the new striving for imaginative self-expression and the resulting search for new means and techniques capable of adequately demonstrating the director's idea on the screen, all caused a considerable intensification of the director's personality in the film.

To quote the prophetic words of Sergei Eisenstein, the whole history of cinema could be divided into three periods: the silent, the sound and the sound-visual one. Without doubt *auteur's* cinema tended towards the latter. Thus, in the sixties *auteur's* cinema made a decisive move towards mastering the sound-visual nature of the screen image and reconsidering all previous systems of relation between the components of the cinematic synthesis, including music. In practice, this meant giving up the tradition of saturating the film background with loud symphonic music (the use of the orchestra in a picture was even considered an anachronism). In general, the use of music was limited, and it was often replaced by different sound effects with a forced level of emotional expression. Films appeared the directors of which deliberately dispensed with music. In this way they tried to get rid of boring clichés and to attract spectators' attention.

Such were two films noted for their outstanding artistic merits: Romm's film *Nine Days of One Year* (1961) and Alexander Stolper's picture *The Living and the Dead* (1963, 2 parts) which fully realized the idea of a film without music which had been thought of since the thirties. The former was devoted to problems of the time and told of young physicists, whereas the latter turned back to the tragic early days of the Great Patriotic War. In spite of the stylistic differences of their directors, they had a lot in common. Both shared a tendency towards documentary and towards being true to life in depicting events and characters. Accentuated realism, severe and graphic visual texture, the verbal element coming to the fore in the drama: all of these helped penetrate into the logic of the heroes' behavior and the motivation of their actions. The absence of the extensive lyrical periods which had formerly been filled with music, and the appearance of a natural sound background, which held a special meaning, left no place for music. In other words, the deliberate a-musical character of Romm's and Stolper's films was dictated by a desire for liberation from the banal clichés of musical film illustration. It transferred the emphasis on to speech and noise, so as to preserve a chronicle-style and a realistic manner of narration.

On the whole, the films *Nine Days of One Year* and *The Living and the Dead* remained an isolated phenomenon in the Soviet cinema, since their technique, both innovative and extremist as it was found no direct support among film-makers. But in a somewhat less extreme form, it found some reflection in many directors' films in the tendency to reject old fashioned presentation and to intensify the functional activity of the verbal and sound structures. Also it meant the taking advantage of the previously unexamined artistic possibilities of silence and quietness. This last had a good influence on film music: being generally reduced in volume, it acquired a tendency to be in closer contact with the other sound and visual elements, instead of merely dubbing and imitating the pictorial and plastic images of the film.

One of the most complex, non-trivial varieties of music function in film was suggested by director Otar Ioseliani in his first full-length film *Listopad* (*Falling Leaves*) (1967, composer N. Ioseliani). At first glance, it may appear simple and unsophisticated, since it was based on the technique of musical compilation, familiar since the days of the silent cinema. But the director and the composer managed to achieve the surprising effect of the music being present within the visual image and appearing, as it were, spontaneously in the course of plot development. There seemed to be no reason for saturating *Listopad* with numerous quotations from the tradition of national Georgian and Russian folk-music. Shot in a 'concealed camera' style and kept close to a documentary aesthetic, the film told the story of a young technologist, a shy and pure lad called Nico, who, having graduated from the institute, was sent to a wine-making works. He did an un-precedented thing: he had a quarrel with the director, and stopped the technological process to prevent the release of bad quality undistilled wine. This 'industrial' story acquired an unexpectedly poetic aspect because it was submerged in a spiritual music/sound atmosphere which filled the every-day life of the characters with special meaning, beauty and charm.

The sound-track of *Listopad* is to a certain extent unique. It is founded on the principle of programmed chance, and consists of a quaint combina-tion of city noises, speech, and snatches of melodies which the film-makers overheard in the narrow streets of old Tbilisi. It is curious that this expressive and motley mosaic of the environment proved so strong and valuable in itself that it showed a tendency towards autonomous development and acquired its own dramatic function without the sound being closely connected to the picture . The juxtaposition of the multilayered polyphonic character of the film's sound-world on the one hand, and the severe restraint of its visual style, on the other, led to a complex counterpoint which was finally meant to create meaningful superpolyphonic complexes and a holistic sound-visual image of the film.

In spite of the seemingly modest input of the composer, *Listopad* is an extremely musical film. For the first time it revealed one of the special characteristics of Ioseliani's individual style, which would find its further development in his later films. This was his ability to employ techniques which brought film material close to the laws of musical form. For example, in its composition *Listopad* reminds one of a programmatic suite, which shows in the division of the action into relatively complete parts — short stories, contrasting in content, mood, tempo, and rhythm. Each of the short stories is demarcated from the others by its own title (the day of the week), its own musical signature and its final climactic shot balancing out its symmetry. Besides, a combination of Debussy's and Glinka's music, the popular Georgian song 'Suliko' and the song 'Valenki' (Felt Boots), both well known in Russia, a Gypsy choir and a fashionable foxtrot, a hearty brass band march and some piano finger exercises, all paradoxical at first sight within the limits of one film, all appear to be originally implanted in the artistic tissue of the picture because of the spontaneous, improvisational manner of story telling. There is nothing unnatural in such a whimsical confusion of 'high' and 'low' genres, for such seems to have been the musical sound-world of the late '60s: it left its imprint on the emotional perception and spiritual life of the heroes of *Listopad*. At the same time, the kaleidoscope of episodes quickly following one another did not produce an impression of incoherence and chaos thanks to the strict 'rationing' of music in each of them, and to its somewhat reduced, unobtrusive presence in the sequence.

It would be an error, however, to assume that directors no longer felt any necessity to co-operate actively with composers, and the above examples should be thought of as exceptions, impressive though they were, rather than the general rule. In the majority of films music continued to play as important a part as before, in creating the dramatic conception of the whole and in emphasizing and bringing to the fore the main thematic idea. On the other hand, it was the '60s that produced a search for everyday documentary reality in the events shown, an increased interest in a psychological approach to, and investigation of, complex human characters, as opposed to false enthusiasm, pseudoromanticism and the static schematic images of personality which prevailed in the Stalinist cinema. Film makers were encouraged to look for any stylistic means adequate to the new purpose and task of renovating cinematic language. Music, being an integral part of the cinematic synthesis, appeared to be involved in this reformation process, which made composers introduce essential reforms into their work. This was furthered by the appearance of a new generation of musicians in the cinema. Among them were leaders of all the trends in modern experimental music, which was created in spite of furious protest from the mandarins of official cultural policy and the machine of the Composers' Union. Here were the Soviet avant-garde, (Alfred Schnittke, Sofia Gubaidulina, Edison Denisov), dodecaphony and serial techniques (Nikolai Karetnikov), and electronic music (Edward Artemyev). Though most of these new composers became famous all over the world for their work in the cinema during the next decade (except for, perhaps, Nikolai Karetnikov and Alfred Schnittke), their film scores of the '60s did exert a definite influence on the radical change in the melodic, timbral and sound-world of film music. This became a character of that period.

21

Song in the cinema of the '60s.
Crystallization of a monothematic model
in the musical drama of the song film

One of the distinctive characteristics of the cinema during this period was its recourse to modern themes and subjects, contemplation of the fate of the country, on youth looking for a purpose in life, a desire to understand the frame of mind of people living in close proximity, their psychology, their moral attitudes[1]. The activist, the ardent fighter for the triumph of communist ideas was replaced by the 'thoughtful man', defending his convictions in heated discussions. The shifting of emphasis from action or event to the state of the hero's inner world, a distinctive intellectual tendency in the best films of the '60s, inevitably resulted in a weakening of the element of spectacle, in the holding up of the action and in a concentration on dialogue and discussion given these conditions, music was pushed to the background and treated with caution. Probably it was feared that its emotionality in conveying the inner feelings of man could cast an undesirable sentimental and melodramatic shadow over the cold rationalist style of such films. At the same time, the Soviet cinema could not bypass the vehement dispute over 'physicists and lyricists', which was accompanied by the increased interest of the technocratic intelligentsia in modern art. This was caused, during the post-war period, by the intensity of the restoration of the national economy, and the powerful development of industry, which had raised the prestige of the technical professions to an unusually high level. As a result, a great part of the Soviet intelligentsia developed a particularly materialist and rationalist view of the environment, and an exaggerated conception of man as master and creator of nature. The priority of technical over humanitarian knowledge seemed a foregone conclusion. In response, 'Lyricists', in open disputes, tried to show that any human existence which denied the spiritual sphere made man defective and inferior, and warned against the danger of science being dehumanized. One of such disputes, shot as a chronicle during the meeting of young Moscow poets with the students and teachers of the Polytechnic Institute, was shown in the film by Marlen Khutsiev,

The Ilyich Gate (1961, composer Sidelnikov). Among its participants were the poets Akhmadulina, Robert Rozhdestvensky, Evgeni Evtushenko, and the poet and singer Bulat Okudjava, whose name became a kind of symbol of freedom-loving aspiration and the very spirit of the '60s.

The same technique of introducing the songs of leading poets into the dramatic tissue of a film was used by Khutsiev in the film *Rain in July* (1966). In those years, poets were in open conflict with official art, and were not recognized by it. Yet they enjoyed popularity among people from different social circles, and of different ages. The sound-track of the film was based entirely on the songs of Bulat Okudjava and Yuri Vizbor. The songs were not merely characteristic of the time: they also infused the film with great spiritual force and ethical meaning. The songs of Galich, Okudjava, Vysotsky, in unique performances by their authors, could be heard in the films *The Girl Running on the Waves* (1967, director Lyubimov), *Zhenya, Zhenechka and 'Katyusha'* (1967, director Motyl'), and *Brief Encounters* (1968, director Muratova). At the same time, the presence of significant-songs occupying key positions in the dramatic conception and forming special centres of force which attracted everybody's attention whether they were on the screen or off it, considerably limited the possibilities for composers working on the films. In fact, the task of Jan Frenkel, Isaak Schwarz, Oleg Karavaichuk was reduced to that of writing background music. When compared to the living, acute sense of the time in the poets' songs, this music looked bleak and impersonal. Yet the cinema of this period produced another category of film which demanded great ingenuity and creativity from composers in their efforts to communicate with the mass-audience.

One of the distinguishing characteristics of film music in the '60s was its return to the song type of dramaturgy, in a modernized form. The changes concerned the image of the song itself, and the victorious, triumphal marches and cheerful sports marches which had reigned on the screen since pre-war days were replaced by intimate lyrical songs, ballad songs, and meditation songs. This seemed exactly appropriate melodramas.

Previously, the musical dramaturgy of the song film could have included a large number of songs belonging to different genres. Now, concentration on the intimate, and on the heroes' psychological drama, made composers use the monothematic principle, which is based on the singling out of a leitmotiv song and its subsequent development in the film. The exposition of the song was given out during the introductory captions, showed the emotional tonality of the action, and expressed its main idea. Then followed a number of variation-style transformations of the central song leitmotiv which reflected all the peripeteias in the story and the dynamism of the development of the characters' moods and feelings. Such a primitive scheme of musical dramaturgy was used in many 'prosaic' films which studied the character and the psychology of people with difficult lives damaged by the war.

One of the examples is the film by Yuri Egorov, *A Simple Story* (1960, composer Fradkin), in which the purposeful use of solo song helped the director give a fine and subtle rendering of the inner tragic aspect of a common everyday story about the bitter, hopeless love of two people, no longer young: the soldier's widow, Sasha Potapova, an energetic and mischievous chairman of a collective farm, and a reserved, terse, and unhappily married man Danilov, secretary of the regional committee.

The device used in this film became very popular, and the cinema was soon flooded with a stream of songs, all of them intimate, heartfelt, balanced on the verge of tearful sentimentality but at the same time possessing a romantic elevation and the civilised pathos of song melodies which became sure-fire clichés as the result of repetition. This occurred especially often and insistently with films depicting the recent war. The reason for such partiality is clear: at the front the song always played an important part, supplying the necessary emotional discharge of inhuman stress which inevitably accumulated under conditions of the physical closeness of death, the shock experienced when friends and comrades-in-arms perished. But the increasing historical distance, the new appraisal of the events and results of the Second World War viewed from the standpoint of the '60s, caused a re-evaluation of function of song in film. The novelty devised by film-makers at that time was the removal of the song beyond the limits of the action, so as to make it the *authors's voice* of the film, its musical epigraph, its thesis. Such was, for example, the interpretation of Veniamin Basner's songs 'On the Nameless Height' and 'Where Motherland Begins' in the films *Stillness* (1964, 2 parts) and *The Shield and The Sword* (1968), directed by Vladimir Basov. The combination of the melodious and recitative elements of musical speech, the melody locked within the limits of short phrases and intonations, the variational development of one motif, constantly renovated by the appearance of different intonational and thematic formations, contributed to the communicative openness of songs. This made them popular. It is not surprising that these songs soon went beyond the limits of their films and became generally recognized hits, just as the very same type of solo dramatic song, so successfully worked out by Basner, for years determined the musical structure of the majority of Soviet 'victorious', military-patriotic films whose climax came in the period of 'Brezhnev stagnation'.

Of course, not all films about the war followed this scheme. A basically different chamber type of musical dramaturgy was not less popular. It will be considered later. Meanwhile let us turn to one more active function of the cinema song in the '60s, which was closely connected with the appearance of the Soviet modification of the American western — the adventure historical-revolutionary film. Its ardent follower and propagandist was director Edmon Keosaian, who created within four years a trilogy about the heroic feats of young Soviet fighters, the heroes of the Civil War.

Anticipating the discoveries of the guiding principles of structural organization in the multi-part film in the '70s, the directors of the series on the elusive Avengers (*The Elusive Avengers*, 1967; *The New Adventures of the Elusive Ones*, 1968; *The Crown of the Russian Empire, or The Elusive Ones Again*, 1971, 2 parts) united all its constituent parts into a single whole by means of invariable musico-visual titles. The disc of the rising sun and the figures of four horsemen appearing against its background in the Red Army *budyonovkas* (pointed helmet worn in the Red Army during the Civil War), slowly approaching, moving in on the camera at the beginning of each film, and the same sequence but with the horsemen disappearing beyond the horizon in the finale — this was the visual solution of the titles and conclusions in the serial. As for its musical aspect, in the first two pictures 'The Song of the Elusive Avengers' ('Don't cry for your son, cursing your cruel fate' by Boris Mokrousov.) was used, stylized as a marching song. But in the third film (*The Crown of the Russian Empire*) the authors replace this musical title which was noted for its gloomy, austere colouring, with the excited, lively, optimistic song by Jan Frenkel, 'Pursuit'. Frenkel's collaboration with Keosaian started as early as *The New Adventures of the Elusive Ones*. It is curious that though writing a song essentially different in its mood, Frenkel reproduced the tonal-harmonic design of Mokrousov's song, and also its distinctive timbre and orchestration. This prevented the destruction of the intonational, imaginative and, eventually, the conceptual integrity of the cycle and enabled the composer to be replaced inconspicuously and painlessly. In spite of this, however, the third film was considerably inferior to the first two in its lack of dynamism, the unpredictability of its plot and in the working out the individual characteristics of its personalities. This demonstrated the genre's 'fatigue', and the exhaustion of the authors' fantasy. To judge the musical dramaturgy of the film more strictly, its main drawback was its cumbersome character. Apart from song titles, which performed significant functions, acting as a sound code, the emblem of the cycle, almost without participating in the dramatic action of each part, the music was replete with a mass of different thematic material. Specially important was the overture, highly developed, expressive and heroic. It contained all the main leitmotivs of each part, subsequently accompanying numerous scenes of pursuits, fights, skirmishes of the avengers with bandits and White Guards. There were also inserted concert items which created a rich picturesque background, close to operetta, and which helped develop a fascinating, dynamic adventure story. Practically all the enemies of the four friends were caricatures. Their behavior and habits strongly resembled those of American Supermen. Incidentally, Keosaian's trilogy contained quite a few musical borrowings from classic Hollywood westerns. On the whole, the music was no more than an illustrative and subsidiary means for urging on the action and working up emotions.

22

The mixed and chamber types of musical dramaturgy

The rehabilitation of the song type of dramaturgy was accompanied by a sharp reduction in symphony orchestra dramaturgy. This was replaced by a more flexible new model, which used a mixed or chamber-instrumental composition of the orchestra. Its birth cannot be considered a spontaneous fact, or even one conditioned only by directors declining to put up with the domination of symphonic music. Besides, there were also other reasons for changing stylistic orientations. Film music is like a fine barometer, responding to all the fluctuations of fashion and the processes directing the development of autonomous musical genres. It was one of the first to put into practice the new systems of intonational-imaginative thinking and progressive composition techniques, showing an increased interest in the expressive potentialities of individual elements, such as rhythm, texture, timbre, dynamics etc. Again in this way it emphasized its special status in musical art, where composers could enjoy freedom of choice and do their creative work outside of the 'sacred' canons of socialist realism without fear of persecution, and acquire a reputation as adherents of western musical conceptions, which were then considered to be 'ideologically alien to Soviet art'. These were dodecaphony and serialism, pointillism and sonoristics, concrete and electronic music. Even such a distinguished master as Georgy Sviridov could not overcome the temptation to see himself in a new role, as a destroyer of stereotypes. Having made his debut in the cinema of the '50s, he earned great popularity as the author of excellent music for the screen versions of Russian classical literature — Tolstoy's novel *Resurrection* (1960–1962, 2 parts, director Shweitser) and Pushkin's story *The Snowstorm* (1965, director Basov)[2]. Nevertheless, in 1966 he surprised his admirers by accepting Mikhail Shweitser's proposal to write music for the film *Forward, Time!*, which was innovative in style and in its principles of montage organization. The film described the strenuous working life and the suffering of the inspired collective labour of the workers on one of the greatest construction sites in the period of the first five-year plan — Magnitogorsk[3].

As the director admitted, in this film taken from Kataev's novel of the same name, a decisive return to 'the Russian montage' tradition of the '20s was made. This allowed the authors to use the arsenal of expressive means of the silent montage cinema, to show the collision of different human destinies, psychologies, characters, and also events of the recent past, all shown in dynamic counterpoint, viewed as it were in the light of the modern world.

The film opened with a documentary prologue, which consisted of a hundred frames from chronicles of the late '20s and early '30s. Like a grandiose epic fresco, it unfolded an astonishing picture of radical ideological and social changes, mass enthusiasm, and the optimistic mood of people busy in transforming nature and society, and considering themselves genuine creators of history. Staccato rhythmical montage, and a fast interchange of sequences to emphasize the feverish swiftness of the tempo of life during the epoch of the first five-year plan, received powerful support from the music of the overture. It was really the overture that gave the power impulse, and channeled the informational, documentary stream which became an integral part of the action. A similar technique of natural transition from the general to the particular, from the impersonal to the individual, was applied in the musical dramaturgy of the film *Forward, Time!*

The musical material of the film widely distributed over the two-part picture, possessed on the whole only a local significance, and was used to describe everyday life, creating the necessary sound background for the development of the action. This toning down of the music could be accounted for by the authors' desire to remove any impediment which could divert the audience's attention from the general theme of the film, which was expressed in a general, concentrated manner in the overture. The latter evoked visual, object-associations with the revolutionary whirlwind which once raised the mass of the Russian people from lethargy and whirled them into the midst of events. The overture opened with masterful, resolute exclamations on the piano: this was concluded by the side drum 'shooting' in dry 'machine-gun' bursts. The total domination of toccata motor rhythms, the indomitable urge to move forward, and an insistent onslaught of the overture's music was considerably intensified by the use of different syncopations, repetitions and the treating of the piano as a hammering rhythmic percussion instrument. At the same time, in the ecstatic and exalted 'calling' phrases of this theme, there was not only heroism but 'the will to win at any cost'. In the piano ostinato formulas, repeated frenziedly within a narrow compass but devoid of any solid basis, and stuck on the discordant second degree of the scale, troubled and tragic touhes notes would at times break through.

When, after repeated and unsuccessful attempts to find inner stability, the piano theme began to lose its novelty and acquired a mechanical character, violins were introduced to inject a new stream of energy into this peculiar *perpetuum mobile*. Their spiralling passages were superimposed on the piano and side drum music, painting the overture music in bright colours and raising its emotional tone by several degrees. But the main purpose of the violin version was to create appropriate psychological conditions which would help the perception of the central theme both of the overture and the film as a whole — the victorious, triumphant fanfare theme. Brave and purposeful, it emerged on the crest of the dynamic wave as a logical conclusion and as the highest point of the preceding development, which had merely served as a spring-board for its freely soaring take-off.

This poster garishness in the melodic profile of the fanfare theme, in which there was something both impersonal and timeless, was used to embody, according to the authors, the eternal dream of humanity about a radiant future, for the sake of which people were ready to perform mighty tasks, to do hard and exhausting work which took them to and sometimes beyond the limit of human endurance. Besides, one could hear in it the beating of the pulse of the modern epoch, of great deeds, a dynamic link between the past and the present.

Powerful muscular energy, and an excited and cheerful world outlook which seemed to permeate each bar of the overture, both determined the intonational system and stylistic of the image system of the picture, imparting to it an elevated and romantic pathos which combined different parts and episodes into a single dramatic conception. In turn, this created an organic synthesis of poetic and documentary — realistic scenes and a smoothly modulated transition from metaphor to the reality of everyday life. And though, after the extensive prologue, music was used economically later on in the film and, being a generalized symbol of time, kept its distance without coming into contact with the film action, the brilliant and easily remembered themes presented in the overture allowed the extension of their zone of direct or subconscious influence to the whole film apparatus.[4]

Thus, in spite of the fact that Shweitser's film belonged to a peculiar category of retrospective films noted for their revolutionary romanticism, political rhetoric and ideological bias, the composer found an original musical solution, rejecting the conventional restoration of the musical atmosphere of the late '20s and early '30s. His music was surprisingly modern and possessed characteristic features peculiar to the artistic and cultural trends of the '60s. In particular, this was shown by the emancipation and personification of timbre, by a drastic activation of the rhythmic factor and its conversion into the most efficient means of musical expression, by the individualization of its texture and its saturation with thematic elements, and finally, by the traditional symphony orchestra being replaced by its genre variant — the *concerto grosso*.

Still greater courage and determination in the radical renovation of the arsenal of expressive means and the language of film music were demonstrated by young composers. One of them was Mikhael Tariverdiev. He shared the director's resolve on the necessity of 'reviving' film music, and in fully accepting the tendency, widespread at that time, for reducing the number of instruments used, tried to create his own stylistic model of musical dramaturgy based on a synthesis of chamber and dance music. Among his works, each of which bore the imprint of the composer's individual manner, the most remarkable was the music for M. Kalik's film *Man Follows the Sun* (1961). In this story about a small boy discovering the endless beauty of the world surrounding him, and of those living in it, it is music that plays the main role in the rhythmic organization, which is made up of a quaint mosaic of varied film episodes, noted for their special elegance and improvisational character. Thanks to its music, the film became surprisingly exciting and at the same time ironic, subtly spiritual and lyrical. This emphasis on music was also assisted by reserve and an extreme laconicism in the use of other sound components (speech and noise). This raised its dramatic level and opened the way for closer contact between music and representation, which brought back the techniques of silent cinema.

The film *Man Follows the Sun* is notable for its use of a principle of timbre linearity, and of small instrumental ensembles which allow unexpected and picturesque combinations (for example, duets for flute and cembalo, French horn and organ, etc.). The bases of the musical construction of the film were two leitmotivs representing, as it were, two complementary aspects of one image, sometimes playfully joking, sometimes lyrically exultant and childishly pure.

In the same year, 1961, Tariverdiev finished work on the music for A. Zarkhi's picture *My Younger Brother*. It is interesting that in this undistinguished film, the composer made a daring attempt to unite into one dynamic process two stylistic devices, quotation and allusion. His overall aim was to remove the time distance between the music of the past and the present. During the time of the relaxation of the hermetic character of Soviet culture, and the appearance together of differing trends in art, which had previously run in parallel or in confrontation, this decision did not seem anything special. But all the same, it did seem to be original and it attracted attention, since it was based on the destruction of a conventional stereotype, in this case, the destruction of the musical and stylistic harmony which had become a distinguishing characteristic of film music in the preceding period.

In the course of the action, which is a modern version of the wonderful and bitter love of Romeo and Juliet, the hero hears the famous organ Toccata of J.S. Bach. Its melody causes a revolution in the young man's soul, makes him adopt a more sensible, and wiser view of life, and starts him thinking about the meaning of existence. For Tariverdiev a quotation from Bach turns into an inexhaustible source which feeds his imagination. Following Bach, he impregnates his rhythms and intonations with 'bachisms', which help him synthesize various episodes via a system of leitmotivic connections. At the same time, Tariverdiev managed to preserve his own individual style in the original music of the film, i.e. its softness, and the vocal plasticity of its melodies; a tendency towards lyrical images, as simple and warm-hearted as Schubert's; an elaborately detailed development and polishing of phrases with 'feminine' endings and touching flat seventh progressions, all of which reveal a connection with the classical tradition. As the result of the use of such different historical styles in one acoustic space, a synthesis of a higher order appeared, which could be decoded at conceptual and philosophical levels. For music containing the characteristics of both the 18th and 20th centuries had a double semantic meaning. On the one hand, it drew the audience's attention to ethical norms and humanist ideas, and the holistic perception of the world inherent in the Baroque epoch. On the other hand, it seemed to clothe the same ideas in modern language and in a freshly communicative form of expression.

A comparable alloy of the languages of old and new music was also demonstrated by the composer Andrei Volkonsky in a two-part picture by director Savva Kulish. As a connoisseur of medieval, Renaissance and Baroque music, the founder and artistic director of the early music ensemble 'Madrigal', Volkonsky wrote music for the film *The Dead Season* (1969). He took a risky step, unusual in the genre of political cinema (though it accorded fully with his own personal partiality). He experimented with music stylized in a Baroque spirit and aesthetic. Formally, the occasion for this unexpected decision was the fact that one of the characters, the fanatical fascist Doctor Hass, for whom the Soviet intelligence officer Ladeinikov is searching, kept his long-standing love for old music, in spite of changing his own name, appearance, and manner of behaviour. This love, which linked the old and the new Hass, helped Ladeinikov find him. But, in reconstructing the life and horrible deeds of the war criminal step by step, the Soviet intelligence officer could not remain indifferent to the wonderful and charming world of music. It caught up with Ladeinikov at a moment of poignant contemplation, when he was trying to track down Hass by comparing some unusual data. When he heard music which seemed to have returned from ancient times, it prodded him into action.

At first hearing, there is much in common between the musical characterisations of the two protagonists, one of whom is a criminal hiding from justice, the other his pursuer, personifying retribution. Though, the music connected with Hass and that characterizing Ladeinikov seem externally similar and belong to the same epoch, there is an abyss between them which makes it impossible to establish any contact. Hass's music is always motivated by the plot and its appearance is made explicit by the pointing out of its source (a concentration camp orchestra, a gramophone record, a TV set etc.) Thus, it is pointedly alien to Hass, and plays the role of some *terra incognita* which neither reveals his essence nor reflects his genuine thoughts and feelings: it only informs the viewers of his almost maniacal passion and humour.

Alongside this 'normal', un-transformed music preserved like a museum exhibit, which functions in the film as the sign of an SS hangman, there is another musical layer bearing the imprint of the composer's individuality, which is very important for revealing the author's purpose of creating an antifascist adventure film. This plays the musical role task of an off-frame authorial 'voice', commenting on the film, and therefore it is logically addressed to Ladeinikov, the positive hero of *The Dead Season*, the indefatigable opponent of Hass. It is surprising that without resorting to any radical change of language, and by frequently making allusions, Volkonsky veers amazingly close to quotation from Bach, Scarlatti, Monteverdi, and at the same time fills this music with the atmosphere of the modern world. Thus, in one musical episode of the film, set against the background of a big Western European city in which Ladeinikov has arrived in pursuit of Hass (part 1), the main theme resembles the *Toccata* from the E-minor keyboard *Partita* by J. S. Bach. But when the delicate and tender harpsichord melody is invaded by an impulsive, nervous percussion rhythm by improvisation, bright modulations, and unhealthy chromatic sequences, it becomes clear that it is a child of the 20th century. This device, which addresses the past via the mirror of the present, it also repeated using other themes, and because it is used throughout the film acquires its necessary dramatic integrity and elegance of design. Unfortunately, sometimes the borderline between quotation material and the author's stylization appears to be rather vague: this makes viewers lose their bearings, and distorts their psychological perception of the film's meaning.

The return role to film music of the experimental creative-laboratory which it had all but lost, can be traced in a number of pictures from the '60s. Proof of this can be found in Alfred Schnittke's music for Elem Klimov's *The Adventures of a Dentist* (1967). Under the strong influence of neoclassicism, and using the polystylistic technique which was widely spread among the young generation of Soviet composers, Schnittke resolved to realize a daring idea. In the film, he took up the structure of the old suite, the succession of whose movements coincided with the succession of stages in the life of the luckless dentist hero. Later much of the films's musical material, as well as its basic conception, became the starting point for the composer's original work *A suite in the old style* (1972).

The advent of composition, 'timbre' which shook Soviet music on the verge of the '60s, also affected film music, which for many composers was a testing ground to study of and experiment with timbre combination. One of the first to begin intensive work in this direction was Edwardas Balsys.

The irrepressibility and inventiveness of his creative imagination sometimes evoked sincere admiration. He was not afraid to introduce into his film scores rare instruments such as the claviolina (the film *Adomas Wants to Be Human*, director Žalakiavičius, 1959) or to create absolutely untraditional ensembles, including objects which seemed to be quite unadapted to music making, such as the axe and the petrol tank, both of which were used as percussion instruments in R. Vabalas's film *Steps in the Night* (1962). At the same time, the composer proved to be a convinced exponent of leitmotiv dramaturgy, which enabled him to make active and varied use of the whole expressive arsenal of timbre music. But picturesque instrumentation was never an end in itself for Balsys, and it was always combined with symphonic development of thematic material, and with classical simplicity and clarity of form.

A wish to find unusual timbre combinations, which could infuse a fresh spirit into and attract attention to the naive plot about a young village women who came to the capital to study singing, may account for the desire of Andrei Eshpai to record his music for Evgeny Tashkov's picture *Come Tomorrow* (1963) on the ANS synthesizer[5]. Several years later, he turned again to the unique sound and timbre possibilities of ANS in Saltykov's film *Women's Kingdom* (1968). Most uninhibited is the scene of fortune-telling and sorcery by Russian women waiting for their husbands and lovers to return from the front, which is filled with mysterious, mythological and unearthly electronic sounds.

In spite of this successful experiment by Eshpai in adapting electronic music to the cinema, contacts between them in the '60s were weak and timid and did not go beyond the limits of a trite and narrow, conservative notion of the specific possibilities of electronic music. Electronic music itself gave grounds for such a prejudiced attitude: at that time it used artificial timbres and synthetic colours. It was not surprising that the sphere of its functional application was strictly limited, and was mainly connected with unreal, fantastic scenes and images.

Unlike timbre and electronic music, the techniques of which more or less affected the film music of the '60s, the influence of *musique concrète*, which also interested composers, showed itself in the cinema more indirectly, via its introduction as background into speech and noise episodes. Among the few instances of the use of *musique concrète* a special place is taken by films about the Second World War, where the most interesting and non-standard varieties of sound correlation were to be found. The best examples are in Andrei Tarkovsky's film *Ivan's Childhood* (1962, composer Ovchinnikov).

During the war, Tarkovsky's age was the same as that of his hero, the twelve-year-old front line scout, Ivan Bondarev. Perhaps that was how he succeeded in showing the inhuman nature of war with such a powerful emotional force, via the child's consciousness distorted by the war.

The war orphaned Ivan, and turned a common, shy village boy into a fearless, tireless avenger, devoid of compassion for the enemy. His soul is submerged in a darkness of unlimited, total hatred which has became the sole aim of his life. The state of Ivan was exactly described by Jean Paul Sartre: 'This militant and crazy child wages war for the sake of war! He lives only for the sake of it, among soldiers who love him, in an unbearable loneliness.

And nevertheless he is still a child. This mournful soul preserves the tenderness of infancy, but cannot feel it any more, and still less can he express it'[6].

Thus two seemingly incompatible and mutually exclusive realities collide in the film: the severe everyday life at the front, and the hallucination-like visions of quite a different world — Ivan's pure, poetic dreams. In the former, gloomy colours reign and there is almost no light. This is the forest at night, illuminated only by bursts of rockets; the basement meagerly lighted with a candle-end in a half-destroyed church, which serves as a temporary shelter for the scouts; the low, ominous sun; a crooked cross on a grave against the dark sky; the dim shapes of the bodies of Soviet soldiers, killed by the Germans with ropes around their necks and wooden placards on their chests, with a mocking phrase in Russian: 'Dobro pozhalovat' (Welcome) outlined in the early morning mist. Such is the landscape of war, and there is no place for music in it. That is why, when one of the soldiers tries to play on a gramophone a record of a folk song performed by Feodor Shaliapin, 'Mashen'ka is not allowed to cross the river', it is always roughly cut short in the middle of a phrase. In the same way, the only lyrical theme of the film is cut short: the budding love between the military doctor's assistant Masha and Captain Kholin. The nearness of death won't allow living human feeling to flower in a world exploding with the thunder of artillery, the crackle of machine-gun bursts, curt commands and orders, and groans of the wounded.

However, in Ivan's dreams (the film's second hypostasis) a transformation takes place. The screen is flooded with the rays of a warm summer midday, washing away the darkness and animosity of the preceding frames. The happy face of the boy, the kindly smile of his young mother, who is showing him a star at the bottom of a well, a horse pecking at apples scattered on the sand, a dark-haired girl laughing in the rain...

This return to Ivan's childhood, possible only in dreams, is accompanied by a surprisingly delicate, tender, pastoral theme, which seems to have been spun out of the transparent, warm timbres of string and woodwind instruments. It is as beautiful as the nature surrounding the boy, full of quiet joy and peace.

All the more horrible therefore is the sudden transition from the harmony of peace to the cruel reality of war. There is only one moment when the director gave the composer an opportunity to show by means of music the distortion of childhood images in memory. In one episode, the scouts are crossing the river. The black smooth surface of the water and the gloomy autumn forest stand still in the treacherous silence, and reproduce the visions of Ivan's first dream as if in a distorting mirror. The resemblance is intensified by the return of the pantheistic musical theme, but in such a distorted, mutilated form! Broken up by pauses and the ominous, spiky *pizzicato* of the cellos, with the melody torn by unnatural leaps, it only remotely resembles the initially beautiful theme.

Gradually the war also invades Ivan's dreams. And when in one of them the hero sees himself as a menacing avenger, his face distorted with fierce hatred, with a huge flick knife in his hand, the music dies, to be replaced by an eerie cacophony which consists of groans, cries, the grinding of metal, scraps of German speech, and the tragic tolling of bells[7]. Thus, the sound track of *Ivan's Childhood* is founded on an interrelation of all the sound components, which does not preclude a clear-cut determination of the dramatic function of each of them. The greatest expressiveness comes from the natural sounds which sometimes form a complicated counterpoint with the visual material. Besides, both their concentration, and their dispersal throughout the film space give abrupt effects of psychological stress and bring spectators' feelings to a head, imposing a feeling of tragedy. Speech (dialogues, sometimes monologues of the characters) plays a subsidiary, explanatory role and is restrained and laconic. In this achingly communicative film, which is extremely severe in its imaginative structure, music plays a leading role, introducing elements of lofty spirituality and a poetic mood, which emphasize that the film is a mournful requiem for a child's soul crippled, tormented and murdered by war.

23

Music by Nadezhda Simonyan and Dmitry Shostakovich in film versions of Chekhov and Shakespeare

Some critics called the '60s 'the golden age' of film versions. Those years saw a massive invasion of world literature by film-makers in search of new themes and subjects. Among the writers who attracted close attention were Leo Tolstoy, Feodor Dostoevsky, Ivan Turgenev, Alexander Kuprin, Anton Chekhov, William Shakespeare, Honoré de Balzac, i.e. writers whose work was connected with the protection of the honour and dignity of man, and with high-minded humanistic moral problems. The authors of the collective monograph *A History of Soviet Cinema* characterized the keen enthusiasm of Soviet film directors for classical literature as follows: 'As a rule, the classics are resorted to and interpreted anew when, on the arterial road of art, new problems of treating the present have been outlined and the views and the atmosphere characteristic of the period in question have assumed a definite form'[8].

It should be admitted that the genre of literary film versions did not allow any great freedom of choice in techniques and means of musical expressiveness, since it demanded from the composer a perfectly straightforward orientation toward historical stylistic models from the epoch reconstructed on the screen. But, the simplest and once most popular method, compilation, did not arouse any particular enthusiasm on the part of directors. They still preferred to use original music specially written for the film, which could become an integral part of the total dramatic conception, and employed to reveal the artistic design of the film. This allowed composers to introduce their own imaginative corrections into stylistic models from the past, which could be reconstructed by them, by using modern intonations and thematic development of musical material. That was just what the composer Viacheslav Ovchinnikov did in Sergei Bondarchuk's *War and Peace* (1966–1967), and Rodion Shchedrin also in Alexander Zarkhi's two-part film *Anna Karenina* (1968). Unfortunately, an unnecessary passion for over expressive melodic and rhythmic means, astringent harmonies, the personification of timbres caused a certain disharmony between the composer's music and intraframe accessory music which maintained the stylistic canons of 19th century aesthetics. Later, each of the composers used his own music for these films as a basis for an independent work of the same name, a symphonic suite and a ballet.

Figure 5 *A Lady with a Dog*

A composer who managed to avoid any contradiction between her own off-frame music and the subject intraframe music was Nadezhda Simonyan, in the fine, spiritual film of Iosif Kheifits *A Lady with a Dog* (1960). It is well-known that at the 13th International Film Festival in Cannes the film was awarded the prize 'For High Humanist Ideals and Outstanding Artistic Qualities'; the music for *A Lady with a Dog* was even praised by Federico Fellini. It is difficult to find in the Soviet cinema of the '60s another film which portrayed such a modest but sincere and warm love. It was not by chance that another master of modern cinema, no less famous than Fellini, Ingmar Bergman, said in an interview for the magazine *Chaplin*, later reprinted in the newspaper *Sovetskaya kultura* (21.09.61) that he took the film as 'a real purification, as a glass of water from a crystal clear spring'.

The free, somewhat amorphous composition of the film *A Lady with a Dog* founded on the parallel development of two dramatic layers. The first outlined the environment in which the leading characters lived. The second revealed the beauty, wealth and inner harmony of the love between Gurov and Anna Sergeyevna which so unexpectedly invaded their dull everyday existence, and changed the lives of these Chekhov characters. The abundance of expressive close-ups of their faces, and also the seemingly uneventful static landscape episodes, created wonderful possibilities for steeping the film in music.

Nadezhda Simonyan returned to the almost forgotten symphonic type of musical dramaturgy, not in its authentic form, however, but modified according to the musical-aesthetic norms and auditory conceptions of the contemporary generation. In particular, the full complement of the large symphony orchestra, too cumbersome for such a deeply lyrical drama, was replaced by a modest chamber ensemble, used so that detailed characterisation was achieved with melody and tone colour.

A specific peculiarity of the musical organization of *A Lady with a Dog* which brought it closer to the traditional symphonic type of dramaturgy, was the strict delimitation between the spheres of off-frame (author's) and intraframe (accessory) music. For a better characterisation of the heroes' environment in Chekhov's story, a number of music quotations was introduced, which made the historical atmosphere and time of the action more concrete. Among the dance-melodies and romances borrowed from once popular collections of salon repertoire, special attention was paid to the music of Jones's operetta *Geisha*, which is known to have been staged in several Russian theatres in the year Chekhov wrote *A Lady with a Dog*.

Unlike other 'passing' quotations, the music of *Geisha* performed a definite function, recording different stages of the relationship between Gurov and Anna Sergeyevna. Its first presentation occurs during a scene in a summer resort restaurant in Yalta, where a seemingly banal holiday romance starts to the accompaniment of a brass band. Later, the same theme accompanies the meeting of the protagonists in Saratov at the first night of *Geisha* in the local provincial theatre, in the lobby of which a serious, passionate and excruciating declaration of love takes place. The music from Jones's operetta appears for the last time in Gurov's house in Moscow. In the company of his wife and guests, listening to their foolish and empty prattle, the hero feels acutely his separation from the woman he loves. When this state of spiritual loneliness becomes quite unbearable, Gurov almost automatically sits at the piano and tries clumsily to pick out the already familiar melody. How tender and heartfelt his performance sounds, sentimental and sugary though the music is; it carries him away from hateful reality into a world of bitter-sweet memories. The tragedy of Gurov and Anna Sergeyevna is that they feel the impossibility of going on with the old life: they cannot find a way out of the impasse they are in, and do not know how to free themselves from meaningless marriages with people absolutely alien to them.

This drama of two excellent people whom love helps to reveal all that is best in themselves who, like two caged birds, appear unable to ignore standards of propriety and prejudice, is reflected in the music of Nadezhda Simonyan. She based the musical conception of the film on the successive development and contrapuntal interaction of two leitmotivs. They could be conditionally called the theme of love, which elevates and inspires a man, and the theme of the all-consuming boredom which breaks and paralyzes a man's life.

Following the director, who tried to preserve the historically true atmosphere of Chekhov's time, Simonyan writes music in which one can easily see typical stylistic characteristics of the end of the 19th century. For example, the love theme of Gurov and Anna Sergeyevna, close to the aesthetics of neoromanticism, contains a number of characteristics which point to its genetic relationship with the Russian city romance, and the best examples of the lyrical and tragic music of Tchaikovsky. The leitmotiv is given to the cello (a rare case of the use of a solo cello in film music) and surrounded with pulsing pizzicato from the strings, which imparts to it an extraordinary expressiveness and sensuality.

Ex. 15 The Leitmotiv of Love, from *A Lady with a Dog*

Ex. 15 (continued)

The antithesis to the leitmotiv of love is that of boredom. A limp, slow, weakly drooping flute melody, deprived of any inner impulse towards development, exactly conveys the dull routine existence which had previously seemed natural and habitual to the protagonists of *A Lady with a Dog*, but which had now became unbearable and excruciating. However, the theme of boredom, as well as the quotation from *Geisha*, has a narrow zone of action, and its main task is to throw the contrasting variations of the leading leitmotiv into greater relief. Thus, the leitmotiv of love plays a determining role in the musical dramaturgy of the film: this makes it similar to a set of variations with some elements of a rondo.

On the whole, the music of *A Lady with a Dog* is one of the best examples of Soviet film music from the '60s. However, its greatest achievement is undoubtedly Dmitry Shostakovich's music for Grigory Kozintsev's film version of *Hamlet* by Shakespeare (1964). Its creation proved again that the boundaries of applied music could be widened, and it could be turned into a special genre of programme music.

Among the numerous cinema versions of Shakespeare's *Hamlet*, Kozintsev's *Hamlet* attracted attention by its director's thoughtful attitude and its modern understanding of the text, from the viewpoint of the tragic 20th century. The assertion of the value of the individual and the defence of his dignity — that was what determined the philosophical conception of the film. Its contents, in the director's own words, read as follows:

'A young man brought up on the noblest ideals of humanism, believing in human greatness and his own noble purpose, his unlimited possibilities, finds himself in the real world where those ideas are being trampled on, desecrated — the state is based on the fact that a murderer is on the throne, the human relations are connected with the fact that a woman forgets her husband a month after his death, a career can be made only by means of murders and denunciations. He is to discover this world and his place in it. His ideas are wonderful but he cannot realize them, which is his tragedy. But with all the force of human steadfastness he rejects the human relations which he faces'[9].

The development of this conception of Kozintsev's can be clearly traced in Shostakovich's music, which was the climax of his work in the cinema. Moreover, following Prokofiev, he came close to the creation of a musical work which was original, finished in form and artistic design, but at the same time organically incorporated within the cinematic space. In point of fact, the music in *Hamlet* is a specific type of programme symphony, possessing an independent value, which is almost unique. Certainly, in order to take the liberty of introducing the laws of 'instrumental drama' into the musical conception, solid reasons were necessary. The composer did have these.

It is well-known that the structural organization of a number of Shakespeare's plays, based on the collision and struggle between contrasting images, sometimes leads Shakespeare scholars to make direct circumstantial analogies with sonata form. Nor is it difficult to see the characteristics of sonata form in the composition of *Hamlet*. This circumstance allowed Shostakovich to introduce naturally the classical sonata allegro, with inverted recapitulation. The role of the principal, the transitional, and second subjects were laid upon the leading characteristics of the protagonists — Hamlet, the Ghost, and Ophelia.

Figure 6 *Hamlet*

The immediate presentation of Hamlet's leitmotiv takes place in the overture, which opens with a severe, laconic epigraph theme. It is the key to the director's treatment of Hamlet's character — a man of intellect, a

Ex. 16 The Leitmotiv of Hamlet from the film *Hamlet*

Ex. 16 (continued)

Ex. 16 (continued)

philosopher who does not want to put up with the cruelty and baseness of his environment, and enters into an uncompromising battle with all that embodies evil. Kozintsev's and Shostakovich's *Hamlet* is not prone to reflection or agonizing search for truth in labyrinths of doubt. He wishes to act, and this property of his nature finds its reflection in his leitmotiv, which combines the excitability of oratorical speech with nobility and manly beauty.

This theme develops through a gradual build-up and modification of its initial phrase, which sums up — Hamlet in a nutshell. This is enclosed within the interval of the diminished fourth, but endowed with great power and will, shown by the springy concentration of the punctuated rhythm. It dominates the sound track in the process of its development. Its expansion is achieved by the addition to its main thrust new tetrachordal links derived from it.

However, while portraying Hamlet as a fighter, the composer does not forget that the life and fate of this hero are inseparable from Elsinore, where his childhood and youth were spent, where his real and false friends and his 'fair Ophelia' are, and where the ghost of his father is wandering without rest, calling for revenge. Turned in Kozintsev's film into an artistically generalized metaphor of a heartless state, into an image of Denmark as a prison cast in iron and stone, Elsinore is perceived here as a symbol of violence and inhumanity. It is not by chance that in its characterisation a chain of sharply dissonant chords comes to the fore. It intrudes into Hamlet's music as an evil fate. The contrapuntal treatment of the themes of Hamlet and Elsinore (the principle of simultaneous contrast) in the overture conveys an important philosophical meaning: in the irreconcilable collision of two conflicting forces, not only animosity can be felt, but also the hero's readiness for open action against everything represented by the castle-fortress which is steeped in a stifling atmosphere of hypocrisy, fear and hatred.

The leitmotivs of Hamlet and Elsinore also lead an independent existence. The former undergoes different intonational and imaginative modifications, due to the pressure of events, the latter retains a static invariable character and the same monotonous formulaic ostinato rhythms which were presented in the overture. The hammering monotonous rhythm of the kettledrums turns into background to the reading of the Royal Decree by the herald (the beginning of the film). The same monotonous rhythmic motif comes through in the formidable flourish of the trumpets while the army assembles for a campaign. Its latent presence is also revealed in the deliberately pompous, but at the same time cold and indifferent, music of the palace ball.

The richly detailed scene of the ball which takes up the greater part of the film's exposition, presents the other main characters and their leitmotivs — the Ghost and Ophelia.

The appearance of Hamlet's leitmotiv is always attended by the physical presence of the hero on the screen. However, the Ghost's theme presents an invisible personage, a phantom which mostly makes itself known through its music. It should be noted that this was substantially the first refusal to show the Ghost, and replacement of a visual image by a musical one, in both cinema and stage versions of *Hamlet*. However, from the point of view of opera and symphonic genres there was nothing unusual here. Portrayal of unreal, non-material characters was not infrequent.

A remarkable characteristic of the Ghost's leitmotiv is its invariability, which testifies to its profound relationship with the themes embodying the impersonal. The rhythmic evenness and cold impartiality of the Phrygian motif which is the core of this leitmotiv, resembles a chorale. At the same time, it is not difficult to notice here connections with Hamlet's leitmotiv, which seems logical enough since the Ghost was Hamlet's father who has been murdered by Claudius.

On the whole, the main purpose of the Ghost's theme in the dramatic conception of the film is the expression of the idea of revenge, which introduces a tragic note and fatal predetermination into the development of the action. Its first presentation, accompanying Horatio's story about the Ghost, already gives rise to a premonition of future evil. This is intensified in the scene of 'the Night Patrol' — Hamlet's meeting with the Ghost in iron armour, in one of the corridors of the castle. That is when the prince learns about Claudius' awful deeds, and his fathers's words make him thirst for revenge: they sound 'a voice of fate' for him. Later on, the Ghost's leitmotiv endowed with all the properties of an abstract symbolic image, will acquire a magnetic power over Hamlet's actions. At the same time, it preserves its general characteristics, except for some hardly noticeable changes in orchestration and dynamics.

The exposition of Ophelia's image is also connected with the ball. In Shakespeare's play there is no dance episode. It was created by Kozintsev in order to introduce the tender and virtuous daughter of Polonius to the spectator, on the one hand, and on the other, to show how the principles and laws of Elsinore trample and corrupt even the beauty and purity which have grown up by a miracle in its gloomy vaults. The movements of Ophelia dancing, so perfect as to be almost automatic, resemble those of a puppet. The music intensifies the association with a mechanical toy. The repetition of motifs, the strictly maintained gavotte rhythm, the cool and un-melodious timbre of the harpsichord[10], all emphasize the submissiveness and absolute subjection of the girl to rules not only of court etiquette but also to the routines, and laws of Elsinore. At the same time, the penetration of refined modal alterations and colourful modulations into the artless and somewhat archaic melody of the dance makes it possible to see that the laced in, delicate girl diligently performing the studied steps of the dance is, in fact, a living, childishly pure and bright creature.

All these qualities, though hidden from inquisitive eyes, reveal themselves to their full extent in the exquisite scene of Hamlet's parting from Ophelia, which is the climax of the film. Ophelia's feeling for the Prince is unsullied and beautiful. There is nothing complicated in it: it is clear and harmonious. That may be the reason why her world of girlish dreams seems so illusory and unreal, remote from the cruel reality surrounding her. In Ophelia's leitmotiv, a fine poetical and sublime spirit, plasticity and inner tranquility, the peaceful character of the diatonic melody, similar to old English ballads, simple harmony, the warm timbres of strings in middle register, all create an atmosphere of openheartedness, sincerity, and loyalty bordering on sacrifice.

Understanding Ophelia's inability to resist, her submission to fate, Hamlet, occupied with thoughts of revenge, resolves to break with the girl he had recently loved so selflessly. But his eyes, sad and sick, full of re-pressed tenderness, betray his great suffering. It is not by chance that in the finale of the scene Hamlet's leitmotiv appears, played by the woodwind instruments *sotto voce*, in 'the tonality of sorrow', D minor.

There is one more curious detail which explains the reasons for Hamlet's strange behaviour in the Parting scene. In fact, this scene brings into movement the allegorical subject of the mural, which can be seen in Hamlet's room and is a copy of a picture by the 15th century Italian painter Pollaiuolo. It depicts a young man who is rushing, with arms outstretched, to a girl who is turning into a tree before his eyes. It is not difficult to see the similarity of this subject to Hamlet's love for Ophelia, though another interpretation is possible, which is connected with dwindling hopes and loss of faith in a world losing its human image.

The middle part of the film — the development — includes Hamlet's monologues, the players' arrival and the performance of 'The Mouse-Trap', the episode in Gertrude's closet and the scene aboard the ship. In this case, where the director uses the rondo principle, the composer chooses a differ-ent way and resorts to a concentric form which helps to arrange the contrast-ing episodes, to impart inner integrity to them, and makes a logical inter-relation between them. Besides, such an unusual polyphonic combination in the parallel development of two different forms endows the whole with dynamism and diversity.

ОФЕЛИЯ   OPHELIA

Ex. 17 The Theme of Ophelia from the film *Hamlet*

In the central part of *Hamlet*, Shostakovich's attention was riveted to the monologues of the hero, which reveal different aspects of his image. The first monologue ('Man is the beauty of the world') is accompanied by a heartfelt clarinet melody, in which an intonational relatedness to Hamlet's leitmotiv is lightly outlined. Following closely the text of the monologue, it acquires sometimes a hymn-like and solemn, sometimes an intimate and melancholy, and sometimes an oratorical and pathetic character. Yet such a synchronisation does not turn this music into mere illustration, functionally second-rate as compared to the verbal and visual material. This is possible because the purpose of the music lies not in emotional dubbing of the content of a certain frame, but in showing 'the second ground of the actors's work' (according to Sergei Eisenstein), penetration into the depth of the subconscious, revealing the gamut of his feelings. The music seems to reflect the hero's thoughts and imparts to his words and actions a philosophic meaning free of vanity and passing moods.

The contemplative element characteristic of the first monologue, appear in the second one ('About my brain') to have been firmly pushed into the background and replaced by a thirst for action. Hamlet, sitting in the cart and watching the Players perform an extract from *Dido and Aeneas*, unconsciously leans upon a drum, and starts tapping on it with his fingers. This muffled sound, sometimes increasing, sometimes fading, excites him, and starts him thinking of the wonderful ability of art to fire passions in people and stimulate their thinking. And as a call to action in the end of this scene the hero's battle-cry resounds: 'we'll hear a play tomorrow': this is followed by a sequential development of the most active motif of the epigraph theme. The appearance of the leitmotiv sums up the agonizing doubts of the Prince. Besides, the rhythmic impulsiveness of the leitmotiv, its persistent intention to take over the sound track in its indomitable movement towards the climax, and its emphasis on the basic tones of the minor mode all convey Hamlet's overwhelming desire to break the bonds of untruth and to stop the overwhelming advent of evil. The confirmation of this choice having been made, and there being no possible retreat, is the last appearance of the epigraph theme in 'the revenge key' — B minor. The rhythm accelerates, and this gives to the leitmotiv special significance and inflexibility.

It is well-known that in the majority of theatrical and screen interpretations of *Hamlet* the key to understanding the main character has always been his famous monologue 'To be or not to be...'. In this screen version it loses its dramatic significance owing to the reconsideration of its conception by the director. This was done quite deliberately, since a reflective Hamlet, tortured by doubts, and equally subject to bursts of strength and weakness, was not suitable to the treatment of the image suggested by Kozintsev: he claimed that 'Hamlet's tragedy is not at all the tragedy of a lonely thinker, this is the tragedy of a man who does not want to put up with the baseness surrounding him'[11] . It is not surprising that, following the director's intent, Shostakovich, when creating the music accompanying this monologue focused his attention on the process by which the Danish Prince turns into a heroic fighter.

It is interesting that the epigraph theme, on which this item is based, gives rise to clear associations with the music of the monologue 'A Man is the beauty of the world': the same subdued, gloomy timbre of the clarinet in the low register, the unhurried, seemingly held back development of the Adagio melody, the gradual transition from a tragic world outlook to lucidity. All this was designed to show the hero's coming to an understanding of the necessity for fighting and resistance, and his resolve to pursue his purpose to the end even if it meant his death. At the same time, the music of the monologue 'To be or not to be...' signifies a new stage in the development of Hamlet's character: he is now brave enough to give up his passive censure of evil and start his active struggle. His first act of revenge was to establish the guilt of King Claudius, who had committed a terrible crime, the second to accuse the Queen, and the third was his cold fury and wish to kill after learning about the king's secret order, according to which on arriving in England Hamlet's 'head should be struck off' (the scene aboard the ship). Each time Hamlet gets new proof of illegal actions committed by Claudius and his stooges, his theme acquires more and more characteristics which bring it closer to the leitmotiv of the Ghost. As the dramatic events unfold, it loses its individuality and turns into a symbol of retribution, formidable in its mercilessness.

In its development through the film, the strained evolution of Hamlet's theme, which rises to the heights of universal tragedy, is set off by everyday genre scenes (the arrival of the players, the play, garden music, and royal fanfares, etc.) which create an effect of alienation, a brief pause. On the other hand, by combining contradictory episodes with genre and psychological scenes, and also using imaginative transformations of the epigraph theme, the composer managed to achieve the feeling of continuously increasing dynamic movement towards a climax which marks the next part of this peculiar musical-cinematic sonata — recapitulation.

This recapitulation opens with the scene of Ophelia's madness, constructed in accordance with the principles of opera dramaturgy. In the brief, sadly drooping viola tune which introduces this scene and performs the function of a leitmotiv one can feel the confusion and perplexity of a lonely, tortured soul. The ostinato-like repetition of the motif, which seems to bring together the fragmented *mise-en-scène* of the action, resembles an 'idée fixe' to which the poor girl's departing reason is stubbornly clinging[12]. But all her attempts to break away from this nightmare of madness fail.

The fact that Ophelia's madness is treated by the film makers neither as a consequence of unfortunate love nor as a disease which afflicted the heroine, but as the result of an inhuman age, influences the visual, plastic and musical synthesis of the scene. The vast space of one of the halls in the royal palace, lost in darkness, is filled with armed soldiers in steel helmets. Among them a beautiful young girl is a wandering like a lost angel with a bunch of lifeless broken twigs, imagining them to be flowers in her hand. Like Martha in Rimsky-Korsakov's opera *The Czar's Bride*, she is lost in memories, singing simple songs in a feeble voice. Especially memorable for its delicate poetic beauty is the first of them: 'How should I your true love know from another one?' in the melodic inflexions of which a connection with Russian song can be observed.

She cannot stay still for any length of time. Soon in Ophelia's burning brain the music of the gavotte begins to sound: on hearing it she starts to dance. The well-known steps of the dance make the girl return to the serene days when she was happy. But these memories also take away the last of her strength. Her reason is slowly ebbing away. Ophelia's last song: 'Tomorrow is Saint Valentine's day', echoing through the resonant arches of Elsinore, tells of her complete and irrevocable plunge into the world of illusion and madness. Peace and lucidity visit Ophelia only for a moment before her death. The artless and naive melody of the folk song 'Robin' (one of the rare cases of Shostakovich introducing a quotation into the musical score of the film) is her leave-taking. Later, the same melody will sound again in the scene of Ophelia's death, in the high register of the violins which gradually melts in the high spring air, while the fragile rays of the sun illuminate the girl's deserted room.

Ophelia's death continues the long list of Elsinore's latest victims. Gertrude dies, having drunk a goblet of poisoned wine. Claudius, brought down by the Prince's sword, dies with a desperate animal cry. Laertes perishes in the duel, and then Hamlet himself dies. But if the king's death, marked by the appearance of the Ghost's leitmotiv, is felt as vengeance, the duel between Hamlet and Laertes returns the tragedy to its starting point — the opposition of the hero and Elsinore, which is achieved by means of music. But not as in the overture, which is founded on the counterpoint of two leading dramatic themes, their hostility towards each other achieves the highest degree of intensity. The prevalence of close-ups in the pictorial composition of the duel also affects the music, as a result of which Hamlet's theme, surrounded by whirlwind passages in the strings, appears with its rhythm augmented two- and fourfold, with an evened out pattern in the tragic B minor key. This severe restraint of the melody's progress, which is emphasized by the balanced, measured rhythm, makes it sound like a chorale, revealing its relation to the revenge leitmotiv. The epigraph-theme, connected with Hamlet's character, is followed by the rigid, ominous theme of Elsinore. But the latter's triumph is short-lived. Pressed by a heroic, life-asserting motif from Hamlet's theme (a variant of its third phrase) it gradually loses ground and retreats, admitting the moral victory of the hero in his fight with Elsinore.

The scene of Hamlet's death is laconic: having left the gloomy walls of the castle, the hero breathes in the air of freedom for the last time, looks at the sea and cliffs of his native Denmark. At that moment, his leitmotiv is played by the strings and the harp, now free from earthly passions and griefs, devoid of its former expression.

The finale of the film, according to the critic Efim Dobin, 'is not an epitaph to a hero who perished in vain, but a baton handed over to future fighters'[13], and therefore the funeral march crowning the film is perceived not as mourning for Hamlet but as a glorification of reason, dignity and the nobility of man. During the funeral procession, the epigraph theme arises in the sparkling timbre of the trumpets, full of force, triumphant and magnificent. This is emphasised its recasting in the major key.

This analysis of Shostakovich's music for Kozintsev's *Hamlet* makes it possible to conclude that it is unique in the cinema of the '60s, since the composer succeeded in fusing the classical form of the sonata allegro with the structural organization of another kind of art, and also in using symphonic method not only in the musical but also in the pictorial composition of the film. The juxtaposition of the leading dramatic themes of the film, and their unification in the inverted recapitulation, the consistent development of leitmotivs characterizing the protagonists, all suggest a possible connection of the music in *Hamlet* with the genre of the programme symphony. This is one more testimony to the interrelation between musical art and cinema and to music's ability to influence the composition and dramaturgy of a film while possessing a definite artistic value.

24

An upsurge of interest in musical cinema. Ways of solving the problem of 'cinema and opera'. *Katerina Izmailova* by Shostakovich and Shapiro

The end of the '50s, and the '60s, appear to have been the most favourable and productive years for the development of musical film genres. The efforts of film makers engaged in this field were mainly concentrated on working in four areas connected with further adaptation to the demands of the wide screen: concerts, ballet, opera, and operetta.

At first sight, the unaccountable interest of directors in the most un-cinematographic genre of musical cinema, the film-concert, may cause surprise, and arouse suspicion of there being material advantage in it. In fact, generous financing by the state of this sort of production stimulated the appearance of a whole series of uniform film concerts, which served as advertisements, aimed at demonstrating the concert programs of opera and variety singers and of the leading professional and amateur groups. Sometimes, these had simple comic or melodramatic plots which helped overcome their fragmentary character and unite the uncoordinated concert items, and, to some extent, facilitated understanding of the film by spectators. However, in criticizing the artificial and un-cinematic character of the film concert, it is necessary to bear in mind one important but little known fact: intensive use was made of film concerts as a special training ground for mastering the techniques of stereophonic music recording and stereoscopic filming. The starting point was the film concert of the director Nemolyaev, *An Evening in Moscow* (1962). Two years later the Armenian director Grigori Melik-Avakyan shot the film *Goar Gasparyan Is Singing*, which proved to be a turning-point in musical cinema. In it, he made an attempt to reveal the meaning of popular arias from the repertoire of Goar Gasparyan, a soloist of the Erevan Opera and Ballet House, by means of staging and performance devices. It is interesting that for this purpose the director used different combinations of documentary film and episodes shot on location, with a carefully chosen cast; the main point is that he gave each novelette item its own colour range.

A combination of feature film and animated cartoon was used in the Tadjik film *The 1002nd Night* (1965, director Makhmudov, composer Babaev), and though it also, as with Melik-Avakyan's film, was far from perfect, a way was paved for mastering essentially new methods of musical and visual synthesis. Moreover, these films formed a technical and creative basis for subsequent experiments, though they were really better adapted to television.

The advance of Soviet ballet, which by that time had acquired world renown, evoked a natural desire on the part of directors to screen the best ballet performances, and so to preserve the art of famous ballet masters for posterity while at the same time acquainting cinema fans with theatrical novelties. As a result, within a decade eight film ballets were released in the Soviet Union. Among them there were both screen versions of such classic ballet masterpieces of Tchaikovsky as *The Sleeping Beauty* (1964) and *Swan Lake* (1968), by the Leningrad directors Dudko and Sergeyev, and cinema versions of modern ballets. The latter were the film ballets of 1960 *The Moor of Venice*, set to Machavariani's music, after Shakespeare's *Othello* (director and ballet-master Chabukiani) and *Leili and Medjnun*, to the music of Balasanyan, after the poem of the same name by Nizami Gandjevi (directors T. Berezantseva, T. Valamat-zade). In their creation, an active part was taken by the ballet companies of the Tbilisi Z. Paliashvili Opera and Ballet House, and the artists of the Tadjik Opera and Ballet House.

Unfortunately, in most cases the director's work on film ballets first of all demanded an ability to adapt the stage version to feature film time-scale. Much rarer were instances aimed at the creation of independent screen versions, distinct from the theatrical performance and based on an organic synthesis of the expressive means of dance, music, and cinema. Among them were the charming screen version of Raukhverger's ballet *Cholpon — The Morning Star*, a collaboration between the Lenfilm studio and the Frunze feature film studio (1959, director Tikhomirov) and the film ballet of Lithuanian cinematographers to the music of Balsys, *The Fir-Tree, Queen of Grass Snakes* (1959, directors Grivickas and Mockus).

The climax of these developments was achieved in the '60s in the genre of the film opera. One after another, screen versions of Russian classical opera of last century appeared: *Khovanshchina* (1959, director Stroyeva), *The Queen of Spades* (1960, director Tikhomirov), *Iolanta* by Tchaikovsky (1963, director Gorikker), *Mozart and Salieri* (1962) and *The Czar's Bride* by Rimsky-Korsakov (1965), *The Stone Guest* by Dargomyzhsky (1967, these three films were directed by Gorikker). In the wake of Russian film makers, interest in the opera film appeared among the directors in the national studios of other Union republics. In the Ukraine, Molostova and Lapoknysh screened the opera *Naimichka* based on the story of Taras Shevchenko and the opera of Mikhail Verikovsky (1963). In Azerbaijan, a screen version of the musical comedy *Arshin Mal Alan* by Uzeir Gadjibekov was made, edited by composer Fakret Amirov (1966, director Taghi-zade). In Georgia, Leonard Esakia completed a screening of the monumental epic work by the founder of the Georgian school of composers Zakharia Paliashivili, *Abesalom and Eteri* (1967). It is curious that the formidable task of editing the musical score for this screen version required the formation of a special committee consisting of members of the Georgian SSR, Union of Composers. This, however, didn't help the film...

In any attempt to describe the specific peculiarities of Soviet opera film during this period, the first fact that springs to the eye is the use of a double actor-singer cast. The performers were very famous actors. Of course, there were exceptions when the film was shot for the sake of one opera star, for example Zurab Andjeparidze (*Abesalom and Eteri*), Vladimir Atlantov (*The Stone Guest*), Galina Vishnevskaya (*Katerina Izmailova*, to be discussed below). Besides, the opera pictures of those days were character- ized by a passion for shooting on location, and filming interiors aimed at destroying conventional theatricality and conveying historical and realistic authenticity to the feature film. It was not by chance that in striving to achieve a correct reconstruction of environment and historical atmosphere for *The Czar's Bride*, Vladimir Gorikker shot the film in the old Russian city of Suzdal, where the frescos and murals of the great icon painters Theo- phanes the Greek and Andrei Rublev have been preserved.

This example was not of course unique. Apart from Gorikker, other directors also showed serious intentions and took decisive steps towards breaking with the vicious practice of shooting 'photographed' film perfor- mances, and adapting opera to the expressive means of cinema. The main obstacle they inevitably faced, and could not always overcome successfully, was connected with the different time -scale of musical and visual processes. The static character of opera action also gave a lot of trouble, as did the hold-up of the plot by arias, monologues and ensemble scenes. For a cinema based on dynamic and spectacular factors these qualities of opera con- tradicted its very nature, and essence. Therefore directors strove to find some means which could reconcile cinema and opera and make their collaboration productive. However, in spite of their good intentions, most opera screen adaptations were too illustrative and decorative, and simplified the plots. Nevertheless, such pictures played a definite cultural and educational role, and helped to bring the treasures of opera closer to the mass of common spectators.

Against a background of fairly ordinary productions, the film opera *Katerina Izmailova* shines like a bright pearl. Its creators managed to come very close to what is referred to as the *cinema opera*. Filmed in 1967 at the Lenfilm studio, by director Mikhail Shapiro, with the active collaboration of Dmitry Shostakovich, *Katerina Izmailova* differed in principle from typical cinema versions of classical opera by being an opera from the modern repertoire, and little known to most spectators. Indeed, it required courage to decide on screening an opera which had been forbidden by the censorship because of an accusation of formalism, which was listed as the number one enemy of Soviet art. On the other hand, the absence of stage clichés and 'politically imposed treatments' did not circumscribe the director's fancy, which in the long run helped to create an original film, based on an organic fusion of music, singing, playing and the use of specifically cinematic devices and means of expression.

A significant fact was that the film script and a new version of the musical score were prepared by the composer himself. Incidentally, for Shostakovich, who eight years earlier had written a film script for Mussorgsky's *Khovanshchina* in collaboration with Abramova and arranged a new orchestration for it, adapting an opera for the cinema was not new, and caused him no difficulty. The success of *Katerina Izmailova* was assured by the sympathetic understanding between the director and the composer, which brought wonderful results. They managed to put aside the theatrical thinking characteristic of most opera films, and proved that it was possible to create an independent audiovisual treatment of the opera which was valuable in itself.

The principal difference between the film interpretation of this opera and its theatrical counterpart was first of all the fact that the tiniest stop or retardation of visual movement could cause the destruction of an opera dramaturgy based on continuous dynamic development. Shapiro resorted to some effective plastic devices: he translated musical images into visual action and made a contrapuntal unification of real and imaginary time within each frame. In practice, he achieved this by using techniques of combination shooting, and double exposition, chromo-key (i.e. dividing the frame into parts, either diagonally or vertically). This device acquired a special expressive and emotional significance on the wide screen. Thus, Katerina's arioso at the beginning of the opera, 'The air smells of spring in the yard', where the heroine's story about her luckless marriage, interspersed with memories of her happy girlhood, was shown by the director in double image which united past and present. If the past had an unreal, idealized colouring, the present reality of Katerina's life was, by way of contrast, shown as deliberately earthly. The camera pinpointed slowly and thoroughly the essential details of the merchant's everyday life: the gaudy popular prints on the walls, geraniums on the window-sill, a pile of pillows on the marriage bed etc.

No less original was the visual solution of the monologue of Katerina's father-in-law, old Izmailov, during which one can see Boris Timofeyevich's secret thoughts materialize. They appear on the screen medallion-shaped or, by daring association, in the shape of a key-hole placed on the left side of the frame. In this way the spectator is given an opportunity to watch both the actual behaviour of the old man spying on Katerina and the birth of his vulgar and squalid dreams of seducing his daughter-in-law. Certainly, in these examples the director chooses a fairly traditional method of visual illustration based on the musical text, but it is so artistically convincing that it seems quite natural and does no harm to the film.

A more complicated musical-visual structure is presented in the scene of the discovery of Katerina with her lover, which is based on the principle of parallel action, in a dynamic crescendo leading to a climax. In a constantly accelerating tempo the sequences of the drinking party at the wedding of Katerina and Sergei are replaced by a running bedraggled muzhik who happens to stumble on the dead body of Katerina's husband Zinovy Borisovich in the basement of the house, by the feet of marching policemen and, finally, by Katerina's face which bears an expression of animal fear at the prospect of the inevitable day of reckoning for the killings committed both by her and Sergei. This swift intensification of montage rhythm is accompanied by shorter and shorter sequences, the nervous, chaotic flitting of which stops abruptly in one long frame — the arrest of the newly-weds. The static character of the opera was also overcome by the device of expanding space, discovered and well-realized by the director. Whereas in the exposition of this film opera the action is restricted to the house and the yard of the Izmailov merchants, later streets of the provincial town sometimes appear, and sometimes the river with picturesque trees lining its bank. Katerina, locked in the house, has only a dim knowledge of the former, and therefore the town appears rarely and does not attract any special attention. But nature, for which Katerina's freedom-loving soul yearns, occupies a considerable space in the film because it is associated with her memories of happy childhood and youth, and happiest of all, her meetings with Sergei. At the same time, the landscape scenes serve as a peculiar bridge for exploring another Russia, whose immeasurable expanse hides so much human suffering, grief, and despair. The tragic fate of Katerina Izmailova is dissolved in this sea without trace or memory. That is why the scene of the heroine's death in the cold waters of a Siberian river, which stopped only for a moment, the movement of a column of convicts deadly tired by their long march, seems to be an unremarkable episode in a long line of lost lives. The naked marker poles disappearing beyond the horizon, measuring the distance to be travelled, the vast empty space, the miserable party of convicts plodding along the snow-covered road, — this is the finale of *Katerina Izmailova*, projecting the drama of one single person on to that of the whole Russian people.

According to the tradition then current in the operatic cinema, two casts, one acting and one vocal, were used. But the part of the heroine was both acted and sung by the Bolshoi Theatre soloist Galina Vishnevskaya. Though she had never performed this part on the stage, nor had ever been in a film, she managed to create on screen a complicated and contradictory image of a woman consumed by passion, capable of overcoming any obstacles and moral standards for the sake of love, and of committing any crime. Vishnevskaya's performance, natural and devoid of deliberate affectation, excited strong emotions. At the same time, she preserved operatic conventions and artistic generalizations in portraying the feelings of the heroine. This helped the revelation of the psychological portrait of Katerina Izmailova in its dynamic development, continuously changing, various in rhythm, plasticity, emotional fulfillment.

In spite of the undoubted merit and originality of the director's approach, the creators of this film made one serious mistake. For this picture, shot in a hard realistic manner, a standard version of the musical sound track was prepared like a recording which excluded any sound but music. When the sound track, cleared of any 'alien' sounds was subsequently joined to the pointedly naturalistic scenic material, the visual element of the film resembled an animated illustration, a pantomime of the recorded opera.

The musical recording was also far from perfect, there being a considerable unbalance between the enhanced sound of the voices and the muted orchestra. It should be remembered that the music recording took place under the wrong conditions, directly from the stage of the Kirov Theatre. It was made with five microphones, all of them connected to one input, which naturally affected the quality of the sound. Nevertheless, thanks to the titanic efforts of the musical editor Yuri Prokofiev and the chief recording engineer Evgeni Nikul'sky, it was possible to achieve a stereophonic effect, and *Katerina Izmailova* lengthened the short list of Soviet films with experimental stereophonic sound.

During the '60s, the genre of musical comedy film and film operetta also went through a period of creative activity. However, directors' attention was focused here not on any search for original forms, or artistic synthesis, but on a simple transfer to the screen of the most popular operettas. This was done, not so much for the sake of prolonging their lives, as for competing with the theatres, attracting mass interest and obtaining high profit from commercial hire. As a result, practically all the box-office operettas of the Soviet musical theatre were screened: *The Wind of Freedom* by Dunayevsky (1961, director Trauberg), *Moskva, Cheremushki* by Shostakovich (the film was called simply *Cheremushki*, 1962, director Rappaport), *A Serf Girl* by Strelnikov (the film *A Serf Actress*, 1963, director Tikhomirov), *Romeo, My Neighbour* by Gadjiev (1963, director Makhmudbekov), *A Wedding in Malinovka* by Alexandrov (1967, director Tutyshkin), *Trembita* by Miliutin (1968, director Nikolaevsky), *Karine* by Chukhadjan (1969, director Manasian). The casting of popular comedy actors, picturesque landscape backgrounds, the bright national colours, entertaining plots, and the abundance of stunt situations all brought these close to the best examples of '30s musical comedy. At the same time, the exploitation of old techniques, the recurrence of old turns from the Russian vaudeville, the classical French and Viennese operetta, the Soviet romantic comedy, in forms more or less adapted for the screen, imparted archaic traits to these films and testified to the stagnation of the operetta genre.

It became possible to see a change in this wretched situation and some sign of new life, an awakening of interest in experimentation, and a search for new models and structures in the musical-dramatic cinema, when the eccentric musical comedy of the director Rolan Bykov and the composer Boris Tchaikovsky, *Aibolit-66* (1967), was released. The picture was based on the famous fairy-tale by Kornei Chukovsky about the kind doctor Aibolit (Oh! It is painful!) who went to far-off Africa to treat sick monkeys, and about the terrible robber Barmalei who did his best to prevent him from achieving his aim. Since the entertaining story about Aibolit and Barmalei was known to everybody in the Soviet Union, the director rejected the idea of retelling it word for word but chose a method of free, *buffo* improvisation 'on the topic', pointing out the exact date of its birth and describing it as 'a film performance for children and adults with songs, dances, shooting, and music'. This ironic focus of the picture influenced the choice of expressive means, and allowed many paradoxical combinations of the simple and the complex, of the comic and the tragic.

The masks appeared to be simple and easily recognizable, as did as the lyrics of the songs and the music, which was based on elementary and instantly remembered melodies. Not one of the thirteen songs in the film was there by chance. All of them were part of the action, connecting the episodes, directing the general development, portraying the characters, commenting on and explaining their actions. Extreme clarity, a democratic and emotional musical language resorting to basic song and dance structures, and effective and decorative orchestration all evoked motley carnival spectacle.

A more complicated tendency towards theatricality was also observable in the visual elements of the film. Using an open structure for the scenes and a continuous development of the plot, the director made his own rules for the game: it would be impossible to understand what was taking place on the screen without accepting these. Abrupt modulations from cardboard scenery, for interior shots, and the deliberately theatrical plasticity of miming actors, to location shots, to traditional 'live' reality; quick transitions from wide screen to a narrow strip of film — all of this was aimed at surprising the spectator's imagination with a cascade of witty attractions, to take him beyond the boundaries of customary stereotypes, to accustom him to strange metamorphoses in the action, where nothing is in earnest and at the same time everything is serious, in the same way as the world is perceived by a child. Though formally this musical comedy should be attributed to the category of song films, it became the foundation of the domestic musical — a genre which appeared in the Soviet Union very late because of obstacles put in its way by officials of the party apparatus who thought it was a harmful bearer of Western culture and ideology.

25

The zenith of musical achievements in the directors' cinema of the '60s: music for the films *The Shadows of Our Forgotten Ancestors, Andrei Rublev* and *No Ford in the Fire*

Besides the above tendencies, which in many ways determined both the intonational image and the characteristic genre and typological traits of film music in the '60s, that period was marked by the creation of number of works, truly innovative in spirit, which had a great influence on the style and treatment of sound in the cinema in subsequent decades. Among such films were Sergei Paradjanov's *The Shadows of our Forgotten Ancestors* (1964, composer Skorik) and *The Colour of Pomegranates* (1969, composer Mansuryan), Andrei Tarkovsky's *Andrei Rublev* (1966, 2 parts, composer Ovchinnikov), and Gleb Panfilov's picture *No Ford in the Fire* (1968, composer Bibergan). The extraordinary and unique talent of these directors, each of whom possessed his own artistic vision, was shown by the fact that they generated the musical ideas and directed the work of their composers. The magnetism of the personalities of Paradjanov, Tarkovsky, Panfilov, and the philosophic polysemy and originality of their designs, demanded adequate forms of expression and, as a result, cardinal reconsideration of the whole system of devices and techniques, and the creation of a unique sound aura and original stylistic models of sound and musical dramaturgy in their films.

Sergei Paradjanov's film *The Shadows of Our Forgotten Ancestors* shook both the public and professional critics. The film is also known under the title 'The Fiery Horses'[15]. Local critics proclaimed it the beginning of a Ukrainian 'new wave', a film which restored the traditions of Ukrainian romantic cinema, one of whose sources was Alexander Dovzhenko, the famous director of the '20s–'30s. The action of the film, made after Kotsubinsky's tale of the same name, took place at the beginning of the 20th century in a small Guzul village in Western Ukraine. The plot of this film, very intimate in character, is as follows.

Clan hatred separates the families of the poor Paliichuks and the rich Tuteniuks; but their children, Ivan and Marichka, have been in love since childhood. When they grow up they decide to marry. On the day before the wedding the bride perishes, the young man leaves the village in despair, wanders for some time, then returns and tries to throw in his lot with another woman. But his wife is unfaithful to him, and Ivan dies.

However, the story of the tragic love of Ivan and Marichka, intertwined with fate and death, is only one, and not at all the most important, dramatic story of this polyphonic film. In reality, it serves as a pretext for showing, both musically and visually the peculiar national atmosphere and customs of the Guzul people, in vivid ritual forms. The use of old folk-song material and reconstructed folk dances and rites, struck spectators' imaginations with their archaic exoticism, as did the introduction of pagan rituals during Christmas observances — all of this, together with the liturgically static montage rhythm, imparted an air of mystery to the film. On the whole, the creation of a specifically 'carnival' musical milieu, which was, as it were, a fragment of folk life, a condenser of national customs and rituals, was of great importance in revealing the philosophic conception and the directors's world outlook, distinguished by heightened expression and sensual picturesqueness. At the same time, in the kaleidoscopic mixture of musical motifs, songs, dances, prayers, folk tunes there appeared to be an inner logic and power governing this seemingly elemental whirlpool by means of leitmotivs: in particular, the sustained sounds of *trembitas* carrying glad or sad news to the inhabitants of the Carpathians. The calls of *trembitas* here measure the course of time like the refrain in rondo form, and mark changes in the fate of the heroes. Besides these, two more leitmotivs play an important organizing role in building the musical dramaturgy. They serve as symbols, and are connected with the themes of love and death (fate).

Both themes were written by the composer, and resemble traditional expressions of love and evil in musical tradition. Thus the theme of love is a plastic cantabile melody which derives a special warmth and excitement from the sonority of the strings in the middle register. A distinguishing characteristic of the death leitmotiv is its series of multiphasic, deliberately amelodic thematic formations, with elements of aleatoric technique and *bloc sonore* which are combined into an integral sound image by ostinati resembling mystic incantations.

Preserving the static immutability, the themes of fate (*trembitas*), love and death form a framework which holds together the dramatic construction of this film which consists a chain of loosely linked episodes. Each of them has its own subtitle caption and a separate place in the structure of the plot. But besides musical leitmotivs, the overcoming of centrifugal tendencies, which could lead to the disintegration of the form, is assisted by the introduction of several plastic symbols into the tissue of the story: a cross, a lamb, an old witch, the fiery horses etc. which, together with the music, impart poetic polysemy and philosophic depth to the film, making into an epic.

It is interesting that Sergei Paradjanov himself thought the main hero Ivanko to be a poet, if not professionally, then at least through his world outlook. The image of the poet caught the director's imagination so much that he devoted his next picture, *The Colour of Pomegranates* (originally it bore another title — *Saiat-Nova*) to the outstanding poet of the Armenian Renaissance, the great folk poet and singer (ashug) of the 18th century Arutiun Saiadyan, better known in history under his penname of Saiat-Nova.

However, *The Colour of Pomegranates* scarcely resembles a biographical film, which would tell the hero's life story chronologically. Thus one will look in vain for historical facts in it. The subject of the director's investigation is the inner theme of the poet's fate, reflected in fifteen miniatures. Each of them, like a pearl from an amazing necklace, adds its colour to this portrait of the artist's life.

The film consists of a series of static frames full of symbolic objects, illustrating the recited poems and the Ashug's songs, set with poetic metaphors and picturesque epigraphs to the chapters / miniatures. Like the film *The Shadows of Our Forgotten Ancestors, The Colour of Pomegranates* has its own sound world and characteristic timbres. But if in Paradjanov's first picture the artistic texture was virtually permeated by *trembita* calls, here the sounds of the *camancha* reign — an instrument associated with the poet's youth and his love for the czarevna. Later they are replaced by the ringing of church bells. With the appearance of the bells his love ceases, and then he takes monastic vows, leaves the world, spends his old age and dies in a monastery. Yet the presence of music in the film is not limited to the introduction of recurring themes and dominant images. The whole atmosphere seems to be woven from the most ancient Armenian tunes, with a fine, almost imperceptible plaiting into the quaint patterns of Tigran Mansuriyan's music. The latter, owing to the use of sonorous and acoustic effects, introduces a feeling of airiness and of free soaring in infinite space.

Although many students of Paradjanov's and Tarkovsky's work express the opinion that there is a certain affinity in their approaches to the theme 'the artist and his time', as well as in their treatment of the leading characters in *The Colour of Pomegranates* and in *Andrei Rublev*, these films differ as regards the attitude of their directors to music. In Paradjanov's film *The Colour of Pomegranates* (and also in *The Shadows of Our Forgotten Ancestors*) the basis of the musical dramaturgy is the principle of collage, which aims at showing a correct musical-ethnographic cross-section of the historical epoch, via the prism of folk ritual and custom. However, the musical dramaturgy of Tarkovsky's *Andrei Rublev* reveals an underlying connection with the tradition of Russian epic symphonism, and also the film heritage of Prokofiev and Shostakovich. Besides, as compared to Paradjanov's films, where the role of the composer in revealing the artistic design was modest, the distinguishing characteristic of the music in *Andrei Rublev* was that its composer, Viacheslav Ovchinnikov, brought the events of the far-off past closer to the present.

Figure 7 *Andrei Rublev*

One of the film's script writers, director and playwright Andrei Mikhalkov-Konchalovsky (in his book *The Parabola of Design*), formulated the main dramatic principle on which the composition of *Andrei Rublev* was based. He wrote:... 'the story is centred around one man, everything is perceived by him. The hero's evaluation of events... never stops'[16]. Proceeding from this principle, the director actually creates an antibiographical film whose hero is not an active participant and the subject of the action, but an observer, a medium. It is not by chance that his presence in most of the scenes, to quote the critic Nekhoroshev, 'is built *not on the expression* of his attitude to what is happening but on his absorption of external events'[17].

Thus, in depicting the calamities and misfortunes which befell Russia at the beginning of the 15th century, the discordant combination, in the space of one picture, of the rude and the cruel, of naturalistically sensual reality and of the immaterial, the highly spiritual, and of the divine which endowed the world with the creative work of the gifted Russian icon-painter, opened the way to the artistic representation of the philosophic idea of the film in its music.

On the whole, the musical composition of *Andrei Rublev* was based on the dynamically contrasted conjugation of three relatively independent imaginative and thematic spheres, which were grouped around condition-ally designated themes of 'cruelty', 'paganism' and 'Christianity'. Their main propose was to set off and emphasize, against a background of general development, the process of the excruciating maturation of the film's central leitmotiv — Rublev's theme. As for their interrelation, it was as follows.

The theme of 'cruelty' was personified by accumulative images of evil, violence, and injustice, which have quite a few analogues in the world musical practice. Evil is known to be inventive and many-sided. Therefore, in *Andrei Rublev* Ovchinnikov used three themes at once, each of which possessed its own individuality. The first theme was based on a deathly, descending movement of brass instruments, and suggested parallels with the chord complexes and roaring of the 'Teutonic trumpets' in *Alexander Nevsky*. The second theme, written for woodwinds with the addition of xylophone, contained only one short angular-aggressive phrase, and evoked associations with the famous 'wicked scherzo' style of Shostakovich. Finally, the third theme arose out of a biting, sweeping movement of muted strings with a constantly changing nervous rhythm abundant in chroma-tism. In the process of active interrelation the themes of 'cruelty' were contrapuntally superimposed, the elements of one theme 'sprouted' in another (one of the examples is an episode called 'Cruelty' in the director's script, a Tartar attack on a Russian town and the siege of a monastery). Not only did this contribute to their unification into one musical imaginative complex, but it also helped to create a generalized, inhuman symbolic image of violence.

It is also possible to attribute to the themes of 'cruelty' the musical links accompanying the episode of the tartar invasion. Their characteristic feature was the use of sound representational devices, and all kinds of exotic timbres constructed with the help of the synthesizer ANS, and the use of non-traditional methods of sound production, such as the frullato of the strings[18] or rolls on the timpani obtained by rotating wire brushes on the drumheads (the episode 'Invasion' — 'the Tartar sound').

'Paganism' was represented in the music of *Andrei Rublev* by several items: 'Festival', 'Consecration of the Bell', 'The Skomorokh', 'Paganism'.

They possessed a number of stylistic characteristics, the most remarkable among these being very simple diatonic tunes; ritual meditation created by multiple repetitions of elementary melodic and rhythmic figures, which make the music resemble a magic incantation, or a primal, archaic pagan act; a frequent recourse to the expressive power of choral singing.

Ex. 18 Common Prayers from the film *Andrei Rublev*

Save, o God, our Lord most gracious,
God, save thy people

The wild manifestations of the life-giving sensual force of 'paganism' is opposed to the severe ascetic images of 'Christianity'. In their most condensed form they proclaim themselves in the scene 'Andrei's dialogue with the ghost of Theophanes' where a problem, highly important and topical in our time, is discussed, that of morality, and the artist's duty to history. Throughout this lengthy scene Ovchinnikov's 'Prayers' can be heard. The functions they perform can have a twofold explanation: on the one hand, 'The Prayers' accompany the scene as an illustrative sound background, with a concrete subject motivation; on the other hand, they help penetrate the spiritual world of the hero, to clarify the depth and sincerity of his belief.

The musical item 'Prayers' was written for mixed chorus *a capella* and is a complete strophic work. It is based on the Orthodox Church prayer 'O dear Lord, have mercy on us!' skilfully stylized in the spirit of 12th century psalmody, preserving all the characteristics of cult singing, i.e. the long drawn-out recitation of the prayer text, the declamatory character of the performance, the dependence of the rhythm on the logical and grammatical accents of the words pronounced, etc.

The functioning of these three independent imaginative-thematic spheres within the musical space of the film, as well as the division of the film's composition into eight chapters representing complete stories, naturally demanded a single form-creating technique capable of shaping the discrete character of the epic story. This task was entrusted to the leitmotiv of Andrei Rublev, which was not only associated with the image of the main hero, but was also the axis of its musical conception. It is interesting that in its composition the graphic sharpness and severe ascetism of the melodic opening were organically combined with the plasticity of its subsequent development, which maintained both tension and drama. The means was the rhythmic and dynamic singling out of the sharp sixth of the Dorian mode, then a descending movement over a diminished seventh chord finishing on the leading note of A minor, all of which seemed to make the theme lose its inner stability and emotional balance, and become distorted by excruciating doubt and suffering.

Appearing in the prologue of the film as a simple folk-tune on a pipe, Rublev's leitmotiv is further subjected to intense modification (melodic, rhythmic, harmonic), which appears to clarify from inside the image of the main hero, to show it in its different aspects, to reveal the spiritual wealth of an artist who felt a profound connection with his people. This theme also obtains a peculiar musical character by deriving subsidiary themes from the main leitmotiv. They appear either as modification of one of its elements ('The flight of the man') or as independent developments of its figures. For example, a substantial musical item ('Ballooning')[19] was based on a tune characterised by the minor third borrowed from the second element of the leitmotiv, reproduced not exactly but in reverse. A still more complex version of this image building by transformation of the leitmotiv is to be found in the scene 'Calvary', the music of which grows out of the concluding figure which consists of a second, and bears the imprint of grief and suffering. Yet, given the undoubted melodic, harmonic, and rhythmical

Ex. 19 The Leitmotiv of Rublev from the film *Andrei Rublev*

relation between the leitmotiv and the theme of 'Calvary', it is not difficult to see in the latter the influence of another, not less dramatically important sphere in the musical symbolism of the film: that which represents images of evil and cruelty. Such an unexpected synthesis of two quite different themes in the music for 'Calvary' can be accounted for by the content of the scene: Andrei Rublev becomes an involuntary witness to the torture of the sacristan Patrikei with fire and burning hot tin. The spectacle shakes the artist, fills his eyes with silent pain and is imprinted on his tortured soul forever.

The gradual and prolonged building up of Rublev's leitmotiv corresponded to the measured 'annalistic' rhythm of Tarkovsky's film. Some similarity to epic narration was further intensified by the juxtaposition of episodes different in character ('The Skomorokh', 'Prayers', 'Consecration of the bell'). At the same time, reiteration of the leitmotiv imparted rondo characteristics, complicated by varied development of Rublev's role in the structural organization of the film.

As the finale approaches, emotional and psychological stress increase, and so does the film's effect upon the spectator. To a great extent this is achieved by the horizontal structure of the picture, which consists of a long series of catastrophes and revivals which shook medieval Russia. The realization of the imperfection of the world and the sinfulness of man made it necessary to look for salvation within man himself. This struggle towards truth reaches its climax in the epilogue, which blows away the ascetism of black-and-white representation by the use of colour and music. Here the immortal works of the master appear for the first time: the purifying, sunlit 'Trinity' and the strict beauty of 'The Saviour'. Here also the central leitmotiv — the theme of Andrei Rublev — appears at last in all its grandeur.

This musical finale of the film is written in a ternary form using polyphonic techniques. It opens with the fourfold repetition of the leitmotiv in the chorus twice in the boys' chorus, and then twice in the male voices, all of which superficially resembles the exposition of a fugue. The only deviation from the norm is the disruption of the conventional key relations between the leading theme and its three answers. A minor   D flat minor F minor – A minor. However, this use of an unusual key scheme has its own logic ground in the symmetry of the keys D flat minor and F minor relative to the key centre of A minor, which contributes to its reinforcement. The same device intervallic symmetry is repeated by Ovchinnikov in the Finale.

One characteristic of the development is that it moves as a dynamic wave unfolding like a spring. The impression of growing tension is mainly created by the continuous thickening of the orchestral texture: the expansion of register, which sometimes exceeds five octaves; the quickening of the rhythmic pulsation within the bar; the intensification of diminution, the figurational division of the themes, which are gradually pulverized in the flood of movement. At the climax of the development the recapitulation breaks in, which starts with a return of the main key, A minor. As compared to the exposition, the recapitulation is more compact, and in it homophonic writing prevails. But when the first pathetic declamatory element of the leitmotiv appears, an emotional turning point suddenly begins in the brass. This quenches the powerful stream of passion, and with a reserved and concentrated intoning of the orthodox choral prayer penetrates the music of 'The frescos'. The appearance of psalmody here appeals to the spiritual, to the divine, to a belief in the triumph of goodness and justice, to the hope which should never leave humanity on its way to the knowledge of truth. 'The frescos' concludes with an imitative recapitulation of the leitmotiv, but presented in a mirror image of its initial form, using first the manly and severe timbre of bass voices sustained by the orchestral double-basses, then the bright, angelically clear timbres of bass trebles, after which figures from the theme dissolve in the orchestra and melt away. The gradual disappearance of the instruments is accompanied by a simplification of the musical texture and by an abrupt drop in dynamic level. Against this background the leitmotiv, as if exhausted is absorbed in the general movement, and imperceptibly transformed into the noise of the rain which streams down the face of 'The Saviour' and soaks the horses peacefully browsing in the green field. In this semantic modulation of music into the natural earthly sound of material reality[20], the outlines of a new attitude to music as part of a sound-visual conception of film can be seen, an attitude which will reappear strikingly in Andrei Tarkovsky's films of the '70/'80s.

At the end of the '60s, the growing interest of film makers in the dramatic, critical stages of the history of the state, as reflected through the perception of a creative personality, gave an impulse to the creation of another film, which was extremely curious in its un-traditional use of music. This was Gleb Panfilov's *No Ford in the Fire*. It tells about events of the Civil War, but its heroes are neither bolsheviks, fanatically convinced of their rightness, nor the red commanders, but a plain, awkward and simple-minded girl, Tania Tetkina, an orderly from a train transporting wounded Red Army soldiers to a hospital behind the lines. Firmly believing in the idea of the revolution, she dreams about universal love, kindness, happiness, and for the sake of this belief goes to her death. The revolution not only takes command of her flesh and blood, but awakes in her a thirst for creation and self-expression.

The drawings of the young painter are not passive copies of reality[21]. In the inexperienced 'uncouthness', naivety and touching openness of her pictures her clear, childishly fresh and idealistically enthusiastic conception of the surrounding world is revealed. The unification of two levels of reflected reality (concrete everyday and generalized artistic) within one cinematic space results in the appearance of a peculiar two-layer drama-turgy in which each of the layers possesses its own expressive means, its own stylistics, and which embraces not only the pictorial but also the sound elements of the film, including the music.

The convincing embodiment of the conceptual design of the film *No Ford in the Fire* is to a great extent assisted by its consistent use of two artistic methods: concretization and generalization, both of which had a great influence on the building up of its musical dramaturgy. Just as with the visual element, so here also a strict delimitation of the two spheres was observed, the music of the real world, motivated by the plot, existing within the frame, and the music of art, sounding off the frame and accompanying the appearance of Tania Tetkina's drawings on the screen.

The sphere of 'prosaic existence' is represented by rough but honest and sincere people — the wounded on the hospital train, with their artless joys and sorrows, heated discussions and reflections on the purpose of life. Music is an integral part of that world, the habitual milieu of these wounded Red Army soldiers. Besides, it is a characteristic mark of the times, and reproduces the atmosphere of the '20s. In such cases composers usually resorted to the rather hackneyed device of quotations, typical of Soviet revolutionary films. Fortunately, Vadim Bibergan avoided this temptation and chose the less widely used devices of stylization and reconstruction of the most typical musical genres belonging to the period of the third Russian revolution and the Civil War, such as the heroic march, the merry chastooshka, the naughty accordion folk-tune and, in contrast to these the drawing-room waltz. In this way he managed to destroy the stereotypes typical of such films, and found his own original musical solution. It is curious that,for all that, the composer did not balk at the use of trivial formulae/clichés which were taken by the spectators as 'signs', of the period, and evoked concrete object-visual associations with those times. Moreover, those 'signs', composed of banalities, stimulated the spectator's perception and served, in a certain sense, as class/ideological, guide-lines. Thus, the banal anacrusis, the blatant 'poster' character of sweeping melo-dies, and the sound of the band left no doubt of the revolutionary origin of the march[22], whereas the waltz was characterized by the softness of 'feminine' endings, melodious lines, and clear harmonization. The change-ability of modes and the thematic variations in repetitions, typical of Russian folk-song music, characterized the accordion tunes.

The chastooshka was represented in the film in an interesting way. Trying to make it sound authentic, and as close as possible to folkloric sources, the composer based the part of the balalaika accompanying the singing on specific chastooshka figures, but added to them his own melody.

But in spite of the fact that they reproduced meticulously features characteristic of this Russian song culture (the question–and–answer principle of
structural organization, the symmetry of couplets-catch phrases, the melodic boldness, the movement in consecutive thirds etc.), the orderlies'
chastooshkas bore the bright imprint of the author's individuality, which
made them unusually picturesque and attractive.

However, the composer asserted himself to a greater extent in
another sphere, which led one away from the vanity of everyday life and
carried the action to another world, that of art. Of course, the film-makers

Ex. 20 Chastooshki of the Medical Orderlies from the film *No Ford in the Fire*

Locomotive, locomotive,
Where are your carriages?
It seems the bandits are but fools
to fight for shoulder-straps.

did not conceal that their heroine was a self-taught artist, and therefore her drawings often resembled those of a child. They lacked composition. They were primitive and poster-like in content. Nevertheless, Tania Tetkina's drawings were surprising and attractive to the Red Army men, who were shown standing in close ranks, with a menacingly raised forest of bayonets over their heads, arresting one's attention not by their angular rigidity and intense poses and gestures, but by their huge, wide open eyes. There was a child's enthusiasm and defencelessness in those eyes, kindness and sacred, excruciating belief.

The drawings in the film were inseparable from the music and the poetry, which all formed a symbiosis of different kinds of art. Its purpose was to express the quintessential idea of the film in a generalized artistic form: the idea of the revolution. To give a poetic foundation to the chorales used in the film, lines from Alexander Blok's poem *The Twelve* were used:

> Once our boys went away
> To serve in the Red Army —
> To serve in the Red Army —
> To lay down their wild lives.

In the first and the last repetition of the 'drawing music' these were supplemented by four more lines, also from Blok:

> To put all bourgeoisie to grief
> We will fan out the world fire,
> The world fire in blood,
> God bless us!

However, the excited and joyful outlook of Blok's overthrowers of the old foundations unexpectedly acquired a different colouring in the film, an exalted and dramatic meaning, through its combination with Vadim Bibergan's music. The reason for this transformation was that the five musical items accompanying the demonstration of the drawings were all based on a severe, ascetic chorale sung by the male voices in *znamenny* chant. Its deliberate lack of emotion, its alienation from a world vain, impregnated with earthly passions, and full of hatred and fratricidal bloodshed, imparted to the music a solemn, cult-like, mystical character.

The structure of the initial phrase of the chorale is interesting. It contains the intonational core out of which the whole theme develops, ribbon fashion. This phrase is a complex alloy of different polyphonic styles. Besides the *znamenny* chant, there are elements of Russian two-part polyphony, a sacred polyphony a cappella which simultaneously introduces the abstract, the impersonal, the 'cosmic' and also a national colour into the chorale theme.

Ex. 21 The music to the drawings from the film *No Ford in the Fire*

Once our boys went away
To serve in the Red Army . . .

Ex. 21 (continued)

Subsequently, the music of the drawings is subjected to intense melodic, modal, and timbral variation. Thus, the second repetition of the chorale theme is in inversion, with a two-voiced splitting of the bass part. The third item, which comes with the appearance of the drawing entitled 'Death of a Comrade' has a tragic note and stands out among the other musical items because of its juxtaposition of different sound levels in the orchestra and mixed chorus (no sopranos), and also, to an even greater extent, because of its introduction into the transparent texture of the balalaika, with its jingling vibrato in the high register. In the fourth item, the composer gives a new, heroically pathetic interpretation to the chorale theme, giving the main melody to a solo tenor and setting it off against prolonged, stiff chords in the male chorus, singing a capella. Finally, for the fifth and last time, the music of the drawings appears at the climax of the film. In this, the leitmotiv connected with the artistic and imaginative overall idea of the film, that of revolution, is proclaimed, confidently and proudly in 'close-up', using both chorus and orchestra. Thus, the final repetition of the chorale, with its resemblance to the first one, forms a gigantic arch, which imparts an architectonic harmony, and a rondo-like compositional completeness. At the same time, consistency and purposefulness in juxtaposing the two musical and imaginative spheres (the music of the drawings and the music of the real world) capable of independent development and transformation, testify to the use of symphonic method. This proved the viability of the traditional symphonic musical dramaturgy, the founders of which were the great modern masters Prokofiev and Shostakovich, and showed that it was possible to adapt genre forms and the structures of autonomous music to the needs of the cinema.

Thus, in the history of Soviet film music the period from 1959 to 1969 should be considered as transitional, on the way to mastery of new models of musical dramaturgy, and to the understanding of the nature of sound and visual images. The increased attention of film makers to representative stylistics, their interest in documentalism and, as a result, their use of a wide range of noise complexes pushed music into the background, making it necessary to reconsider the purpose of film music. On the other hand, the reserve shown by some directors towards music was combined with its rejection as mere background, part of the general phonosphere of the film. This greatly influenced its perception, and helped to form the emotional atmosphere of the action.

This coming into closer contact with representation and natural noises was accompanied by intensive research in the field of timbre dramaturgy. Thus, as before, cinema continued to serve as an experimental laboratory where the latest stylistic trends in modern music were tested and approved, such as concrete and electronic music, which had been censured and banished from the field of autonomous music. Finally, the '60s entered the history of film music as a period when a masterpiece not only of Soviet but of world film music — Shostakovich's music to Kozintsev's film *Hamlet* — was created. Once more, this proved the possibility of the existence in applied music (to which film music undoubtedly belongs) of an original, highly artistic work, equal to the best examples from academic musical genres.

At the same time, the appearance of the directors' cinema in the '60s showed how strong the influence of the personalities of the composer and director could be on the language of film music, and on the principles of its structural organization. In the '70s, distinguished by the flourishing of the *auteur* cinema, and its recognition beyond the boundaries of the Soviet Union, brilliant results were achieved in this field because of the formation of stable partnerships, the most famous of which were the creative collaborations between director Andrei Tarkovsky and composer Edward Artemyev, and between Dmitry Shostakovich and Grigory Kozintsev, in their last joint work.

Part 4

1970–1985

26

The rise and fall of film music
in the period of stagnation.
The problem of choice:
the semi-official film, the commercial 'hit' or
auteur cinema

The next stage in the biography of Soviet film music is connected with that period which was subsequently called the epoch of stagnation by Soviet historians and political commentators. Yet, in spite of the absence of any obvious movement in the political and social life of the country, this period was marked by developments in the arts, which were intense though extremely contradictory in their ideological and moral orientations. Music and cinema were no exceptions. Moreover, the process of cinema stratification, at the end of the '60s and the beginning of the '70s, led to the appearance of official 'all-union' films which yielded to the pressure of the party and state structures; main stream commercial films which had monetary success and exploited the genres of the hit and the melodrama; and *auteur* films, intellectual and poetical, which appealed to the philosophical, spiritual problems of human existence. This process was accompanied by an inner differentiation of stylistic language models, and the formation of stable musical images for each of the above tendencies. At the same time, the acquaintance of Soviet film directors with the works of the leading foreign masters (Visconti, Fellini, Bergman), who paid much attention to music, also had a certain influence upon the extension of musical expressive means in cinema. This forced coexistence, within the same period, of mutually exclusive trends caused a quaint and often paradoxical combination of the outdated clichés of socialist realism with the latest advances of modern music, which had made the music of the '70s and the early '80s motley, eclectic and unbalanced.

The specific characteristics of film music at that time included the crystallization of stable musical clichés. The sphere of their functional application was as a rule limited to the strictly regulated category of film created according to state demand[1]. According to the implicit, but nevertheless strictly observed genre and thematic hierarchy of films within this sphere, the first 'privileged' ranks were occupied by the monumental military epic and the grand historical peasant saga. It is not surprising that work on these blockbusters, which promised material profit, high state awards and honoured titles, was entrusted only to 'the most deserving'. This very soon led to the usurpation of this genre by a small group of directors. If some changes in the list of directors' names could sometimes be observed, the monopoly for music composition was practically held by three men: Yuri Levitin (the epic *Liberation*, 1970; the diptych *The Soldiers of Freedom*, 1977; the diptych *The Taste of Bread*, 1979), Veniamin Basner (the diptych *The Red Square*, 1970, the tetralogy *The Siege*, 1975–1978, the serial *The Front without Flanks*, *The Front Beyond the Front Line*, *The Front to the Rear of the Enemy*, 1974–1981), and Evgeny Ptichkin (the diptych *The High Title*, 1973–1974; the diptych *Earthly Love — Fate*, 1975–1978; the two-part epic *Victory*, 1984).

What was it that made directors resort to these same composers with such astonishing constancy? These musicians, by the way, never took the trouble to offer different musical solutions, and were mostly engaged in copying a universal scheme which was a hybrid of the song and symphonic types of dramaturgy. From the above, it follows that the motive for the conservative directors' stable preferences should be sought primarily in the music which was offered by those composers. This corresponded perfectly to the pathos and heroic atmosphere of these grandiose descriptions of Soviet historical events, and fixed in the people's consciousness a generalised image of the collective hero which was devoid of individuality.

As happened before, the fulcrum of the ideological directives for these epics, and at the same time the axis of the meaning of their slightly modernized musical construction, was the song. In the opinion of their directors, its marching step and volitional energy combined both the heroic and the lyric principles, a poster-like garishness, as well as a sublime and humane poetical text. These were used to introduce a charge of good spirits and optimism into the film. The leitmotiv song, endowed with the properties of a symbol did not have to come into direct contact with the action, and could keep some distance from the events developing on the screen: it could 'work' for the final result, the crowning final chord of the whole film. In a number of cases the heroic-patriotic slogan song was accompanied by a lyrical song which set it off, and was usually associated with the love story in the plot, or with the generalized theme of love for one's Motherland, one's native country. Such a song possessed melodiousness, sensitivity, and usually a source in Russian folklore.

The repetition of song leitmotivs alternated with extensive orchestral episodes which accompanied battle and collective work scenes. Usually such musical episodes were based on development of a neutral background theme of a generally dramatic character, and resembled the illustrations from the silent and early sound films. On the whole, they did not play any outstanding role in the musical dramaturgy of the film. This allowed the composer to concentrate the spectators' attention on the song, which served the central idea and was subjected to various transformations in accordance with the plot. All this gave the film's musical form some resemblance to a set of variations.

This unified scheme became almost a norm for the musical dramaturgy of the majority of monumental epic films, which were intended to record the mass heroism of the Soviet people in both fighting and working at all the stages of its history. Only in one film and by only one composer was a determined attempt made to escape the iron vice of the worn-out music-song dogmas, and to find a solution adequate to the director's conception, by leaving aside the conventional cliches. This was Edward Artemyev, in his music for Andrei Mikhalkov-Konchalovsky's many-sided epic film *The Siberiade* (1978), which covered a wide range of periods and events.

This film, the action of which stretched over half a century, told of several generations living in a far-off Siberian village: a dynasty of well-to-do peasants, the Solomins, and their poor neighbours, the Ustyuzhanins, of the love and hatred connecting them, of dramatic breakdowns in the history of the state, and of individuals' fates. The extended panorama of events shown in this picture, the mosaic character of its structural organization, where acted episodes were intertwined polyphonically with chronicle and documentary sequences — all this set the composer the complicated task of synthesizing the heterogeneous pictorial material into whole by means of his music. As a result of discussing the possibilities with the director, Artemyev chose a method according to which musical conception was to be based on three structure-forming elements connected with the central symbolic images. These were provisionally entitled the theme of Fire, the theme of the People and the theme of Time.

Each of these musical leitmotivs had its own striking stylistic character. Thus, the explosive emotionality and expressive impulsiveness of electric rock-music served as a basis for the theme of Fire. Though constantly changing in colour and moving freely in the acoustic space, it kept its melodical invariance, which created associations with the famous *Bolero* of Ravel. Opposed to it, the theme of the People developed from the folk tradition, and was based on authentic Siberian solo and choral singing. This eclectic combination of rock and folklore within one space, which leapt to the ear, revealed one of the main ideas of the film — the eternal struggle between man and the elements. Certainly the film needed some unifying factor. This function was taken by the theme of Time (also called the theme of the Course of History). It seemed to have been born out of an abundance of sounds from the environment, taking in the noise of the forest, the mysterious whispers and rustlings of nature by night, shell bursts, fragments of song, marches, and hymns intertwined with impetuous passages of electric improvisation in the style of Bach's organ preludes personifying the inexorable endless race of Time. Unfortunately, the biased attitude of the critics to Mikhalkov-Konchalovsky's film did not allow them to grasp the originality and innovative character of the composer's work. He had created a complex, multifunctional sound equivalent to the visual elements, and to their artistic and imaginative treatment. For example, in the first part of *The Siberiade*, entitled with the name of one of the characters *Afanasy*, the dynamic montage of newsreel sequences shot during the First World War, — the workers' demonstration, Lenin's speeches, the taking of the Winter Palace was accompanied by highly organized music composed of two layers developed in parallel. The first was a severe organ melody, submerged into a throbbing, intense and excited rhythm of percussion and electric 'sparks' from synthesizer SINTI–100. The second layer contained several different musical and noise complexes, intended to concretize and reconstruct historical events: shots, shell bursts on the battlefield, fragments of the hymn of czarist Russia and *The Internationale* etc. Subsequently, the polyphonic superimposition and juxtaposition of different music and noise layers were used by the composer to divide the film composition into separate parts and activate the dramatic development. Later, the discoveries made by Artemyev in *The Siberiade* were to be reconsidered and fully realized in Alexander Sokurov's films of the '80s.

Besides monumental epic films, mostly dealing with the tragic events of the Second World War, at the end of the '70s and early '80s (the period when the USSR started its military action in Afghanistan) a whole series of propaganda films devoted to the Soviet armed forces, and demonstrating the power of different branches of the services appeared. Those films were brimful of music which was clearly illustrative and designed to create an elevated and romantic atmosphere in the manoeuvres episodes, training scenes and rare scenes of soldiers and their commanders resting. The musical apparatus of most of these 'army' films was on the whole primitive, and was bound to contain an invocatory-heroic theme with an excited punctuated rhythm and ascending trumpet fanfares surrounded with string passages, and also its lyrical antithesis, which resembled a variety stage hit. Together, both themes created a dialogue, for which the stock reference of leitmotivs, and their non-conflicting comparison according to the principle of complementary contrast, seemed to be quite natural and regular. This device was used most consistently by composers

Afanasyev in *Blue Lightning* (1978, director Shmaruk), Volkov in the film
Entrust It to General Nesterov (1984, director Galkin), Minkov in the film *In
the Zone of Special Attention* (1977, director Malukov) and especially by
Babushkin in the series by Mikhail Tumanishvili *An Answering Move* (1981),
An Incident in Square 36–80 (1982), and *Solitary Sailing* (1985), the musical
dramaturgy of which was a simple succession of static items, mechanically
connected as a suite.

The same standard schemes, with uniform sets of expressive means
and devices, were cultivated in the genre of the revolutionary film, which
became a best-seller in the '70s–'80s owing to its turning into a 'Soviet
variety' of the American Western. The prolonged exploitation of the
revolutionary theme canonized by the socialist regime, its gradual
mythologization and, as a consequence, its alienation from reality was
bound to cause either degeneration or mutation in this genre. But since the
organs supervising culture could not admit the former, the latter remained,
— 'a reanimation' of the revolutionary film, which was made by transforming
it into an adventure, transferring the centre of gravity from 'the struggle of
ideas' to 'the struggle of muscles', where the main argument in class differences and in proving the rightness of political convictions was not verbal (as
before) but physical. In practice, the modernized revolutionary Western,
with its free, entertaining manner, which tickled spectators with a well spun
plot, kept to the old legends of the new power conquering different regions
of the former Czarist empire, and of the Cheka fighting the White Guards
and nationalist gangs during the Civil War. Specific features of the Soviet
Western were a passion for national exotica, which transferred the setting
to the Asian and Trans-Caucasian republics, to Siberia and the Western
Ukraine, and also an excessive use of pursuit scenes, fights, and skirmishes
carefully copied from American originals with the addition of purely
'local'ethnographic details.

A swiftly developing plot based on abrupt changes in psychological
tension demanded activation of all the components of screen synthesis,
including the music, which was allotted a very responsible role as co-ordin-
ator and stimulator of the spectator's emotions. The peculiar conventions of
the revolutionary Western and its approximateness in depicting the realities
of everyday life in the stormy and tragic period of the Civil War which were
turned in the cinema of the 1970s into mere thrills, affected film music
strongly, and the choice of musical expressive means was arbitrary. Understanding that these films were intended for the mass audience, which
wanted breathtaking spectacle, composers had to cater to dividtaste and
gave up completely any attempt at reconstructing the musical milieu of the
1920s by using stylization and quotations: they turned instead to rock and
electronic music, which were just becoming fashionable.

Rock music, with its impulsive character, emotionality and sensual cognitive openness to the world, and possessing well expressed psychedelic properties and great explosive power, entered organically any dynamic adventure story saturated with physical movement. Moreover, the rhythmic ostinato which had become an integral part of the revolutionary Western's music was also borrowed from rock. This became popular as a universal means of intensifying and bringing to a climax the state of increased nervous stress connected with feelings of anxiety and fear, and the agonizing waiting for the tragic outcome in scenes preceding attacks, murders, or fights with the enemy. For the same reason, the device was adopted of modelling discrete sound zones, static and at the same time apparently galvanised with invisible energy borrowed from electronic music. Their seeming stillness, emphasized by a deliberate lack of visual events and by frequent panorama views of landscape, was fraught with deadly danger which proclaimed itself by the sudden appearance, and equally sudden disappearance, of electronic clusters, which were interrupted by melodic fragments which used meditative and *pointillé* techniques of treating thematic material. Of considerable importance also were the finely graded nuances of electronic instrumental sound. The total simplification and paucity of melody in these sound zones were generously compensated for by the intense textural development of specially organized acoustic layers with sharply outlined boundaries for high and low frequencies, which left room for speech and noises. Like a 'light relish', the synthetic timbres of electronic instruments were sometimes interspersed with the natural sounds of ancient national instruments and archaic folk tunes. These contributed their ration of exotica to the film sound world, in case the spectator forgot where the events on the screen were unfolding.

The music for the majority of these revolutionary adventure films of the late 1970s and early 1980s was based on the contrast and juxtaposition of advancing movement, and moments of sinking back into the sound aura, and on episodes of activity switching over to die realm of the subconscious. Very soon these devices lost their novelty, and turned into annoying, automatic clichés which were used by many composers, including Vildanov (*The Extraordinary Commissar*, 1970; *The Seventh Bullet*, 1972; *The Fiery Bank*, 1975; *One Shouldn't Shoot in a Hurry*, 1983); Lazarev (*The Last Heyduck*, 1972; *Following the Wolf's Track*, 1976); Zubov (*Forget the Word Death*, 1979; *Bread, Gold, Revolver*, 1980; *The Sixth One*, 1981); Rakhmadiev (*The End of the Ataman*, 1970; *The Trans-Siberian Express*, 1977); Stankevich, (*The Train of Extraordinary Destination*, 1980) and many others. Superficially, these works differed little, and were more or less professional hackwork.

It is curious that the revolutionary adventure film of this period was on very cool terms with the song, which stopped performing the function of 'ideological focus' as it had in the days of Dunayevsky, and was pushed aside to the 'episodic parts', sinking to the level of a mere accessory element. In some cases, its presence could be accounted for only by the necessity of holding up the plot to prepare for the climax. Sometimes the song formulated the general programmatic idea, but this was rare, even though it made a stronger impression than the other music of the film. Such were the title songs of *At Home among Strangers, a Stranger at Home* (1974, director Mikhalkov, composer Artemyev), *The End of the Taiga Emperor* (1978, director Sarukhanov, composer Krylatov) and *Come When You Are Free* (1984, director Mastyugin, composer Zhurbin). At the same time, the rejection of the song signified not so much a wish to get rid of outdated clichés or a crisis of trust in song, as the fact that the revolutionary Western had lost its former ideological militancy, its ceremonial and official and openly propagandist character and turned into a genre exclusively of entertainment.

On the whole, this situation of the revolutionary Western was dangerous for film music. The same could be said of the military-patriotic, and the 'peasant-collective farm', the so-called 'production' genres[2] which followed the directions and resolutions of the party and government organs. Continuous repetition of monotonous plots, and the appearance of a special 'strictly limited contingent' of composers specializing in particular genres, were bound to affect professional levels and allow hackwork to predominate. However, this process was not universal, and collaboration with composers of the highest rank helped prevent music from becoming a utilitarian convenience in the cinema, or its becoming mere 'aural wallpaper'. At that time, the most famous composer was Dmitry Shostakovich, who accepted a proposal from his steadfast partner Grigory Kozintsev to write the music for the screen version of Shakespeare's tragedy *King Lear*, though his creative interests had long abandoned the cinema.

27

Human tragedy as reflected in film music

In the extensive cinema output of Shostakovich, the music for *King Lear* appears to be unique. Here for the first time, obeying the director's wish, the composer does not create a developed programme-musical conception resembling a symphony or an orchestral suite: he restores the main purpose of music — that of being art. The theme of art becomes the theme of truth and, according to the director's design, it 'does not accompany the sequences but transforms them'[3]. The sad melody of the Fool's fife which frames the picture, and his caustic songs, full of sarcasm, sound like the voice of Conscience which insistently tries to get to people through silence locked in fear, through the howling of the wind, the clanging of arms, the web of lies and shamelessness, the cries and groans of the dying. The Fool's songs, like Brecht's *Songs*, reveal the hidden and evil designs of false friends and flatterers. There is something here akin to a philosophic parable. At the same time the *piccolo* E flat clarinet melody of the fife is astonishingly simple and artless, like a folk tune. It combines lament with dancing lyrical scherzo, sorrow with a lucidity which leaves hope for purification through suffering, the possibility that the king may understand the real values of life. Unfortunately this comes too late for the octogenarian Lear.

The cruelty of the pictorial black-and-white texture, where two elements reign — fire and stone, the metaphoric language, the laconic and profound characteristics of the hero, is peculiarly reflected in the music. King Lear is different from the composer's earlier pictures: the duration time of its performance in this two-part film is limited to only twelve minutes, which made Shostakovich resort to strong means for emphasizing the most dramatically important images and symbols. One of these is 'the Call of Life'.

At the beginning of the film the hoarse, long-drawn sound of a horn sets in motion a dejected procession of beggars, tramps, wanderers heading for the King's castle to find food and shelter. In this 'call', full of anguish and pain, played by the French horn, the way is prophetically shown along which King Lear is to follow, freed of illusions and sinking into the boundless sea of human suffering and grief. In the course of painful wanderings within a collapsing world, he will come to know what is good and what is evil, what is human and what is inhuman.

Ex. 22 The Fool's Fife from the film *King Lear*

The 'Call of Life' is opposed to the frightening 'Call of Death' the music of which was associated by the critic Alexander Lipkov with the sound of a falling coffin lid[4].

This 'Call of Death', expressive and at the same time fatally inevitable, catches up with Shakespearean heroes just a moment before their death. The roaring of the brass instruments and the convulsive rhythm of the percussion resemble waves of nervous trembling, which deafen and paralyse the will, whereas the sudden drop in volume and the subsequent dynamic intensification to the utmost limit of loudness in the last chord, impart almost physically a state of horror at the approaching death agony, a feeling of the end of life.

Besides the 'Call of Death' there is another death sign in the music score of the film: the bellicose trumpet fanfares which precede any death. Their sounds burn out hearts, and turn soldiers going to battle into killers, hunters pursuing beasts; they make Edmond blind with rage, and remove the remains of his humanity in the single combat scene with his brother Edgar. But in this bloody mess and the insanity of fratricidal wars the music is unexpectedly estranged from the violence, cruelty and chaos, illuminated by fire, which reign on the screen: it may be possible to comprehend their monstrous consequences which bring the people only endless grief and despair. An appeal to modern expressive means[5], the co-existence of pure diatonicism with refined chromaticism, the frequent use of dissonant

Ex. 23 The Call of Death, from the film *King Lear*

intervals and chords, viscous polyphonic tissue together with the emotional and spiritual singing of the chorus a capella, elevated the requiem which concludes the film to the heights of a universal lament for the innocent souls of the killed, independently of the concrete time and place of the tragedy. Actually, Shostakovich's requiem in the finale of *King Lear* expresses the consciousness and memory of modern humanity shaken by the world cataclysms of the 20th century.

One of the most dramatic cataclysms in Russian history was the production of the film *Flight*, shot in 1971 by directors Alov and Naumov after Bulgakov's novel[6]. The composition of this two-part picture was complex and somewhat heterogeneous in style because of the large number of events and characters. The revolution, the Civil War and the forced change in the fate of millions of people connected with it, the defeat of the

Figure 8 *Flight*

White Army and the flight from the Crimea and the fate of the Russian emigrés — such is a brief account of 'Flight'. The mosaic structure of the plot, the contrapuntal combination of large-scale epic scenes with chamber lyrical episodes, and the real, everyday life and somewhat farcical situations contrasted with the fantastic hallucination-like dreams of the White General Khludov, all demanded a strict delimitation of the musical sphere: the distinction of the music in the frame, participating in the action, from that *out-of-frame*, expressing the director's position, his vision of the artistic conception of the film.

According to the tradition current in Soviet cinema, the intraframe music played the part of 'the mark of time'. Its main task was to bring the tonal and imaginative atmosphere as close as possible to the historical reality of the epoch portrayed on the screen. Abandoning direct quotation, composer Nikolai Karetnikov wrote a number of original items stylized in the spirit of the march songs popular with 'the White movement' (the song of the cadets), the waltz (Charnota's waltz), galop (the scene in the circus) and the march hymn (the episode of cockroach races). Using the 'intonational slang' characteristic of these, he, using the 'absurd' device of unbalanced instrumentation and by deliberate harping on the hackneyed trivial tunes, imparted to those songs an ironic, sometimes sardonic air, expressing the contemptuous attitude of the newborn system to the 'ideologically alien' classes of the old Russia. Of course, such a demonstratively disparaging portrayal of the enemies of Soviet Power occurred frequently in film music (and not only in film music). At the same time, the composer managed to avoid dogmatic thinking in the musical solution of General Khludov's vision dreams. He is one of the central characters, formerly a talented battle commander and now a man inevitably sliding down into an abyss of senseless cruelty and sadism, and feeling the approach of his day of reckoning. The music accompanying Khludov's terrible hallucinations is astonishingly powerful. This power was mainly achieved by means of the symphonic device of polyphonic superposition of several stylistically diverse thematic layers. Their apparent incompatibility showed the irreversible psychic destruction process, the disintegration of a human consciousness.

Ex. 24 A prayer for being saved (Khludov's dream), from the film *Flight*

> Prelate, Father Nikolai,
> Pray to God for us.
> Have mercy upon us, Lord,
> Have mercy upon us.

The musical basis of Khludov's dreams is a dodecaphonic development of several melodic phrases. This incoherent pile-up of sounds conveys the highly-strung state of the former czarist general, bordering on madness. The chordal exclamations of the brass are sometimes drowned out by a frenzied, hysterical polka, sometimes by a funeral chorale. This prayer appears in the most nightmarish of Khludov's visions, when he sees his own execution at the bottom of a huge pit filled with water, under the blind stare of the private once hanged by his order. Long silent ranks of soldiers for whose death he was also responsible bear witness to the execution.

For the second time the memory of this awful dream occurs to Khludov in the finale of the picture: his freezing stare, like that of a lonely madman, follows a ship departing for his Motherland, while he himself stands on the seashore in a foreign city in a foreign country. He himself cannot even hope to return: his army has left too bloody a trail in its feverish retreat and flight from its native land. That is why the severe prayer sounds again over the head of a man who is still alive but actually long-dead. The prayer sounds as a just retribution, and at the same time as a mournful burial service. This man has lost everything: above all, the land where he was born and where he will never be buried.

Ex. 25 The theme of the Motherland, from the film *Flight*

But not only the life of General Khludov appears to be crippled and disfigured by this revolutionary whirlwind which rushes over Russia like a tornado, destroying families, and people's fates. Few of those who left the country during the Civil War survived without losing themselves in the brutal conditions of emigrant existence and, moreover, or found the courage to return to the frighteningly unknown Soviet Russia. Only those managed it who kept faith with two notions sacred for all Russians: those of the Motherland and Love. It was not by chance that the film opened with a quiet melodious chiming of the Rostov bells, which introduced the leading musical leitmotiv — that of the Motherland. Its connection with ancient Russian folk songs is clear. This pointed not only to its national origin but also made it familiar and easily recognizable to the spectator.

It is interesting that both the exposition and the development of the Motherland theme seem to be locked within that action which develops within Russia and finishes at the climax — the final sequence of the first part, where it becomes an inconceivably beautiful farewell lullaby. Softly, and at the same time powerfully absorbing the chaos of sound in the seaside town which is seized with panic and crammed with refugees and troops of the White Army retreating in disorder, the Motherland theme seems to soar over the sinful land, and becomes a symbol of the Motherland deserted in headlong flight. In the second part it also appears as a symbolic image, as a secret, cherished dream evoking agonized fits of nostalgia.

The initiative, as well as the ability to influence the course of events, the behaviour, and the actions of the characters, partly lost by the Mother-land theme in the second part, is taken by the theme of Love, which slightly resembles it. Unlike the contemplative and majestically calm Motherland theme, this leitmotiv of Love, sadly drooping, romantic and arising in the transparent crystal timbre of the vibraphone, gives a feeling of childlike defencelessness and the purity of a deep, sincere emotion. The tonal kinship and emotional interrelation of the main musical themes of the film, and their interchangeability, allow the composer to avoid monotony and to use leitmotivs as powerful focuses of force, as centres of attraction for stylistically diverse material, and to unite the numerous plots of the film. He manages to create a strong spiritual atmosphere around the film which is severe and pitiless in depicting the psychological breakdown of people who found themselves in critical and dramatic states of spiritual and physical existence.

28

Extending the expressive means of film music.
A search for new models of stylistic interaction between music and the other components of screen synthesis

The 1970s were marked by the increased attention given by artists to moral problems, to eternal philosophical questions about the meaning of man's existence, the purpose of personality, its relations with society and the state, and on truth in the modern world, which seemed full of unsolvable contradictions. These years coincided with the beginning of director's collaboration with young composers, with the appearance of new leaders and changes in artistic orientations. As before, the arrival of new musicians in the cinema can be accounted for by prosaic rather than creative reasons. One should not be surprised that the most talented, who made a great contribution to Soviet film music in the 1970s–1980s, started working in the cinema only because they had got onto the 'black list of the politically unreliable' because of their adherence to 'bourgeois', 'modernist' trends. These included, according to the ideological censors of the time, avant-garde, dodecaphonic, and electronic music.

Banished from concert halls and the opera stage, their music practically never performed, they tried to break through this dense curtain of silence via the only channel left open to them, i.e. film music. Among the now famous names of Alfred Schnittke, Sofia Gubaidulina, Viacheslav Ganelin, Ghedris Kupriavičius, whose flight of creative activity in the cinema was connected with the period of stagnation, the name of Edward Artemyev stands out especially. It so happened that for him working in the cinema proved not merely a forced occupation which enabled him to earn his daily bread, but a true calling, which allowed him to take a leading position in Soviet film music, not only because of his huge productivity and his collaboration with outstanding masters, but also because of his creation of a unique 'Artemian' timbre-colouristic manner of composition, his natural feeling for the screen, his ability to 'catch' the musical correlative of the visual material. Certainly, the revelation of the merits of Artemyev's original music, his universal stylistic and organizing gift, and also his supreme skill as a cinema composer came through his meeting with two original and talented but quite different cinema directors, Andrei Tarkovsky and Nikita Mihalkov.

Andrei Tarkovsky invited Artemyev in 1972 to collaborate on the film *Solaris*. This happened almost by chance, because of Tarkovsky's differences of opinion with Viacheslav Ovchinnikov. The director's initial design for the sound dramaturgy of the film, shot after Lem's science fiction novel of the same name, presupposed a multicolour palette of natural noises, and the use of J. S. Bach's Chorale Prelude in F minor. When he offered this task to Artemyev, the director saw in him first of all a man capable of perfectly organising the film's sound world, and designing its sound track. Moreover, Tarkovsky also knew him as a professional composer of electronic music, and therefore relied on his help in the treatment of timbre and rhythm and recreating the 'live' natural sounds on the synthesizer: he believed that Artemyev would impart to it emotional expression and individual distinction. As it turned out, this first meeting was a prologue to one of the brightest creative partnerships in the history of cinema and led to the creation of one of Tarkovsky's most 'musical' pictures. The distinguishing feature of *Solaris*, as compared to his other films, was its developed programme-musical conception, which synthesized and author's main ideas, and gave his answer to the social and philosophic question, which was extremely important for the fate of human civilization, of the relation between science and ethics.

It is interesting that four years before, the American director Stanley Kubrick had made his *2001: A Space Odyssey*. When Tarkovsky's film was released, many reviewers tried at once to compare and juxtapose them, in spite of the extreme differences in the ideas and aesthetic principles underlying them. The most exact and laconic characterisation of those differences came from the critic Yuri Khaniutin, who wrote: 'if Kubrick's picture is a look from the Earth into the Cosmos, Tarkovsky's film is a look from the Cosmos at the Earth'[7]. But this vision of the Earth from the Cosmos was also possible for Artemyev, who composed the music for *Solaris*.

The musical dramaturgy of the film is based on the opposition of two absolutely distinct tonal and imaginative spheres: the sound images of the Earth and of Solaris, which is frightening because of its mystery and unpredictability of behaviour. The film starts with Kris Kelvin's last hours on his native Earth, and his leave-taking from it. Getting ready for his long-distance flight, Kris tries to imprint in his memory all the beauty and uniqueness of the scenery surrounding him: the babbling of the brook, the singing of birds, the rustling of the forest, the noise of raindrops. For this man who has to say goodbye to what has been familiar since childhood, these natural sounds acquire a special poetic colouring, which is turned into an 'earthly symphony' incorporating the finest timbre nuances, a barely noticeable transfer of natural noises into music (for example, as a result of processing bird cries by means of the synthesizer, it acquired their crying intonations). To create the desired effect, the composer used the principle of 'living statics', changing the inner structure of sound complexes, 'playing ' with space sensations but strictly preserving the invariance of their timbre parameters.

However, modern man's conception of the Earth is not only that of an idyllic natural landscape but also that of the glittering tentacles of octopus-like cities which have became the peculiar characteristic of Civilization. Therefore the lyrical metaphors at the beginning of the film (a quiet pond, a gentle rain, a bunch of autumn flowers on the table) are replaced by a winding, roaring, howling motorway flaring along in blinding lights (this episode was shot in Tokyo). This image of a gigantic City created by man and swallowing him up is splendidly revealed during the 'long' passage of pilot Berton through the tunnel. The main purpose of this long and static episode is the alleviation of the abrupt transition from audiovisual images of habitual earthly existence to unreal images of the Cosmos.

The suddenness of the alternating patches of light and darkness, against the background of the car's monotonous movement through the labyrinth of the empty tunnel, is set off by a quaint aleatoric mosaic of electronic sound strictly controlled and directed by the rhythm of the percussion (a device borrowed from rock sound-recording, and characterised by repeated superimposition of solo percussion parts upon the basic rhythmic structure). The spinning out in time of 'Berton's passage' and its pictorial monotony are also of great dramatic importance, because they exert powerful pressure upon the spectator's psyche, provoking tiredness, irritation and, as a consequence, an impatient expectation of denouement. When tension reaches a critical point, the incoherent piling up of 'strange', unintelligible sounds gives birth to a beautiful female *vocalise* which sounds both like a wail, and like a cry of loneliness in this stream of continuous crazy movement, when the massive night City, in garlands of coloured lights, blazes up on the screen. This image is immediately followed by the next sequence: a space ship shooting up into a black sky. With these appearances of the City and the ship, the musical development seems to condense into a very complicated, but brief and terrifying wailing chord. This accompanies the roaring of tanks, the booming of a volcano, and the tolling of farewell bells.

The arrival of Kris at the space station, without any smooth transition, transfers the action to another world, hermetic, closed-off from human cognition and repulsing all attempts at contact. The planet Solaris, covered with an ocean of intelligent energy, keeps close watch over the people living in the space station. Moreover, it creates extreme psychological conditions for their existence. By penetrating into the most intimate corners of their consciousness, where the memory of sins and mistakes is deeply hidden. Solaris makes the inhabitants of the station pass through moral tortures of repentance again and again, driving them into traps, then leaving them alone with their conscience.

Outwardly, Solaris is mysterious and incomprehensible, but it is not horrible, and resembles a sighing, frothing plasma mass. Its formidable force and, above all, its animosity to human beings is mainly conveyed through the music, which takes an active part in the modelling of both its sound and visual aspects. The music of Solaris is based on an electronically generated theme which is a ninefold chord complex capable of folding and unfolding horizontally.

Ex. 26 The Solaris theme from the film *Solaris*

The Solaris theme possesses a number of individual characteristics which determine their invisible presence in the frame immediately. First of all, there is the invariable position of the theme in the low bass register, approaching infrasound in its frequency; there is also an intense heterophonic development, which imparts to the leitmotiv both its special density and richness, and its variability of texture and timbre, which allow it to delineate the finest shades of 'mood' and response to what is happening on Solaris.

The Solaris theme enters the film from the moment of Kris Kelvin's arrival on the mysterious planet. At its first appearance, its outlines are still devoid of precision. It has neither melody nor rhythm, and is perceived as a compressed clot of sound energy. Subsequently, as Kris gets acquainted with the 'strange' events happening at the station, the Solaris theme comes to the fore more and more. Its behaviour is quite unpredictable and change-able, because it serves as a matrix for several groups of themes derived from it. One of these groups is formed by themes connected with fantastic processes, inaccessible to human reason, which are observed by the inhab-itants of the station both on the surface of the planet and in the cosmos. Their peculiarity is their hypertrophied, phasic development of some technical compositional device, either pointillism ('The Cosmos Landscape'), or mul-tilayered cluster formation ('The Electronic Ocean'), or a dynamic wave design ('The Wind Ocean'). Each of the themes belonging to this group lacks any precise beginning or end, and is an arbitrary combination of movement phases, which allows a free rearrangement of its elements.

Solaris not only lives its own life: it actively affects humans with mysterious sounds, rustlings, signals. The musical background seems to come from nowhere, and introduces vague feelings of alarm, uncertainty, and fear arising from the subconscious. This state of spiritual discomfort is mostly induced by the use of aleatoric techniques ranging from totality, entirely relying upon the performer's fantasy, to limited freedom, which places the performer within a clearly defined context of non-fixed im-provisation set by the composer. Special emotional expression is conveyed by this group of themes through whimsical play with timbres. The 'pure' timbres of brasses, woodwind, strings, percussion, dispersed in acoustic space along with an a capella chorus (singing different combinations of vowels and consonants in arbitrary rhythm on random pitches), intertwine with the artificial timbres of synthesizers ANS and SINTI-100. From all the musical fragments belonging to this group the strongest impression is produced by the sequence 'The Solaris station — the round corridor' com-posed by using a technique of 72-step temperament, where the starting point is the fundamental tone of the counteroctave split by the synthesizer into primary and secondary overtones. The task of the primary overtones is limited to that of modelling the rhythmic pulse, whereas the secondary overtones help build up the sound mass by aleatoric manipulations of multi-track chord complexes. The movement of overtone streams is controlled by sharply outlined sinus tones filtered through modulation. The main purpose of these technical contrivances is the creation of an emotionally unstable sound world which conceals an incomprehensible, inexplicable threat, and which envelops and paralyses Kris's reason and will while he aimlessly wanders along the stations's corridors.

Finally, the third group contains phantom themes which characterize the station's 'guests'. Each of their appearances is preceded by low melodious chimes of little bells, crystal rods and goblets, and the sound of the vibraphone. And this delicate, disembodied music does seem the best way of conveying the unreal, unearthly origin of the mysterious spirit guests ('Kris's Dreams').

Thus, Solaris studies the uninvited strangers impartially and almost indifferently, sometimes resorting to cruel experiments. But of the three members of the team, only Kris appears to be capable of withstanding these in his intense, excruciating search for contact with the powerful intellect of another planet. The first successful attempt to break through the deliberate incommunicado and alienation of Solaris occurs in the scene 'Kris's Illness'; which starts after his encephalograph has been taken. The proof of Solaris having accepted this 'message' is a change in the timbre of the theme which unexpectedly arises in the organ — the instrument firmly associated in the film with J. S. Bach's Chorale Prelude.

Andrei Tarkovsky is known to have had a great predilection for music and art, and in each of his films there are episodes where the canvases of great artists appear and also the music of great composers, which supply clues to the understanding of the author's conception. In *Solaris* these 'signs from art' are Bach's music and Pieter Brueghel the Elder's picture 'Hunters in the Snow'. The Chorale Prelude in F minor appear in the film three times: firstly, with the captions (in its original form), secondly at the golden section point — the scene in the library (combined with Artemyev's music) and lastly in the finale (dissolved in Artemyev's music). Such a clear semantic and dramatic emphasis is far from accidental, for Bach's Prelude is not only a symbol which has absorbed the greatest timeless values of human culture, but also represents the highest level of exactness known to man, and is used by the author as a spiritual argument defending his moral conception. This philosophic and imaginative interpretation of Bach's Prelude was also congenial to the composer who chose it as a theme of Expiation. It could also properly called the theme of Conscience. It is this theme that starts the agonizing process of Hari's resurrection, which reaches its climax in the scene of weightlessness (the scene in the library), when out of the sound chaos of this unreal fantastic world (different devices of concrete and electronic music), the powerful and wonderful sounds of the Prelude F minor sprout as Kris's memory of the Earth, Home, Father, overcoming the chaotic "Brownian movement". However, Bach's great music not only awakes nostalgic images in Kelvin's consciousness, it also miraculously influences the state of the inanimate phantom Hari to whom his pain, his feelings have been imparted. Moreover, listening to the music and looking closely at Brueghel's picture, Hari suddenly begins 'to recollect' her human past. Then, under the influence of her 'returning memory' the sound of the Chorale Prelude is interspersed with the noise of the forest in spring, the singing of a folk chorus, and the chimes of the Rostov bells, in which the outlines of the *Dies irae* can be discerned, which seem to predict Hari's subsequent fate.

The Chorale Prelude in F minor appears lastly in the finale of *Solaris*, where it seems filled with profound philosophic meaning. Having hardly recovered from a severe disease, Kris receives another blow: news about Hari's suicide. Afraid of losing his reason, quite desperate, he appeals to what was most dear and pure to him and bound him to life, to his thoughts about the Earth, to pictures of his native land, and his family house. The frames of Kris's memories resemble a silent amateur film, and appear on the screen without the habitual sound accompaniment: this deafening silence makes them look like a mirage. When his feeling of horrible loss is about to cast Kris's consciousness into the gloom of loneliness and paralyse his will, on the surface of Solaris the model of a familiar and beloved earthly world appears to him. This is not real but, is as it were, a mirror image. To the sounds of the electronic organ, with the addition of the chorus performing Bach's Prelude, Kris sees himself standing by the window of his house, sees rain falling in the room; its streams are running down the shoulders of his father who comes to meet him, and he kneels before this dear and precious man in the pose of the prodigal son.

Here, as compared with its use in the preceding scenes, the music of J. S. Bach's Chorale Prelude undergoes a considerable transformation. It becomes more sensual and is brought closer to the Solaris leitmotif by the use of richly coloured timbres. On the whole, Bach's music has the function in this finale of a clear-cut *cantus firmus*, which is superimposed on a freely improvised, limited aleatoric texture from the chorus, synthesizers ANS and SINTI-100, and instrumental groups from a reduced symphony orchestra. The main peculiarity of this Finale is that there, for the first time, a variation of the Solaris theme is played, unfolded horizontally and, as it were, 'humanized'; it has lost the frozen didactic character of a thesis-theme and has turned into a passionate bass guitar solo monologue played in counterpoint to the Chorale Prelude. This parallel simultaneous development of the two, at first entirely distinct, leitmotivs of the film shows that Solaris is ready to establish contact with humans, and trust them. Thus, Edward Artemyev creates here an original composer's programmatic conception equal to the director's philosophic conception by using a complex system of expressive means, and applying symphonic method in the juxtaposition and subsequent fusion of two stylistically heterogeneous imaginative spheres.

Figure 9 *Mirror*

In the next collaboration of Tarkovsky and Artemyev – the esoteric, refined and highly personal film *Mirror* – the limits of the active functioning of composed music appear very narrow, and the resulting 'free zones' in the sound-track are filled with noises and fragments of classical music. In the choice of quotations, music of the preclassic period was preferred (J. S. Bach, Händel, Pergolesi) because of its emotional balance, integrity, and harmonious world outlook.

Similarly to *Solaris*, the film opens with the majestic, elevated sounds of the Organ Prelude in D minor by Bach (Tarkovsky's favourite composer).

It is an important component of the sound and visual images of the prologue which is based on a complicated associative musical and the pictorial montage. On the screen, a doctor cures an adolescent of an agonizing stammer by making him overcome his fear and pronounce clearly and distinctly the short but difficult phrase: 'I can speak!' The presence of music in this scene is perceived as a deep metaphor, which signifies more than the fact of a man set free from an awful disease. The music gives us an opportunity to see in this everyday episode a reflection of a world process, a universal aim for Soviet society, of man acquiring the right to be a person, to be autonomous. Later, this device is repeated in the film, imparting to it a philosophic, multidimensional character and depth. An especially strong impression is produced by a portrait frame showing the father who has returned from the front and with his two children, who are starved and exhausted by the long years of the war, clinging to him. This is accompanied by the agitated, passionate tenor solo from J. S. Bach's *St. John Passion* (Recitative No. 61) which purges the image of its concreteness and gives it a universally human, symbolic meaning. On the whole, classical music, as well as other cultural layers (verses by Arseni Tarkovsky, painting by Leonardo da Vinci, prose by Feodor Dostoevsky) exists autonomously in the artistic space of the picture, sometimes being consonant, sometimes dissonant with the visual elements. But independently of its artistic and semantic connection with the visual sphere representation, Baroque music preserves a certain distance and alienation from the correct objectivity of the screen images, which often happens when events of the recent past and modern times are correlated with the spiritual heritage of past centuries.

This shifting of the weight of the film's musical conception to classical music resulted in the composed music being reduced to a minimum, and limited to a background presence which intensified the emotional reactions of the spectator at moments of climax. An exception was made for the leitmotiv – the theme of the child's fears. A simple, artless melody played on a common toy pipe, it continuously appeared in Aleksei's dreams, sometimes blissful, sometimes alarming, evoking memories of early childhood and adolescence. Besides this leitmotiv one other musical item was of first importance though it had not been planned beforehand by the director, but was written on the composer's own initiative. This is an extensive episode called 'Sivash'. According to Tarkovsky's design, it was 'a long march of soldiers' created by a montage of documentary shots belonging to different times. It embraced events from the Second World War to the incidents on the Soviet-Chinese border at the beginning of the 1970s. It is curious that the musical solution of this 'Sivash' episode was wholly made by using the technique of 'variations on one chord'. As the building material of this prolonged musical sequence (it lasts ten minutes, throughout one

whole episode of the film), the C sharp minor triad was chosen, variously
recorded and kaleidoscopically orchestrated.

   In spite of the absence of any obvious premise for inner development, the music in 'Sivash' is extraordinarily dynamic and expressive. It is
achieved by gradually increasing the volume, density, saturation of texture,
all of which creates a feeling of continuous *crescendo*. This is all that can be
said about the composed music in *Mirror*. Yet the director's reserve concerning this original music is to some extent compensated for by 'the musical'
structure of its screen form, which relies upon the varied development of
several symbolic images (water, fire, wind, milk). These visual leitmotivs
play the part of a peculiar *basso ostinato* which helps establish an inner
cause-effect relation between the otherwise unconnected links of the story
which consists of several temporal streams — the past and the present, and
sometimes the future.

   The polystylistic principle underlying the musical dramaturgy of
Mirror interested many film-makers, and paved the way for 'the wave of
collage' which came from concert music. A passion for collage flooded the
Soviet cinema in the late 1970s and the early 1980s, only showing signs of
abatement in the late 1980s. The pretexts for the appearance of this 'collage
wave' were not only Tarkovsky's films but those of such Western masters,
as Visconti, Bertolucci, Wajda, Coppola, and Bergman. To a certain degree,
this appeal to collage technique and stylistic synthesis may be correlated
with similar processes observed during that historical period in the development of poetry and painting.

   The most common musical practices in film were two ways of using
quotation material. One of them was a return to the compilation principle,
but at a new level. Unlike the silent and early sound period of film development, where classical music was mainly used as a utilitarian background
illustrating the film contents, this 'playing with strange styles's in the cinema
of the 1970s and 1980s was directed at an activisation the spectators associative and imaginative thinking. Its main purpose was to carry the hidden
meaning of the inner psychological action into the public realms of history
and culture, and to help the spectator to decide correctly the film's system
of moral, aesthetic and ethical ideals and values.

   On the whole, the sphere of directors' musical preferences was
extensive and varied, and embraced different musical epochs from the
Baroque to the modern. At the same time, among composers whose works
were used by directors, priority was certainly given to Shostakovich,
Mozart, Vivaldi, Mahler, J. S. Bach, Purcell, Gluck, and Penderecki. Attention was also paid to music by Glinka, Tchaikovsky, Stravinsky, Händel,
Bartók, Schumann, Chopin, Albinoni, Bizet, Schubert, Ravel, Reger, Franck,

and Rakhmaninov. However, the presence of Russian composers in this list certainly did not mean that they held some special place in the hierarchy (with the exception of Shostakovich). Much greater popularity with directors was enjoyed by Western European classics which were mostly used because they provided the same sign code, i.e. general symbols of humanism and moral purity, and eternal longing for the ideal, which gave hope and belief to humanity steeped in blood, suffering and vice. Frequently a mix of 'different musics' (the expression is Alfred Schnittke's) imparted to musical dramaturgy the character of a mosaic. This was not always happy and convincing. Sometimes the limited possibilities of quotation, their deliberate pretentiousness turned into mere illustrativeness, and simplification of the imaginative interpretation in the film context. This happened to the music of Mozart, Beethoven, Mahler, Shostakovich, Sviridov, Schwarz, Tishchenko, and Castro, by means of which director Sergei Solovyev tried to create the musical world of his picture *The Elite* (1983, 2 parts). Just as ineffective and pretentious proved to be the result obtained by the directors. Alov and Naumov in *The Shore* (1984, 2 parts, music by Vivaldi, Tchaikovsky, Händel, J. C. Bach, J. S. Bach, J. Strauss) and Ritenbergas in *The Longest Straw* (1981, music by Albinoni, Reger, Sukhon'), who used the trite technique of musical compilation as a universal emotional means. On the contrary, however the history of the cinema of that period contains other instances of a dramatically justified introduction of classical fragments into the artistic texture of a film. Perhaps the best of these is the Georgian film *Repentance* directed by Tengiz Abuladze, with music compiled by Nana Djanelidze (who was also a co-author of the script)[8].

The genre of this parable film, which investigated the tragedy of personality cult, was defined by the director as 'a sad phantasmagoria', 'a grotesque tragicomedy', 'a lyrical tragifarce'[9]. It proved that evil, on coming into power, killed everything — people, honour, dignity, friendship, conscience, talent, and goodness. It showed what horrible damage philistine hatred could wreak on culture, spirituality and the history of the people. The unusual, polyphonic, and multilayered character of the director's design for *Repentance* evoked parallel associations with the recent history of the country and required the use of expressive means which were powerful in their action and artistic generalization. In order to solve this difficult problem the directors of *Repentance* decided to use quotations from musical works, which were well known and therefore easily 'read' even by an inexperienced spectator and could carry important semantic information. It is interesting that almost all the quotation fragments yielded to semantic decoding only when superimposed on the visual elements of the film, and when motivated by the plot and presented as in-frame 'musical items'. The choice of 'item' depended to a great extent on its connection with one or another imaginative sphere.

Figure 10 *Repentance*

For example, to characterize the epoch and the main character of the film, Varlam Aravidze (the name is derived from the word 'aravin' which means 'nobody') bravura Italian arias were used, cheerful, bright marches intended to deafen and paralyse the will and reason of the people. Manrico's aria from *Il Trovatore* and the march from *Aida* by Verdi, the spirited sword dance from the ballet *Gayane* by Khachaturian, the Wedding March by Mendelssohn, the Georgian song 'Mravalzhamier' sung in honor of a guest (*Long life*), the Finale of Beethoven's Ninth Symphony (the famous *Ode to Joy*) were deliberately used loudly and demonstrated the terrible metamorphosis, 'the transplantation of culture' (a term belonging to the cineaste Neya Zorkaya) of conditions under the totalitarian regime.

The shadow of the tyrant left its imprint on his son Abel, who, like his father, was not without a taste for high art. But his grotesquely over-exalted and over-emotional performance of the first part of Beethoven's *Moonlight Sonata* at the banquet, in the presence of bored powerful guests, is nothing but a theatrical sham, a necessary and carefully calculated com-plement to the antique furniture and shelves of old books which decorate the walls of his luxurious flat. Yet, love for art is only the external, visible part of Abel's life. Left alone, he and his wife feel much more at ease in their own world of pop songs flooding from the loudspeakers of video recorders, audiosystems, and transistors. Here, suddenly, the aggressive rhythms of rock and lively disco tunes show a distinct resemblance to the equally pushy, self-assured and energetic music of Varlam. A shot which sounds out to the music of the group Boney M is the closing link in the vicious circle of the evil father's and son's corruption: this shot ends the life of Varlam's grand-son Tornike, who has decided to pay in this awful way for the monstrous doings of his grandfather.

But there is another kind of music in *Repentance*. This is represented by the astonishingly beautiful piano piece by Debussy, *Steps in the Snow*, which is permeated with sadness and loneliness, and which signifies the parting from home, family, and freedom of the artist Sandro Barateli. The delicate poetic waltz from René Clair's film *Sous les Toits de Paris* accompanies one of the most tragic scenes in *Repentance* — the scene by the prison gate, with a mournfully silent queue of women and children who come there in the secret hope of learning at least something about the fate of their relatives. The use of this quotation can be accounted for not only as a wish to define the time of the action (the 1930s). Morett's waltz bears the echoes of a former happiness which now seems ephemeral and illusory.

The ironic and at the same time sad guitar melody of the Venezuelan waltz by Lauro frames the memories and visions of the heroine of the film, Ketevan, the daughter of Sandro and Nino Barateli killed by the dictator's order, and imparts harmony and logic to the dramatic conception of the film. Of great semantic importance here is also the music of the concerto *Tabula Rasa* by the Estonian composer Arvo Pärt. Arvo Pärt's music, permeated with unbearable suffering and pain, appears in the film twice: in the scene with the logs (the women look for messages from their lost husbands and sons on logs brought from Siberia) and in the episode where Nino Barateli learns about the arrest of her friend Elena, who was a firm believer in communist ideas but nevertheless joined the number of innocent victims of the regime. But in the finale of *Repentance* a new theme appears — an uplifting theme of life from the oratorio by Charles Gounod, *Death and Life*, which gives hope for redemption, for goodness gaining victory over evil, and the possibility of repentance.

Another method of appealing to the associations of quotation material resembled collage technique. This was stylistic synthesis, which was based on the interpolation of a strange musical text into the composer's music, with different proportions between them. For example, in director Vadim Abdrashitov's *Parade of Planets*, 1984 (where via a group portrait of the heroes a generalized image of Time and social life and man's existence in it are shown), alongside the original music by Ganelin two extensive fragments from the *Allegretto* of Beethoven's Seventh symphony and the *Toccata* from the Eighth symphony of Shostakovich are introduced. In spite of this stylistic heterogeneity, the quotes from Beethoven and Shostakovich which appear at the dramatically connected climaxes of the film brought about the artistic conjugation, which seemed to be the purpose of the film makers.

Ganelin's music, in which modern techniques are used, is 'clothed' in electronic timbre, and easily erodes the borders of the real world and transfers the five nameless heroes the (only their professions are indicated in the film: butcher, scientist, architect, deputy of the district Soviet, worker) into a conditional world, so as to immerse them in History and thus to reclaim some sense of a freedom which seemed to have been lost for ever. Besides, though seeming to perform pointedly applied and subsidiary functions, the composer's music shapes a strained and psychologically intense atmosphere, and prepares for the appearance of Beethoven's and Shostakovich's music at dramatically decisive moments. The classical music is presented here in its original form, preserving the full text and the instrumentation of the original. It appears in sound 'close-up', dominating the sound track which is cleared of speech and noises. If, in the exposition of the film, the quotation from Beethoven opens the way to another dimension, giving the heroes an opportunity to become 'ghostly', to get out of the customary course of life into the open air, leaving their families, homes, everyday work, Shostakovich's music, placed at the golden section point, makes them both mindful of the tragedy of the Second World War and fearful of the prospect of a new apocalypse (the scene in the old people's home — 'The Town of Old People'). An especially strong impression is produced by the musical and visual counterpoint at the climax of 'The Town of Old People' scene: the combination of aggressive and hysterical exclamations from the trumpets, against the background of an orchestral *tutti* reduced to automatism with the frames of a documentary, where the Earth has been shot from space. Its frightening disc, with black hollows for the oceans and yellow patches for continents, seems to be crying for help.

Yet the heroes of *Parade of Planets* cannot stand the test. The burden of personal responsibility is too heavy and unpleasant for them. They get tired of freedom too soon, and seeing in the distance the familiar outlines of featureless multi-storied blocks of city houses, they race toward the place where their sleepy everyday existence is awaiting them, where the voices of doubt and conscience will be muted by the noise and jangle of trams, the whine of cars, the swearing in queues; where everything is clear, understandable, material, and there is no room for spirituality and therefore, no room for music . . .

A paradoxical polyphonic synthesis of quoted material and composed music also underlies the score of Elem Klimov's film *Go and Look* (1985, 2 parts, composer Yanchenko), which is terrible and cruel in its frankness and naturalistic representation of war horrors. As if in some phantasmagoria or kaleidoscope, fragments of Mary Dixon's song from the popular pre-war film *The Circus* flash by, Wagner's 'Ride of the Valkyries' mingles with the nightmarish sound chaos and the crackle of the fire in the village set alight by the fascists, and the melody of the Russian song 'Pedlars' appears beside a merry Tyrolean motif and the naive children's song 'Augustin'. All of this impinges upon the shaken consciousness of the common village boy Fler, a living witness to the occupants' massacre of the Belarus people. He manages not to become embittered, not to turn into a wild beast, to balance on the edge of madness, and at least just to survive despite inhuman conditions, only because he feels his people's roots. These are symbolized by Oleg Yanchenko's music, which is tuneful, as if spun out of Belorussian folk song. It is this foundation which holds together the stylistically motley musical composition of the film, and prevents it from fragmenting. As a result of the sufferings experienced and a sign of purification from total hatred, and as a lament for the innocent victims, not only Belorussians but people of other nationalities who perished during the war, the beautiful and tragic *Lacrimosa* from Mozart's *Requiem* appears.

Besides these devices of contrasting polystylistics based on the remote and independent functioning (without inner interrelation or opposition) of collage materials, in the cinema of the 1970s and 1980s there occurred other methods of combining original music and quotation (mainly classical). Not infrequently, the music of past centuries was adopted by composers as a starting point, and served as a guide-line for 'impression' of a set theme. For example, this device was used in several screen versions by the stable creative duo of director Nikita Mikhalkov and composer Edward Artmyev, such as *An Unfinished Piece for Player Piano*, shot in 1976 after early plays by Chekhov, and *Some Days in the Life of I. I. Oblomov* produced three years later, after Ivan Goncharov's novel *Oblomov*.

Figure 11 *An Unfinished Piece for Player Piano*

If in the earlier joint works with Mikhalkov — the revolutionary western *At Home among Strangers, a Stranger at Home* and the (retro) film *The Slave of Love* (1975) — Artemyev was not so much bound by the necessity of an exact reconstruction of historic period realities, in the *Player Piano*, according to the director's plan, his duties now included a stylistically true modelling of the musical atmosphere and musical tastes of the end of last century. By looking through a mass of music collections of that time, Artemyev chose pieces popular and fashionable among the Russian provincial gentry, such as romances by Bulakhov, Medtner, Liszt's Hungarian Rhapsody in C minor, Rakhmaninov's Italian Polka, the Georgian lezghinka, and the charming romance of Nemorino from Donizetti's *L'Elisir d' amore*, which became a leitmotiv and served as the basis of the composer's music. Thus, in their choice of musical quotations, the director and the composer pursued the concrete aim of reflecting in the music of the film characteristic stylistic features from the end of the 19th century.

Naturally, this variety of musical material needed an organizing compositional element. This was the above mentioned music by Donizetti. Sometimes it seemed that it permeated the whole artistic texture of the film. The melody of this romance repeatedly invaded the action, sometimes intensifying the emotional tension of the characters, bringing them close to nervous breakdown, sometimes slackening it, interrupting the budding quarrel between them. In the first case (the refusal of doctor Triletsky to visit a sick woman, which causes an outburst of rage from Platonov) a gramophone record of Nemorino's romance, put on by somebody during an oppressive pause, suddenly clears the atmosphere, leading the action to merry masquerade and carefree dancing. At another time, again via the gramophone, Donizetti's music burst upon the protagonists after a large supper scene — the psychological climax of the film — which consists of three monologues. The scene opens with the lordly complacent reasoning of the landlord Pavel Petrovich Scherbuk, who expounds his own home-made notion of dividing people up into 'the blue blood' and 'the niggers'. This is followed by the highly-strung, tragic confession of Nikolai Triletsky on the uselessness of his miserable existence in an out-of-the-way province. The scene concludes with Platonov's story about 'a girl and a grammar-school boy'; it is no more than the youthfully romantic story of his love for Sofia, which ended in his disappointment and degradation into 'a common man'. After the end of this story, a painful silence reigns, which cannot be dispelled by the timid, inappropriate remarks uttered by those present, but seems to be suspended in mid-air. Yet again, some invisible hand lowers the needle on to the gramophone record, and the frame is filled with the sweet sounds of *L'Elisir d'amore*. After this, the action starts to gather monstrous speed in its movement towards the dramatic finale.

On the whole, this supper scene is based on opposing episodes, different in character, which head towards the final point, the passionate explanation between Platonov and Sofia. It is given out against the background of a waltz played by an outdoor band on the other side of the river. Its melody is connected with the initial phrase of the romance, but is more liquid, rhythmically levelled, devoid of sensuality and, as it were, lifeless, just as the long-ago love appears to be lifeless in reality.

Donizetti's music appears several times in the film. Its motif is almost cried out by Platonov as he runs away, choking with pain and exhaustion, from his talk with Sofia Pavlovna. During the concluding sequences it appears again, in its original beauty, in the scene of the main hero's unsuccessful suicide. Fresh like morning dew, it sounds pointedly alien to the wet, ridiculous miserably babbling Platonov, and to the little group of people pottering about in the early morning fog, not seeing the sun rising behind their backs. The contrast between this fine example of *bel canto* and the bustling human figures gives rise to a sense of frustration and of the tragic discrepancy between the life which has been dreamed about and that which is being lived now. 'Everything remains as it was', says one of the characters, Anna Petrovna. But the film does not finish with this sequence.

The camera slowly retreats from the people approaching the house, and the screen shows the face of a sleeping boy lit by the sun's rays. It is on him that the film makers pin their hopes for another, truly happy life. It is this awkward, shy adolescent Petechka who makes them believe that not all their dreams and ideals have been crushed by their collision with cruel reality.

Ex. 27 The leitmotiv of Hope from the film *An Unfinished Piece for Player Piano*

The image of Petechka is musically characterised. In those few moments when he manages to escape the surveillance of grown-ups and feels free and unrestrained (the episodes 'Grass', 'Rain'), tender and delicate music appears in the film. Like the Waltz, it is based on Nemorino's romance, but at the same time differs from it in its unconstrained and spontaneous character, helped by light and transparent orchestration which sets off the melodious flute solo[10].

As compared to *An Unfinished Piece for Player Piano*, the musical solution of the film with the equally lengthy title *Some Days in the Life of I. I. Oblomov* was notable for its much greater complexity and refinement. In general, the music for *Oblomov* was a consistent development of several leitmotives. These were: the love theme of Olga and Oblomov (*Casta diva* by Bellini from the opera *Norma*), the theme of dreams and nostalgia for childhood (born out of acoustic play on the tetrachord of the psalmody) and the leitmotiv of the earth, of Russian spirituality, for which the composer used the *Vsenoshchnaya* (The Night Service) by Rakhmaninov. There were invisible but strong links between them because of an original device used by the composer. Artemyev encapsulated Rakhmaninov's scale in a cluster, and recorded it on tape, subsequently adding specific sound colour — the prayerful singing of the church choir seems to grow out of the depths of the earth. In the finale of the film where a summing up of the leitmotiv development is effected, the earth and dream themes are polyphonically superimposed on the music of *Vsenoshchnaya*, revealing their kinship.

Thus, in the 1970s, Artemyev obviously preferred openly quoting and not concealing his use of immortal works of musical art as sources for his own improvisations (which were both correct and stylistically close to the originals). However, in the following decade this composer discovered for himself vitally new forms of creative contact with the spiritual heritage of the past, turning to stylistic *symbiosis*, and the implantation of alien texts into his imaginative thinking. This is demonstrated by Tarkovsky's *Stalker* (1980, 2 parts), the last picture shot by this director in his own country. It is based on a complex counterpoint of music and representation.

29

Breakthrough into the future:
film music in the work of Artemyev, Schnittke, and Gubaidulina in the 1980s

The peculiarity of *Stalker* is its use of the minimalist principle in its choice of visual expressive means to accompany the rich and multidimensional sound elements. This allowed the filmmakers to carry out their almost imperceptible transformation of the perfectly real, everyday objective world of human civilization ('The Town') into the fantastic, conditional world ('The Zone').

The plot of *Stalker* is simple and tells of an unfinished expedition into a forbidden Zone (the place where some unknown cosmic body had landed) by three people: the Writer, the Professor and their guide Stalker. The cherished aim of the expedition is to get to the magic room, where one can realize one's greatest wish. But the path to this goal proves a difficult and agonizing path of self-knowledge. As the director explained in an interview, when 'they come to that place, having experienced and re-thought so much, they cannot bring themselves to enter the magic room. They have come to understand that their morals are probably not so perfect. And they cannot muster the courage to believe in themselves.

'So it seems till the last scene, when Stalker's wife appears in the café where they are resting after their travel. She is a tired, worn woman. . . . It is difficult for them to understand the reason why this woman, who has suffered a lot from her husband, who has born a sick child by him, still loves him with the same abandon with which she loved him in her youth. It is her love, her devotion that is the miracle which can be opposed to lack of belief, to frustration, cynicism, that is, to all that was the essence of the heroes' life until that moment.

'In this picture I will try for the first time to be unambiguously clear in defining the main positive value which is said to make man stay alive'[11]. For Tarkovsky the understanding of this value was inseparable from the theme of dignity, which was shown in the film in the light of that moral conflict which a man experiences when he is suffering from the lack of it.

The tragic wanderings of the heroes, searching for their lost faith and hopes, and their desperate attempts to conceal their spiritually damaged personalities in verbal labyrinths of scholastic discussion, found an original interpretation in the musical conception which was strongly influenced by Zen-Buddhism which at that time interested both Tarkovsky and Artemyev. According to the director's plan, the overall task of music in *Stalker* was to portray Kipling's thesis on the incompatibility of the West and the East, which cannot comprehend each other and have to exist within the straitjacket of indoctrinated cultural systems. Yet Kipling's principle was accepted by the authors of the film not as a dogma but as a doubtful starting point. To show the possibility of a different approach to the artistic and philosophical problem of the West and the East, Artemyev chose the medieval psalm *Pulcherrima Rosa*, composed in honour of the Virgin Mary by an anonymous fourteenth-century Italian, with which, by complicated manipulations of its orchestral timbre, he showed European music being 'implanted' into Eastern music.

The foundation of this musical solution for *Stalker* was the isolation of basic tonal material from Indian music, which was then usually allotted to plucked string instruments like the vina or the tampur. By means of this

Figure 12 *Stalker*

basic material, whose timbre was close to that of the tampur, the composer modelled a specific musical-acoustic space into which he placed a contrapuntal combination of the flute rendering of *Pulcherrima Rosa* and an improvisation on the *tar*, a multinational Asiatic instrument. But to avoid a too straightforward and illustrative impression of European and Eastern instruments, he invented a host of different modulations and transformations on the synthesizer of the old transverse flute timbre and of the ancient *tar*. It allowed him to achieve a state of inner harmony, a psychological balance through their combination. The composer's procedure was as follows: for example, the *tar* was at first recorded at the proper speed, which was then slowed; this allowed 'the life' of each string to be heard and the harshness and dryness of sound peculiar to the *tar* to be softened and made more European.

No less interesting was the metamorphosis of the flute music. Its first appearance, during the film captions, was accompanied by harpsichord reconstructed on the SINTI–100 at its nearest approximation to the original. But as the heroes delved deeper into the Zone, which frightened them with its mysteriousness, the antique psalm gradually lost its architectonic harmony and proportions, and disintegrated into separate phrases and motifs, surrounding itself with resonant chords and rhythmic bass ostinato movements. Yet the most surprising changes happened to its intonation and timbre. The saturation of the diatonic melody with delicate microchromatism and ornamental embellishment, and its transition from the regular periodicity which is normal for European music to an arbitrary rhythmic organization, testified to its gradual national transformation. This feeling was intensified by the transfer of the psalm to the lower register, which changed its overtone composition and distinguished in the flute timbre those subsidiary formants which, after special treatment and proper grouping, evoke unexpected auditory associations with the Asiatic drum (with the psychoemotional modus of perception characteristic of it). The symbiosis of the two cultures reached its climax in 'meditation' (the finale of the picture) where identical improvisations on the *tar* and the flute (in the manner of the *magam*) intertwined at the fifth[12], symbolizing the long-expected unity of the East and the West.

When speaking of the music to *Stalker*, one should also mention that it exposed the conflict of City and Nature (the Zone), traditional on modern civilization. This theme is extremely important in our understanding of the artistic and philosophic conception of the film. Its most remarkable manifestation is 'The Way to the Zone'. The plot is very simple: the heroes are travelling on the trolley and at a certain moment they understand by a change in the landscape and deformed natural sounds that they are already beyond the real world. 'The Way to the Zone' occupies a whole episode and is distinguished by its extremely complicated sound organization. The composer's idea was to transform everyday noises into music, and in this way to carry the spectator simply to an entirely different atmosphere of action, to another acoustic realm.

The scene starts with the playing of the theme *Pulcherrima Rosa*, rhythmically augmented. Similar to a medieval *cantus firmus*, it is placed in the tenor voice of a polyphonic structure, the upper and lower voices of which are natural noises – the rumble of trolley wheels and the humming of rails. As the heroes approach the Zone these natural noises are replaced by synthesized sounds similar to them in timbre, with constantly changing acoustics and a strictly regulated rhythmic basis. Replacing natural noises with their musical 'sound-alikes' creates a special multidimensional space, which seems to be an integral part of the strange, ghostly, unreal landscape that unfolds before these invaders, who represent a bitter parody of the Christian Trinity[13].

An important step toward the destruction of dilapidated stereotypes of film music function and comprehension of the nature of the audio-visual image was made by Alfred Schnittke in the film of Larisa Shepit'ko *Ascent* (1976). It is interesting that the plot of this film, shot after the well-known story *Sotnikov* by Vasyl' Bykov, contained several direct allusions to the Biblical story of Christ and Judas who betrayed him. Significantly, the director herself called it a neo-parable.

The chief characteristic of this picture was the fact that its visual elements, as well as its sound-track, were presented deliberately in newsreel fashion: in black-and-white and with carefully selected war-time shots. This made the composer give up traditional methods of using music in its habitual role of commentator on the screen events, and look for new techniques of constructing the film's sound aura.

Schnittke's solution for *Ascent* was the idea of 'the crawling over of the sound cloud' (his words), of a gradual transformation of real noises into music which appears in its basic form in the two final parts of the film: at its tragic climax — the scene of Sotnikov's execution, and in the epilogue. Thus, the development of the sound image is a *crescendo*, from an exposition saturated with sharp sounds signifying danger (the crunch of snow under the feet of the partisans sent on a reconnaissance party, the howling of the blizzard, the short cry 'Germans! . . . Punishers!' the roaring of a car engine, the clack of the breech-blocks of machine-guns, loud German speech, the pursued partisans trying to escape) to the finale where the music, working itself free from noise, acquires thematic expressiveness and lucidity, shaking the spectator with its grandeur and spiritual power.

Figure 13 *Ascent*

In the scene of Sotnikov's execution, where there is almost no speech and no noise, the music supports the hero, who is exhausted by torture but not broken, whose spirit has already left the all-too-solid flesh and approached the boundary of immortality. This treatment of music makes the image of Sotnikov, initially realistic, turn in the finale into an idea, a symbolic image which transforms the concrete story of his life into a parable[14].

Schnittke's next important work in the cinema was his music for Elem Klimov's *Leave-taking* (1983), adapted from Valentin Rasputin's *Taking Leave of Mater*. It is interesting that together with Schnittke, Viacheslav Artemov, Sofia Gubaidulina, and Victor Suslin all collaborated on this film (the names of the last two artists were not mentioned in the credits at their own request). Their task was to create an unusual musical sound world which could harmonise with poetical landscape shots of Siberia, and create a special feeling for and image of the primal matter of living nature. Artless tunes played on folk and children's instruments, colourful flecks of sound, tone clusters appearing seemingly out of nothing, the use of isorhythmic serial modules representing 'the rhythm of the natural life currents': these were the powerful sources feeding and uniting different poles of this film's universe. Any attempt to leave the zone of their action resulted in the hero finding himself sinking either into rough everyday materialism and earthly reality, or else into depths of the spirit purified from petty vanity, and feeling at one with national sacred objects, with his forefathers, and with his native land.

The creators of *Leave-taking* separate those two poles as much as possible, deliberately placing at one of them everyday noises, fragments of trivial 'musical wallpaper' devoid of poetry or aesthetic beauty, and at the other beautiful, inspired symphonic music by Schnittke. Each of this music's appearances, like a powerful force-field, absorbs all other sounds reminding one of eternity. Accumulating powerful humanist potential, the symphonic music becomes here a repository of high moral and ethical ideals in that meta-language in which the director tries to address the spectator. On the whole, the musical conception of *Leave-taking* seems to relate philosophically to vital modern problems, such as ecology, the horrible consequences of the rupture between man and nature, of people forgetting their past, their fathers and grandfathers and great-grandfathers, and the style of life which had been created over the centuries. It is not by chance that the dominant image, the metaphor of the film, is a powerful giant larch, which cannot be destroyed by the Martian-like workers in quaint white plastic overalls who come to flood the island. They look alien to virgin nature, which desperately resists destruction. Therefore the tree, in spite of all the invaders' attempts to saw it down, to blow it up, to uproot it with a bulldozer stays standing, and irradiaties energy. This energy is 'eternity' represented by Schnittke's music.

One of the finest achievements of Soviet film music in the '80s is that by Sofia Gubaidulina for Rolan Bykov's *The Dummy* (1984). It refutes the banal conception of accessible film music as a product of mass subculture. The composer turns to the most modern means of expression, maximally intensifying the emotional effect of this acute, socially observant 'teenage' picture, which tells about the far from childish games of a young generation growing up as predators and hypocrites, and about the spiritual beauty and courage of a girl, thin and helpless at first sight, who can not only pardon other people's weakness, but also challenge the whole school form which tries to humiliate her and strip her of dignity.

Figure 14 *The Dummy*

The musical dramaturgy of *The Dummy* consists of two tonal and imaginative spheres, both absolutely independent in style, genre characteristics and communicative level. These spheres develop in parallel, in non-contiguous planes of simultaneous counterpoint. They are also quite different in the formal methods by which they are introduced into the sequence: this allows a diversity of style and culture in the juxtaposition of quotation material (in-sequence) and the composer's original (off-sequence) music.

The first of these tonal and imaginative spheres is wholly dependent on the action, and demonstrates the material environment of the collective hero — the school-mates of the new pupil Lena Bessoltseva. In this milieu, genuine human feeling is replaced by primary, highly-strung, nervous emotion, nourished on the surrogates of mass culture and aimed at the satisfaction of only one need — that for mindless entertainment (almost at the physiological, reflex level).

Pouring from the transistor, loudspeakers and tape-recorders, from screens of TV sets and video recorders, the hits of the Soviet pop star Alla Pugacheva and even the music of the Beatles are no more than irritations to the ear, intended to fill the vacuum in the teenagers' souls. At the same time, it intensifies their aggression and cruelty to one who appears to be unlike them, and does not belong to their pack. Their standard, featureless tastes, habits, hobbies make them react together, turning them into a herd living according to its own dark laws, and giving short shrift to any manifestation of individuality.

In principle, the attempt to connect mass culture with the processes of dehumanization and the moral and intellectual degradation of modern society can be repeatedly found in the cinema. It is sufficient to remember Artemyev's music in Mikhalkov's *Relatives* (1981) where commercialized pop and rock music symbolize a horrible destructive power capable of tearing up kinship ties, and turning people into irrelevancies devoid of national roots. But if this device is made grotesque by Artemyev, in his surrealistic metamorphosis of the *Moonlight Sonata* by Beethoven into a catchy rock hit (in the scene with the motorcyclist), here, in the tragic corrosion of the Russian folk song *The Steed was Frolicking* in Gubaidulina's music for the finale of the picture, this device establishes the very fact of complete social mutation.

Sofia Gubaidulina's original music forms a second layer devoted to the main character of *The Dummy*. Avoiding existing methods of presenting positive heroes by tuneful and melodious leitmotivs in lyric theatre style, the composer chooses an unusual way of creating a portrait based upon an alloy, a synthesis of the heroine's outer appearance with her inner spiritual essence.

Ex. 28 Lena's leitmotiv from the film *The Dummy*

Lena's youthful angular movements, her slender girlish figure, her face unendowed with natural beauty and attractiveness — this superficial impression is soon forgotten, and one remembers only the trustfulness and kindness shining from the wide open eyes which make her plain face beautiful; and, of course, the music, so strange and touching. The trembling flute and violin solos are surrounded by transparent string *tremolos* which draw a tender and delicate, seemingly defenceless image of a teenage girl.

At the same time, in the concentrated meditation upon and rhythmically varied repetition of the tiny characteristic turn of the theme, in the intense pulsing of the percussion, one can feel oneself not only entering the inner world, but also the powerful moral conviction which reveals itself at the tragic climax, where a dummy clad in Lena's dress is burned by her form mates. By repetition, the crescendo with its gradual accumulation of new orchestral groups imparts to the scene, entirely by musical and plastic means, a great dramatic tension which approaches a state of temporary insanity. The entry of the chorus and the organ arouses almost intolerable despair and pain which, having reached their highest point of development, are squeezed into a horrible lump pulsing in the girl's heart. In the score, this is expressed by a *glissando* gelling of separate instrumental and choral parts into a chromatic cluster which seems to shudder under the strokes of the tam-tam and the rolling of the timpani.

This basing of the musical conception on the opposition of two antagonistic imaginative spheres developed in parallel, without any direct contact, demanded the presence of some element which served as a mediator. This was the march played by a band, whose appearance in the prologue and the epilogue of the picture conveyed an architectonic balance and compositional completeness to the cinematic narration. Indeed, Lena's arrival in a small motor-launch at the town where her beloved grandfather meets her on the bank, while nearby a rehearsal of the Suvorov military school band is taking place, and their final departure on the same launch from the same deserted landing stage to the same sad and solemn sounds of the march, imparts to the action and to all the events of the film a logical finality and balance of proportion. At the same time, the march written by Gubaidulina has a sort of double undercurrent, which opens up the possibility of a natural modulation both into the 'composed' and the 'quoted' musical and dramatic layers of the picture. Belonging to a mass democratic genre, it could formally exist at the same level as the hits of pop and rock music, while on the other hand, it bears such a powerful imprint of the composer's individuality and shares so many tonal characteristics with Lena's leitmotiv that it could be considered as an additional element in the portrait of the heroine.

Sofia Gubaidulina's music for *The Dummy* was one of the most striking and significant events in the history of Soviet film music in the '80s, and was certainly the best of the composer's film work. Probably this fine achievement came about because the film's central ideas lay close to the main themes of the composer's creative work, her concerns with the philosophic conception of the genius, the victim, and the idea of resurrection. This was a situation quite rare in borderline genres of art.

30

The cinema musical: a change in orientation. A transition from the classics to the revue film and the musical. The first Soviet screening of a rock-opera

Interesting changes in the musical cinema, not always unambiguous in their artistic results, were noticeable during Brezhnev's stagnation period. In the early '70s the genre of film-opera finally ceased to exist. The monumental and tasteless screening of Borodin's opera *Prince Igor* (1971, director Tikhomirov) and two chamber films. the Azerbaijani lyrical-psychological drama *Sevil* by Amirov (1970, director Gorikker) and the Georgian lyrical-social opera *Daïsi* by Paliashvili (1971, director Sanishvili) were its last appearances in the cinema[15].

Two outstanding and star-studded ballet productions of the Bolshoi Theatre *Spartakus* to Khachaturian's music and Prokofiev's *The Terrible Age* (based on his music for *Ivan the Terrible*), gave rise to a plan conceived by the ballet-master Grigorovich and the director Derbenev to film those ballets for screening in the USSR and also abroad. However, the modest merits of those films did not inspire anybody to continue such experiments, and they caused no further development, remaining isolated events.

The great public success enjoyed by Western musicals in the Soviet Union at last elicited a response from Soviet film-makers. The first step in this direction was taken by Georgi Shengelaya in *The Melodies of Veriisky Block*, with music by G. Tsabadze (1973). This was hardly surprising: Georgian masters were the originators of the Soviet cinema musical. The specific peculiarity of Georgian cinema had always been its plasticity in visual forms of movement derived from the silent film, and its accent on expressive gesture and music. In the long run, this helped the creators of *The Melodies of Veriisky Block* create a lively, entertaining, idiomatic musical spectacle work, rich in songs, dances, ensemble numbers and colourful crowd, chorus and choreographic scenes.

МЕЛОДИИ ВЕРИЙСКОГО КВАРТАЛА

Figure 15 *The Melodies of Veriisky Block*

The film is based on a fairly traditional vaudeville situation: the laundress Vardo loves the widower Pavle and his two charming daughters, and to give the girls an opportunity to take dancing lessons she steals an expensive fur-coat. But all ends well. Vardo is released because there has to be somebody to wash linen. She and Pavle decide to marry, while the girls go to study dancing.

Georgi Tsabadze's music, spun from Georgian melodies and presented for the stage in a delicate arrangement, became the ornament of this musical, imparting to it a lush national colouring. Of special importance was the sound-image of Vardo, which set off both the lyrical and comical features of her character. At the same time, in treating the other characters the composer and director could not avoid operetta clichés and stereotyped personae. Unfortunately, there were other, more annoying flaws in the film, mainly concerning the weakest aspect of the Soviet musical — choreography. The long-term absence of show-culture in the USSR forced the film makers to use their foreign colleagues' experience. As a result, in *The Melodies of Veriisky Block* whole scenes appeared which copied almost verbatim the style and direction of the crowd scenes in the English *Oliver!* (1968, director Reed, composer Bart) and partly (in the scene with the laundresses) those of the American *Fiddler on the Roof* (1970, director Jewison, composer Bock). Nevertheless, the way was paved and other directors started along it with the assurance and courage of pioneers. It should be noted that, since in the Soviet Union the film musical was born earlier than its theatrical counterpart, directors felt free not only to choose plots, but most importantly, the expressive means and forms of presentation for the material. This stimulated a search for non-standard solutions which took into account the specificity of both arts — music and cinema. Only one film, Gorikker's *The Screen Star* (1974) shot after Eshpai's operetta *There is Nobody More Beautiful than I*, maintained to some extent the traditions of the genre. In others, directors demonstrated considerable imagination and invention in avoiding the inevitable comparison with the best examples of the classical musical, and tried to find their own new methods of shaping an effective musical spectacle.

In 1976, the Lithuaninan director Arunas Žebriunas furthered the work of Georgi Shengelaya and shot *The Devil's Bride*, the music for which was written by one of the USSR's most talented jazz composers and pianists, Viacheslav Ganelin. The plot, created after the novel of Kazisa Boruta *Baltaragis' Mill*, re-told the old Lithuanian legend about the Devil banished from Heaven by God, who settled down among humans and decided to marry miller Baltaragis' beautiful daughter.

The main driving force of this amusing story about the devil's intrigues on Earth, which is full of unexpectedly comic and sometimes dramatic collisions, is the music. This is based on a symbiosis of ancient Lithuanian folksongs (the sutartines) with the latest trends in 20th-century music (aleatorics, sonoristics, jazz, rock music), which strongly affects the representational style of the film, the montage rhythm, and the actors' behaviour in each sequence. Moreover, the considerable amount of music in the film makes it almost an integral musical work, a rapprochement with opera buffo, where the spoken dialogues are replaced by recitatives, and there is extensive use of national songs and dances. It was not casually that the director, who absolutely denied that *The Devil's Bride* was a musical, called his creation a rhythm-opera, probably meaning the rock-opera which was just becoming fashionable in the West at that time. However, in my opinion, *The Devil's Bride* is not a rock-opera: both in its choice of theme and the manner of its presentation, and in its choice of musical social genre, it remains within the bounds of the musical.

For the rock-opera proper, we must turn to *The Star and Death of Khoakin Murieta* by composer Alexei Rybnikov (1983, director Grammatikov), which was the screen version of the disc of this work recorded by Melodia. Despite the tremendous success of the Moscow Leninsky Komsomol Theatre stage version, Vladimir Grammatikov's film of the same name was received with reserve both by critics and spectators in spite of the active participation of the composer. The reason was the difficulties encountered by the film makers when transforming the musical score into visual images, and also the director's unhelpful passion for stage effects, and his evident inability to find visual equivalents for the music in the static lyrical episodes. This often created considerable artistic failings, and caused either an unbalance between music and representation or, vice versa, their cartoon-like literal coincidence ('Mickeymousing')

In this same year, 1983, one more musical film appeared whose makers decided not to tempt fate with risky experiments but simply to make a good musical. Its initiator was the popular film actress and singer Ludmila Gurchenko, who saw a starry role for herself in Karel Čapek's popular comedy *The Makropulos Case*. Taking up this idea, director Evgeny Ginzburg and composer Georgi Garanyan made *The Recipe of Her Youthfulness*, in which the methods of operetta, musical comedy and review were all creatively reshaped. The film turned out to be spectacular, and emotionally expressive because of its skilful combination of two independent topical action streams. One of them is connected with the eccentric buffoonery of the adventure story, which puts an end to the long-lasting law suit "Prus vs Gregor" and includes both the musical characterisation of the protagonists and accessory music. The other appeals to a magic fairy tale world which carefully guards genuine art, treasures which, along with the great Marty, are immortal. Tired of her three-hundred-year wanderings along the byways of life, she has found peace only among actors in carnival masks well-known from childhood stories, among clowns and acrobats. Her monologues reveal her feelings, her doubts and bitter contemplation of the absurdity of eternal life, where man loses any ability to be surprised and rejoice, to despair or fall in love.

In spite of the wonderful cast, sound direction and Garanyan's effective music, which developed through facile jazz improvisation, *The Recipe of Her Youthfulness* was not an outstanding event of musical cinema in the '80s. This can be easily explained: the time for the musical was over, the public had lost interest in it. Now public interest was directed at the concert film, the revue which returned in a new, re-vamped shape, with the indispensable participation of leading pop and rock stars.

This gala parade was opened by Alla Pugacheva who became a leading 'symbol' of Soviet variety in the '70s–'80s. Her first appearance on the screen occurred in director Orlov's *A Woman Who Sings* (1979, music by Zatsepin, Pugacheva, and Garin). Unfortunately, the script written by Stepanov specially for the singer was not original and was designed as a 'biography film of a great actor'. It was based on the story of a Cinderella, who made her way in the world by hard work and by untiringly perfecting her talent and who became famous, but sacrificed worldly joy and even personal happiness for the sake of her art. The strongest parts of the picture are undoubtedly the sequences showing Pugacheva in her natural role as singer, which allowed her to demonstrate her musical and dramatic mastery. Probably this surprising gift of Alla Pugacheva for scenic reincarnation and for turning every song into a solo tour-de-force induced another director, Nikolai Ardashnikov, to shoot a new film with her in a starring role six years later.

Remembering his predecessor's failure, Ardashnikov decided to dispense with plot and turned to the genre of the concert-film, which allowed a certain freedom in the structural organization of the musical and visual material. In fact, the picture *I Have Arrived to Say* (1985, composer Pugacheva: the author of the song 'The 20th Century' is Morozov) was a screen version of one of the singer's gala-concerts. This took place in the arena of the 'Olympiisky' sports complex (besides Pugacheva, the 'Recital' ensemble and the 'Expressia' dancing trio took part both in the concert and in the film). The suite principle chosen by the director, according to which stylistically diverse songs alternated with one another, linked by arbitrary plastic and feature interludes, made the film resemble a TV show; while improvisation, colourful effects, kaleidoscopic, dynamic montage, all made the film resemble the video-clips which were just coming into fashion.

Further collaboration by the film-makers with Pugacheva was restricted to the more or less justified inclusion into the action of song inserts and shots of the singer surrounded by lesser stars by means of which the directors wanted to impart greater attractiveness to the film in spectators' eyes. So, for example, did director Berezantseva in her screen version of Shakespeare's comedy *Much Ado about Nothing*, entitled *Love for Love* (1983, composer Khrennikov). She inserted into the action two concert items as 'entrance arias', performed by Pugacheva and the well known operatic bass Evgeny Nesterenko. A similar technique was also used by director Youngwald-Hilkevich in the film *The Magic Season* (1985, composer Chernavsky), the finale of which showed a colourful carnival performance. This resembled a folk fete with a whole 'bunch' of popular actors, including Mikhail Boyarsky, the group 'Zemliane' and, of course, Alla Pugacheva 'herself'.

After Pugacheva, the cinema started making commercial profit by using other musical stars: Sofia Rotaru (*Where Are You, Love?*, 1980, director

Gageau, composer Mazhukov; *The Soul*, 1981, director Stefanovich, composer Zatsepin), Larisa Dolina (*Jazzman*, 1983, director Shakhnazarov, composer Kroll). It is curious that Shakhnazarov's film *Jazzman* resembled the famous jazz comedy of Alexandrov and Dunayevsky *The Merry Fellows* in its plot, peripeteia and characterisation. It was not by chance that the film's makers included in it songs from Leonid Utesov's repertoire and called their hero Kostya, choosing the same name that the creators of *The Merry Fellows* had used. Nevertheless, it would be wrong to relegate the film *Jazzman* to the category of screen remakes since another principle, unlike the song dramaturgy of Alexandrov and Dunayevsky's comedy, was used in the later film, according to which the music was moved to the fore and gave rise to different subject collisions, some of them funny, some of them romantic and amorous, and some of them dramatic. This eliminated any division between the real and the imagined, and introduced to jazz art an important element of unpredictability.

Another remarkable event in the cinema of the '70s and '80s was director Urbla's and composer Rannap's *This Summer's Hit* (1982) in which two very famous Estonian actors made their debuts, the variety singer Els Himma and the brilliant jazz pianist and rock musician Gunnar Graps[16]. Besides these two, the film featured the group 'Magnetic Band', Tõnis Mägi and 'Musicsafe', Anne Vesci and 'The Golden Trio', the groups 'Ruja', 'Rock Atelier', 'The Office', Ooel Steinfeldt and 'Doctor Friedrich', and the disco-group 'Eurhythmia'. Such a representative forum of musicians, in which the best representatives of Estonian variety and rock came together, created a dynamic background for this story of the private and artistic fate of a singer who, on reaching adulthood, went through a serious breakdown because the public had tired of her, and she was faced with the necessity of competing with younger rivals; nevertheless, she still found the courage to struggle for the right to stay on-stage. However, it was not this rather common story, but the colourful panorama of Estonian light music of 1981, shot in the manner of a newsreel, that became the most valuable element in Peeter Urbla's film and made it distinctive and unique.

Thus, in the development of the musical cinema in the '70s and early '80s a clear re-orientation of interest can be observed, from the academic genres of opera and ballet to the spectacular, mass, democratic genres of the musical, the concert film, and the revue. In this way, Soviet cinema tried to attract the public under conditions of approaching crisis, given the steady fall in cinema attendance, and also the severe competition from television. However, real success was not frequent: there was not enough relevant experience, professional skill or proper production method. But the main problem which musical cinema faced, and which it could never solve, was that most producers only shot musical films occasionally and, as a rule, did not care either build on to their successes or correct their mistakes.

Nevertheless, during that period two films did appear which could be referred to as musicals though with certain restrictions, since neither of them had any analogue in cinema where music provided the main dramatic axis of the ideological and artistic conception. One was director Andrei Mikhalkov-Konchalovsky's and composer Alexander Gradsky's film *A Romance about Lovers* (1974, 2 parts), and the other director Sergei Ovcharov's and composer Igor Matsievsky's *Unlikely Stories* (1983).

The very title of the film *A Romance about Lovers* points to a connection with music, which addresses man's inner world with all its psychological nuances. This picture was designed on the principles of a musical two-part form based on contrast. It is a modern fable of love, made by its creators with powerful feeling, and with striking inspiration.

Male and female. A Boy and a Girl who love each other. Then he is called up, and during military training he goes missing. She waits, not wanting to believe that he has perished. But life takes its own, and the Girl marries. When the Boy returns, strong, sure of himself, and tries to take Her

Figure 16 *A Romance about Lovers*

away by force She refuses because she is another man's wife. Then he dies before the eyes of his shaken parents, friends, neighbours, and the whole town, for man cannot live without love. Thus the first part of *A Romance* ends. It resembles a romantic opera seria. There is no place for everyday, prosaic, concrete things in it. The world which appears on the screen is beautiful and festive. The heroes living in it speak in blank verse, and express their feelings in songs which seem to emerge freely and easily out of the action itself.

The film starts at its highest point, bringing to its audience a powerful stream of joy and happiness which fill the souls of the young heroes to the brim. 'There are only you and I, yes, only you and I, only us two, yes only us two', they either sing or cry to the whole world. This ecstatic, inspired and hymn-like song determines the level of the first part of the picture. Emotionally and sensually uninhibited characters from the modern rock scene, with long hair, motorcycle helmets and guitars, and all the accessories of '70s youth culture, gradually form the general image of the world as seen by the lovers.

The love uniting them is beautiful, but as critic Alexander Lipkov wrote: 'it is only a small part of something else, much more general. You and I have the bonds of the family, friendship, home where we live (home in *A Romance about Lovers* is an extended family, a vibrant unity of different human characters, types, professions, and ages), companions-in-arms, the whole country'[17]. This change in the scale of outlook gives rise to such songs as a ballad about birds flying to their native land and perishing from the bullets of hunters; the Boy's brave parting song by the entrance check-point before leaving to serve in the army, and the solemn chorale 'Oh, Mothers' Hands' which becomes the symbolic image of the Motherland.

The second part of *A Romance about Lovers* is non-musical and in its stylistic solution is sharply dissonant with the first. After the tragic and beautiful scene where the Boy's corpse is carried away on the raised hands of his friends through the yard of the house in which he had grown up and lived, all the people present freeze in mournful silence, and after a darkening still, he appears again in black-and-white, in impersonal and depressing colours. He is chewing something in the dirty, dilapidated canteen. Now his name is Sergei, he is working as a trolley-bus driver and leads the regular 'common' life of a 'common' man. But how dull and monotonous the world surrounding him is, for his soul's death has killed everything in him: the ability to see and feel, to appreciate colour and music, and poetry. The death of music in him (as well as colour) is felt especially acutely, since its place appears to be immediately occupied by a ghastly sound of clattering plates which is painful to the ear, by the screeching of brakes and hissing of opening doors in the trolley-bus, and by the tired and monotonous announcement of stop-names by Sergei, etc. This visual reality is also muted on the sound-track which is devoid of emotional colouring. It resembles a depressing lethargic sleep into which the hero has sunk and from which he cannot awake after his almost random marriage. Only the birth of his daughter returns him to life: colour and music return, and also hope for happiness. Then, to the sound of a rising lullaby, the camera leaves the earth, and the audience is given a bird's eye view of the land below, the fields, the rivers, the cities which represent the Motherland, Russia.

Thus, the structure the of *A Romance about Lovers* contains two contrasting parts — a colour and a black-and-white one, a musical and a sound/noise one, and has an unusual shape resembling an arch; its base points (the songs 'Only I and You' and 'Oh, Mothers' Hands') are the climaxes. They give an impulse to the action, and complete it. This allows the stylistic unification of heterogeneous parts into a single artistic narration, and helps demonstrate the external world changing with the inner state of the hero.

Unlike the modern explosive rhythms of rock music, which shaped the special, elevated and romantic sound world of *A Romance*, another type of music reigned in the film *Unlikely Stories*, which originated in ancient folk games. *Unlikely Stories* resembled a gaudily painted, Russian popular print, built up from motives from fairy tales, legends, games, fables, all related to the deep layers of humour in folk culture. In the film, merry chastooshkas, catchphrases, and dancing folk-tunes all serve as an excuse for the appearance of a whole cascade of wonderful tricks and metamorphoses and practical jokes, which end in a mass Shrove-tide carnival scene — a celebration of spring's arrival.

Unlikely Stories was designed by the director as a montage of attractions, totally disconnected at first sight. Each of them was preceded by its own musical motif. Yet, to avoid the disintegration of the film's construction, Ovcharov introduced three characters: the foolish duffer Neznam (an abridged variant of the common expression 'who knows?', that is 'nobody understands what'), the unlucky village inventor Bobyl (a poor, landless peasant), and the smart and brave Soldier. The comparison of these three different characters gives, as the critic Vladimir Fomin wrote, 'a constructive basis to the whole film, sets going the pendulum of the plot'[18].

The presence of these contrasting protagonists who resemble living copies of popular heroes from folk tales and who constantly find themselves in the most improbable comic situations, induces the composer to resort not only to the song and instrumental forms of skomorokh art, but also to parodied genres of city culture. This is exemplified by the exaggeratedly melodramatic, heart-breaking romance sung by the affected, smart dandy

Figure 17 *Unlikely Stories*

to guitar accompaniment in the scene where he seduces Neznam's wife, and by the Russian dance tune which accompanies the fussy attempts of peasants to retrieve a barrel from the river. At the same time, the practically continuous music never comes to the fore: it is not connected with the plot, being somewhat alienated in the construction of *Unlikely Stories*. Its main purpose is to create a special musical/sound aura of mass, spontaneous, authentic folk performance. The use of authentic instruments, which reproduce a specifically folk-like style of singing with the help of a folklore ensemble, imparts to the film a unique colouring and a gripping emotionality, brings it close to improvised skomorokh performance, and creates an atmosphere of ancient national festivity. There is something enchanting, pagan, sensual in the rushing alternation of melodies. However, there is nothing chaotic in this whirling carnival of themes. The cementing element is a mischievous nonsense chastooshka which appears repeatedly like a refrain in the course of the film. This nonsense chastooshka is not only a uniting factor: its absurd text (e. g., 'A cow is swimming down the river, there is a suitcase on its back') gives rise to equally absurd situations and stories, all of which made Fomin call *Unlikely Stories* 'a marvel film, a riddle film'[19].

Thus, the biography of Soviet film music through the fifteen years of 'stagnation' cannot be assessed simply. On the one hand, increasing pressure from state officialdom caused the propagation of standard and cliché schemes of musical/sound mounting in the genres of the military epic, the historico-revolutionary adventure, the 'collective farm' and 'production' films, where music (mainly song) continued to play the role of an important ideological loudspeaker for communist ideas. For the state, music's task was to form in the people's consciousness a poeticized heroico-romantic mythologized image of 'developed socialism'.

On the other hand, besides the regressive tendencies of the 1970s and early '80s, there were also gratifying positive changes effected by a considerably enlarged arsenal of expressive means, and by a renovation of film music language through the mastering of modern composition techniques. The establishment of *auteur* cinema stimulated a search for original methods of synthesising music with the other components of the sound track, as well as with the visual material: the aim here was the creation of an integral audio-visual image for each film. This became possible through the enlistment of the younger generation of musicians for work in the cinema. Among these were pioneers of the Soviet avant-garde, dodecaphony, and electronic music, who infused a fresh spirit into the film music organism, which had become tired of self-repetition.

At the same time, in the late 1970s and early '80s, a tendency appeared which was to flourish during the concluding stages of the history of Soviet film music. This was a lessening of interest among directors in composed music, and the restoration of the aesthetic principles of compilation. One of the reasons for this giving up of original music was an enthusiasm for documentalism, which demanded the exact historical reconstruction of not only representational but also musical quotations as 'signs of the time', of the information codes of one or another epoch. This tendency was most clearly displayed in director Alexei German's film *My Friend Ivan Lapshin* (1984, composer Gagulashvili) which stunned both professionals and audiences. The detailed reality of the '30s was revived before their eyes in an everyday unobtrusive style. Earlier, almost the same principle of constructing the sound-track by means of roughly reported speech and noise, the in-frame music being in an arbitrary superimposition and counterpoint, and with the minimum of composer's and sound engineer's interference into the natural acoustic texture, could be found in the Estonian picture *A Nest in the Wind* (1979, director Neuland, composer Sumera), the Ukrainian film *The Rooks* (1982, director Ershov, composer

Silvestrov) and the Belorussian film *Others' Patrimony* (1983, director Rybarev, composer Alkhimovich). Here composers faced a complicated task: without damaging the natural sound environment they were to impart to a film an architectonic balance, and to intensify the processes of audience perception by brief sound-superimpositions and by aleatory formations which enforced states of alarm or psychological stress. Reserve shown by composers was balanced by a detailed elaboration of the noise element, with the aim of creating an integral sound-world for each film. Subsequently, the technique of a 'rough copy sound-track', and a 'reporting' style in recording speech, music and noise became all-important and was used in the films of the perestroika and post-perestroika period, the last stage of the existence and development of Soviet art. This proceeded during the incipient disolution of the Soviet empire.

Part 5

1986–1991

31

'Black wave' aesthetics and music.
The crisis of film music under conditions
of intellectual and spiritual depression
in society, and the development of tough
naturalist cinema in the period of the
disintegration of the Soviet Union

The advent of the last General Secretary of the Central Committee was accompanied by a radical reconsideration of policy and a declaration of democratic reform. In practice, this new way, to which Mikhail Gorbachev gave the beautiful name of 'perestroika', drew a line under the history of the USSR, and stimulated the centrifugal process of the destruction of the state, which ended not only in the fall of the largest empire in the world but in the crash of the whole Eastern European socialist system. It was quite natural that this revolution in politics and ideology left its mark on all spheres of the country's activity, and on the consciousness of the people.

The stream of horrible exposures made by declassifying data on the crimes of Stalin's regime, which had been carefully kept secret for decades, and the truth about the years of Brezhnev stagnation, revealed the sores of modern society to the people, and caused a state of deep shock. Much of what had been thought secret and closed for ever became known and accessible to common discussion, and thus open to art. It was not surprising that film makers, who were as always in the vanguard of ideological struggle, followed the publicists and writers, and rushed to assimilate the previously forbidden themes, competing for the most naturalistic and repulsive representation of past and present horrors.

The troubled times of disintegration of this once mighty nuclear super-power were characterized by emotional unbalance, a riot of passion, a burst of hatred for the totalitarian regime and for national differences, a rise in criminal offences, and an unhealthy interest in sensational scandals. All those 'isms' in what recently had seemed quite a healthy Soviet society, very soon came on to the screen, and prepared a favourable basis for the appearance of 'the black wave'.

The aggressive and anti-humane tendencies of the 'transition' period films in which, according to critic Igor Lukshin, 'slums, basements, and garbage heaps are rhymed with restaurants, hard-currency hotels, and underground dens'[1], are depressing. In these films, a man is either the object or the subject of physical violence. In fact, he becomes an anti-hero, turning into a puppet in somebody's criminal game, a beast trying to escape from cunningly set traps, or a lonely fighter settling accounts with his opponents, depending on the story created by the film makers. As for music, there is no place for it in conditions where 'actions are motivated by non-civilized, primary instincts of fury, revenge, thirst (for alcohol, drugs) etc. and where such relations as friendship or real love are almost lost'[2]. The moral and spiritual emasculation plot pushes music into the background, and brings it down to the level of a needless, accessory element performing the role of irritating sound-garbage. Its presence in the 'black' films of the late 1980s, which are full of scenes of fighting, pursuit, and beatings, as well as episodes of violent sexual acts and rape, not infrequently seems to be a mere formality, a tribute to tradition.

Against this characterless background of frame-per-frame illustrative musical commentary in 'black wave' cinema, rare exceptions are Edward Artemyev's music to Sergeyev's film *The Executioner* (1990) and Edison Denisov's to Khubov's *The Body* (1990). It is curious that both these pictures belong to a category of films, extraordinarily 'fashionable' in the late '70s and early '80s, of revenge for outraged honour, trampled human dignity and injured pride. The themes of love/hatred, passion/revenge, which gave directors excellent opportunities to string together a whole series of montage attractions of shocking cruelty, suddenly inflamed the fantasy of composers. The point of attraction was the possibility of investigating the behavioral reactions and psychological states of people in extraordinary situations. But the way chosen for the musical expression of these themes appeared to be new.

A young woman, the heroine of the film *The Executioner*, falls victim to a gang rape and decides to meet evil with evil and hires an executioner to take her revenge. This gives rise to a horrible chain of violence, and drags the heroine into a vicious circle from which she can only escape by putting an end to her own life. This intricate and eerie story, with its elements of mysticism and fatal predestination, made the composer turn to the expressive techniques of psychedelic music. The modelling of static-state zones which absorb and emit sounds, and sometimes explode in a nervous rhythmic pulsation resembling a perpetuum mobile, the dominance of low frequency electronic timbres which cause a feeling of approaching catastrophe, and the concealment of open threat, all contribute to the emotionally dense sound-atmosphere which oppresses the audience's subconscious.

Unlike the heroine of *The Executioner*, who perished, Sveta, the heroine of *The Body*, finds the courage to stop on the brink of the precipice. She takes responsibility for another person's crime, and tries to break the chain of misfortunes and troubles so as to save her soul, and to rid herself of the hatred which gnaws at her because of her profaned love. Not by chance is the musical introduction to the film a penitential prayer addressed to the Virgin Mary, written by Edison Denisov. Appearing also in sequences which show a deserted, half-destroyed church, it is 'the key' to the perception of the picture, and imperceptibly introduces the action, revealing its connection with the main theme of the film, that of the expiation of sin.

The basis of the musical structure of *The Body* is the varied development of two leitmotivs which can be referred to as the theme of Fate and that of Love. The first, squeezed into the narrow range of a diminished fifth and permeated by 'crawling' chromaticism and painful minor seconds, is based on the imitation principle and creates the effect of an endlessly moving 'ribbon' melody. The theme of Fate ensnares the actions and thoughts of the

Ex. 29 The theme of Fate from the film *The Body*

characters in an invisible but strong net, paralyzing their will and making them do mean things verging on crime, one after another. Throughout the film this theme is gradually transformed, and it acquires a darker and 'gloomier' sound-colouring. As the climax approaches, the tone of tragic doomed feeling becomes more and more apparent. In the final prison scene, which completes the development of the Fate theme, this colouring appears in two clarinets against a background of ghastly French horn chords, framed by measured, funereal strokes of the timpani.

The antithesis of this Fate theme is the theme of Love. Its unbridled expression, filled with passionate youthful feeling, reminds one of the bright, impulsive and enthusiastic lyrical themes of Sergei Prokofiev. On the whole, this Love leitmotiv occupies a modest position as compared to the gloomy and tragic Fate theme, but each of its appearances is like 'a ray of light in the kingdom of darkness' allowing the audience to see the best aspects of the heroine's nature. An outrage upon her feelings and her lover's perfidy both soon cut short the theme of Love, and it dies. Only the return of the prayer in the finale brings a faint hope for the expiation of sin and the saving of the heroine's soul.

Films shot in the 'black wave' style included director Pavel Lungin's *Taxi Blues* (1990). Its music was composed and recorded by the outstanding jazz saxophonist V. Chekasin. The plot is a very intricate story of animosity/friendship between the taxi-driver Shlykov and the talented musician Seliverstov, who has become a drunkard. The makers of *Taxi Blues* found almost subconsciously the necessary means for narrating this story, using the classic jazz principle of spontaneous improvization, 'playing without rules' in the spirit of exquisite, fanciful free-jazz composition.

The saxophone fills the artistic texture of the film. Sometimes it seems heartfelt and trembling, sometimes screamingly loud, either touched by nostalgic sadness or carelessly joyful. It transfers the fairly common subject of human fate crippled and broken by the inhuman and unjust world into another philosophical dimension.

Taking advantage of the fact that one of the heroes of *Taxi Blues* is a musician, the director and the composer turn the saxophone, this once forbidden, 'dissident' instrument, into a character in its own right, and make it an almost animate being around which the intrigue of the plot is centered: a rapprochement of two entirely different people, who met by chance, takes place. Extensive monologue confessions from the saxophone create its own aura within the picture, alienated from the scenes of everyday life, which are deliberately earthy in their representation, texture and sound[3]. This aura helps the audience perceive traces of Christian kindness, love and forgiveness, seemingly lost forever, deeply hidden in the protective egocentrism, indifference, meanness and cynicism of the heroes.

There is one more important detail which should be noted. The title *Taxi Blues* contains not only an indication as to the profession of its main characters. The filmmakers' broad interpretation of the word 'blues' leads to the introduction of blues songs, with their typical question-and-answer formal structure, high emotionality and appeal to social themes, into the compositional model of the film (the taxi-driver and the musician are two extreme variants of one broken fate). One should respect the brave decision to base the sound track exclusively on saxophone timbre and to maintain the dialogue with the spectator in the complicated language of jazz avant-garde, giving up the old reliable method of quoting popular hits. However, Chekasin dealt brilliantly with the task facing him. His music, created naturally and easily, possessing astonishing magnetism and exciting in its sensuality, effects all increased by the consummate skill of the performer and his virtuoso technique, made *Taxi Blues* stand out from the mass of mediocre films shot in the late '70s and early '80s.

One last point. A special means of exciting interest in the picture among the young people who constitute the majority of the cinema audience, was to cast as the jazzman Lesha Seliverstov the soloist from the then popular Moscow group Zvuki Mu, Piotr Mamonov. In general, since the middle of the '80s, when as the result of the social and political liberalization of the country, the alternative culture which had long existed underground became legal, cinema underwent a period of enthusiasm for rock music. The massive recourse of film makers to the musical underground resulted in a number of films which exploited in different ways the creative work of the leading rock groups and the visual musical image of their leaders. Film credits contained the names of Andrei Makarevich (Time Machine), Boris Grebenshchikov (Aquarium), Victor Tsoy (Kino), Garrik Sukachev (Brigade S), Yuri Shevchuk (DDT), Konstantin Kinchev (Alisa) and other less famous rock stars. Frequently they were not only the composers of the music and its performers in the film, but were also filmed as actors.

A great stir, followed by vehement discussions (often with a negative bias), was caused by director Sergei Solovyev's film *Assa* (1987, 2 parts, composer Grebenshchikov). The multi-genre structure of this picture, which the reviewers called 'puff-pastry', resembled a quaint pattern which para-doxically combined a bloody melodrama, a detective story and a historical anecdote. Of considerable significance for the decoding of this 'tragic kitsch' (Sergei Solovyev's own definition) was the presence of yet another dramatic layer in the film, the culture and aesthetics of the youth underground. As with the film itself, this was not stylistically homogeneous, and included three independent language elements: representative, textual and musical.

The first (representational) element could be observed in the whimsi-cal dreams of 'a boy from the restaurant', nicknamed Bananan. These were created in the manner of the absurdist compositions in socialist art, used illustrative fragments from the so-called 'parallel cinema', and showed an illusory world of dreams, 'the yearning of the soul' of young post-punk intellectual, indifferent to material blessings. The second cultural language element was based on a kitsch combination of the low/coarse and the high/spiritual: explanatory captions with translation into 'normal' rock slang and quotations from Eidelman's fundamental work on Czar Paul I were juxtaposed. Finally, the third (musical) element was formed by songs from the leader of the Aquarium group Boris Grebenshchikov, and three more leading Russian rock groups, Kino, Bravo, and The Composers' Union. Incidentally, it was the music in *Assa* that caused the heated discussions. These started from general opinion that the director had insulted rockmen's dignity by placing their underground rock music in a 'restaurant' cultural environment, with which this music had nothing in common. Surprise was caused by the choice of Grebenshchikov's songs, mostly written much earlier, and therefore seemingly antiquated. It was amusing that the most melodiously remarkable of them proved to be the song 'There is a Golden City', the music of which was actually by . . . Francesco di Milano (this was certainly never mentioned in the film). Besides, the work of Boris Grebenshchikov, who is considered one of the founders of 'the Leningrad new wave' which absorbed all the new-wave traditions, can be assimilated to rock culture only with certain reservations. On the whole, the method of introducing this composer's 'bardic' songs into the film texture evoked associations with collage insertions. It was aimed at holding back the dynamic, impetuous movement of the absurdist plot, in order to outline another temporal plane of development, and to give the spectator some respite, to catch up and comprehend what he sees.

The next Solovyev picture — pretentiously titled with the first line of a 'cruel' romance sung by the main heroine Alexandra, *The Black Rose is a Symbol of Sorrow, Red Rose is the Symbol of Love* (1989, 2 parts, the songs written and performed by Grebenshchikov)[4] — reproduces almost exactly the multi-genre composition of *Assa*. This electronic mixture of traditional melodrama and non-traditional love story, political farce and musical comedy, circus turn and theatre of masks, variety and ballet, gives the impression of a rich cocktail in which, however, there is a certain topical logic. As in the preceding film, there is a lot of music in it, which creates an atmosphere of carnival, with elements of play or practical joke sometimes bursting into the action as unexpectedly and sometimes as inopportunely as do the Aquarium musicians, with Grebenshchikov himself at their head, when they appear out of the wardrobe in the middle of the family quarrel.

Figure 18 *The Black Rose is a Symbol of Sorrow, Red Rose is the Symbol of Love*

But there is also 'quiet' music in the film, connected with the one romantic hero, the descendant of an aristocratic family, Mitya Lobanov. The appearance in the noisy, densely packed sound-track of *The Black Rose* of the wonderful melody from Gluck's *Orpheus* in the cool, fresh timbre of the flute, seems to appeal to a harmony and purity which are scarce in this frenzied world, torn apart by lies and callousness.

Thus, the musical score of the film, spun out of a mosaic of quotation fragments, reflects in its own way the worn-out consciousness and the loss of moral bearings of the generation living in the late 1980s, which tries to hide behind surface bravado and busyness its tragic sense of spiritual deterioration.

32

The innovative experiments of Alexander Sokurov and Andrei Chernykh: creating a multi-layered polyphonic sound score and a 'musical' film without music

Its last five years were one of the most difficult periods for Soviet film music. Against a background of feverishly increasing film production, it entered a phase of lingering crisis (which soon hit the cinema): this was caused by uniformity of suggested subject matter and a disdainful attitude of directors to composers' music. They supplanted it either with compilation or with the surrogates of mass culture. The fact that a number of the best composers went to live abroad (Schnittke, Gubaidulina, Korndorf, and later Artemyev) which reduced their creative activity in the cinema, resulted in the quick redistribution of vacant places between hacks and second-rate composers, ready to write anything for anybody in record time.

Expansion of the sound-world by means of exaggeratedly naturalistic noises also stimulated this process of forcing music out of film and of turning it into an unnecessary attribute of screen action, which existed only within a given sequence and carried no structural burden. All this in the long run told on its artistic quality.

However, in the late '80s and early '90s two pictures appeared in which a non-traditional, extraordinary solution of the problem of synthesis between music and cinema was outlined, and a new approach was proposed to the practical realization of Eisenstein's theory of audiovisual montage.

Alexander Sokurov's film *The Days of Eclipse* (1988, composer Khanin), shot after the Strugatsky brothers' novel *A Billion Years before the End of the World* and permeated with a tragic premonition of pending revelation, is astonishing in the intricacy, informational richness and expressiveness of its sound-track in all aspects: speech, music, noise. The music appears in it in a contrapuntal interlacing of several stylistic layers, which form a polyphonic construction.

The prime layer is determined by the place of action. The film was shot in western Turkmenia, in the small town of Krasnovodsk, close to the frontier between Europe and Asia. Sokurov himself spoke about Krasnovodsk as follows: 'This is one of the most complicated regions of our country, both in the economical and humanitarian sense of the word. There is no stable, settled cultural situation, everything is mixed up. A Russian does not understand that he is a Russian, a Turkmen that he is a Turkmen. Here not a single national group has a chance to realize itself to the utmost through its spiritual national heritage. Everything exists in parallel with everything else, in conditions of meaningless interrelation and mutual inhibition'[5].

The sounds of the dutar, the monotonous singing of the *bakhshi*, the improvisations of musicians — *mukamo*, exquisite in its beauty and intricate in its Oriental style — all interweave in the sound texture of the picture. They serve (for the European consciousness) as some exotic background which gives rise to a feeling of vacuum, the heroes' alienation from the natural environment. At the same time, Oriental motifs are part of everyday life in this Turkmen town lost in the sands, in which centuries-old traditions are strangely compatible with stereotypes of mass culture devoid of national characteristics.

A disharmony in the combination of past and present, in the images of ancient East and modern West, is especially evident in the scene of the competition between musicians playing folk instruments (this scene, as well as the episode of the Turkmen wedding, was shot on location with synchronised sound recording). The recitals of the amateur musicians take place in a space circumscribed by a semi-circular wall. People are squatting by the wall, and above their heads there are words written in black paint: *rock, break, disco*. The culture suggested by these words intrudes like a sharp dissonance into the ancient songs, aidyms, and magams and evokes an acute feeling of the irreality and fantastic nature of what is happening, while the people represented within the sequence perceive their environment as something habitual, normal.

The shades of meaning set up by the authors at this initial level of audiovisual imagery are many-sided, and reveal their presence later on in the more complexly organized sound-score of the main structure-building element of the film. The invisible neighbours of the main hero Dmitry Malyanov speak Armenian, and the soldier/driver answers the military engineer Snegov in Latin, while a woman says something in sing-song Buryat. She is the wife of another character, Glukhar. The radio, sometimes invisible, sometimes actually in the frame, sends waves of multi-language speech, and fragments of melodies in Italian, Russian, English, German, Finnish[6]. All these people seem to exist in some chaotic Brownian movement, without finding any natural, harmonic form of sound interrelation.

Sometimes a strange music, 'alien' to the Turkmenian environment, is included into the film not as a generalized metaphor but as a direct commentary on the events shown in the frame. In the episode of the deserter, for example, a quotation from Mokrousov's song *Sormovskaya Liricheskaya* supports, as it were, Malyanov's assertion that he is from Nizhni Novgorod, as well as Gubar's reply that they are then from the same district. An especially complicated associative connection between music and sound appears at the moment of meeting of the two friends, Dmitry Malyanov and Sasha Vecherovsky, and the latter tells a story about his mother. This scene is based on a parallel development of Vecherovsky's monologue and the radio broadcast of a request concert. One of the items in the concert (we Gather from the announcer's text) is addressed to an unknown mother and Granny Kovchenkova. Her loving relatives request for her the folk song *I will come out into the Street*. Thus, unexpectedly, two human fates meet: that of a Russian woman who brought up children and grandchildren, lived her life without great trouble, into a quite old age; and won general esteem and respect; and that of a Crimean Tartar woman, Vecherovsky's mother, banished from her native land, deprived of work and then accused of idleness. One cold winter night she was driven out to the steppe and left there. After this she was ill for a long time, and died. A similar fate befell Sasha's foster parents, Russian Germans exiled to Central Asia. The combination of Vecherovsky's confession and the smart, optimistic song *I will come out into the Street*, sung by Alexandra Strelchenko, seems both outrageous and unnatural, but such is historical reality, such is the drama of national relations, usually hidden under a cloak of silence.

Finally, one image-layer crowns the sound score of *The Days of Eclipse*. This comes from the original music by Yuri Khanin. Like a giant funnel, it draws in not only the sound-world of the film but also the visual scale. Holding the visual elements in its power, the music determines rhythmic movement of the visual-plastic element in the purposely unified succession of scenes.

Against the rich warm timbre of the strings comes a waltz-like, nostalgic, piercing accordion melody in '50s retro style — this is the tonal basis of the film's leitmotiv. It appears as early as the prologue. In this introduction, which is unusually extended for a feature film, music seems to become the main character: a deliberate intensification of the sound volume brings it close to the spectator and induces the visual material to tune into it. At the same time, its measured character and strained aloofness help the filmmakers convey with surprising reality that breath-taking feeling of weightlessness which appears when the camera approaches the ground, and then headlong shoots up again. Besides, the leitmotiv reconciles

certain sequences scattered through the film with the overall artistic con-
cepting and given them highly dramatic meaning. These sequences show
the patients of a psychiatric hospital, views of the *kazakh-aul*, the streets of
the Turkmen town and its inhabitants, and camels grazing in a deserted
graveyard.

This 'weightlessness', however, is not isolation from reality but only
a state provoked by reality. Further, the sound of whirling obscure bitterness, the sorrow of the leitmotiv melody when it accompanies intense
monochrome newsreel frames, is pierced by suffering human cries, by sharp
blows of a whip, and by ringing, screeching noise. Sometimes all musical
development stops abruptly, stands still at prolonged chords with interwoven
crying or laughter, which cause contradictory feelings, and an uneasy
expectation of approaching catastrophe.

Further, the texture of the leitmotiv, based on a string meditation,
becomes richer and more mobile. Gradually, the leitmotiv turns into
primary musical matter, a macrocosm which contains all the genres and
forms of musical art from folklore to the classical works of Glinka,
Schumann, Offenbach, and Schnittke. Thus a catastrophic compression of
world culture seems to be happening at one moment, giving rise to a
premonition of universal cataclysm.

Thus, in *The Days of Eclipse* it is sound treated comprehensively that
is the strong artistic means which expands the boundaries of the sequence,
and takes the action beyond current events and problems, up to the level of
general concern about the fate of our civilization.

It may seem somewhat strange, but among the best films of 1991,
honourably concluding the annals of Soviet film music, there was a picture
where music as such was absent, but which nevertheless created a musical
impression. This was Andrei Chernykh's film *The Austrian Field*. E minor,
which evoked associations with the work of the brilliant Russian composer
Alexander Skryabin, and especially with his poem-symphonies. Indeed,
motifs of yearning, of the search for ideal harmony, and of heightened
sensuality, which bring the visual and aural elements of the film close to the
images and symbols of the composer's late works, permeate every sequence
of *The Austrian Field*, which maintains throughout the *art noveau* style of the
beginning of the century. A major role is played by the colour scheme. The
prevalence of deep green and blue shades in most episodes explains
the appearance of the key of E minor which, in the opinion of Ch. Meyers,
a professor of Cambridge University, who met the composer in 1914, was
associated by Skryabin with the greenish-blue colours (earlier he had treated
this key as whitish/blue). The hidden presence of music is also suggested
by the shots of musical instruments (the cornet, the bayan, and the piano)

Figure 19 *The Austrian Field*

which are used in the compositional and decorative shaping of some
sequences.

The plot of *The Austrian Field* resists retelling, and is wholly geared
to sensual perception. There are two anonymous heroines in the film, who
exist independently of each other. Their only significant meeting, which
happens secretly and without obvious consequences, is shown in the opening sequences, and occurs in a place called *The Austrian Field*, which is no
more than a bus terminus, i.e. a final point, the stop where all movement
ends, where life stands still.

These heroines seem to display two aspects of the woman whom
'man cannot understand', a woman dreaming of, looking for, but never
finding love in this dead, unspiritual world. One of them is a refined
intellectual, who treats love as an amusing puzzle worked out with the help
of the opposite sex, and who tries to sublimate her sexual desire in abstract,
rationalistic judgements. The other is impulsive, infinitely female, very
vulnerable, unprotected, and passionately wishing to love and to be loved.

The film starts with a loud and powerful sound mass of great
density, consisting of different everyday noises, steps, doors creaking, fragments of speech which become unnaturally loud owing to the use of
reverberation effects, frequency distortion, transformation, all of which
make this noise hyper-expressive. This emotional sound burst in the opening sequences of the picture is so strong that all further development
proceeds *decrescendo*, first as a gradual dying away of sound, then its total
disappearance and dissolution in the silence of the final scene.

Rejecting the use of music, the creators of *The Austrian Field*, director
Chernykh and sound engineer Vladimir Persov (he also worked with
Sokurov in *The Days of Eclipse*) instead focused their attention on articulating
the subtlest elements of their preferred sound world, in particular those of
human speech. The range of its colour in the film is extremely wide, from
the nobly sublime, inspired by the melodious beauty of poetry, to the
mechanically distorted, distorted by the loudspeaker; or from impres-
sionism to obscure humming. Twice the film is invaded by foreign speech:
first by Italian, which imparts a sweetly melodramatic character to the scene
of the first heroine's talk with the young man, then by English, which
introduces into an autumn landscape a motif of indifferent and idle tourist
curiosity, that of detached observers of a life unknown to them.

The film-makers' experiments with sound reach their climax in the
scene where the Blind Man talks to one of the secondary characters, Serafima
(a friend of the second heroine). The black-and-white texture of the image,
in the style of French 1930s cinema and the externally static outlook of the
episode, shot without montage, in which through the windscreen of a car
only the faces of two people speaking can be dimly seen, both create a

splendid background for one of the most complicated polyphonic devices, rare anywhere in cinema, the speech canon. It is interesting that the impulse for this imitative appearance of characters, conversational rejoinders is not part of the in-frame but the off-frame text which, after some delay and in a somewhat different semantic interpretation, is later spoken by the actors from the screen; this gives to the dialogue between the Blind Man and Serafima a definite strain, and the artificiality of a badly learned lesson. Besides, the use of four actresses with different vocal timbres when recording the part of Serafima introduces elements of tension and uncertainty, caused by the continuous modulation and fluctuation of the words she speaks.

Traces of the influence of these principles can also be found in other episodes of *The Austrian Field*. For example, the episode of the conversation between the first heroine and the young man is a three-part structure with a contrasting middle section, whereas the scene at the station resembles a rondo in its rhythmic organization.

Thus, both the music and the noise in Chernykh's film are unpredictable, daring and astute. They bear the stamp of mystery and betoken a coming tragedy of silence. But before this silence happens, before the heroes' vocal chords stop sounding, music itself materialises. The simple melody of a small rural band playing in the street appears in the finale of the film, isolating its dramatic climax from the general context. In combination with verses which sing of the elusive charm of female beauty, it brings forth the alien graphic severity of the autumn landscape, with green-blue-black clouds portending misfortune, the abominable grimace of the Blind Man, and the second heroine's face, shaken and hardened with inner pain. The emotional tension of this scene is so great, it comes to such a critical point, to such a very final point of development, that there can be no further movement, no life. After the death of sound people turn into shadows, and disappear in pairs beyond the horizon, going nowhere.

It is a very complex task to sum up this last period in the history of Soviet film music. The reason is not its brevity, but mainly the forced interruption of its most interesting stage. This was the attempt to discover new possibilities in the meeting of the two arts: music and cinema. Now it is difficult to predict whether the experiments with sound and music carried out in the 1990s will be continued, or forgotten, for the critical situation in which all film makers in the former USSR without exception find themselves, and the dominating presence of second-rate American westerns and porno films on their cinema screens, may result in the loss of the best traditions of the local cinema. If this really happens, and the Russian cinema, in pursuit of commercial profit, engages in mass production of average pictures, film music will be deprived of one of its main merits: it will stop attracting both famous composers and creative young people. Meanwhile, the experience accumulated, through more than sixty years of Soviet film music, shows that it was the collaboration between directors and leading representatives of academic tendencies in modern music which yielded the best artistic results, stimulated the search for non-traditional solutions to the problem of the interrelation between music and representation, and enriched its language with the newest devices and expressive means.

Practically all the leading composers — Prokofiev and Shostakovich, Sviridov and Khachaturian, Karetnikov and Karayev, Schnittke and Gubaidulina, Ganelin and Artemyev — submitted to the cinema test and passed it with flying colours. There are many instances where the music written by them broke the screen barriers and continued its life in the theatre and on the concert stage. Thus, Soviet film music was never an exclusive phenomenon, passively serving the cinema, but developed vividly and dynamically, without losing touch with autonomous genres of art. Besides, being a borderline area of creative work, it was for a long time the only resort for composers who were out of favour, and was hardly ever subjected to any ideological purging of 'pernicious Western influences alien to Socialist art'. Not surprisingly, it was in this field that many experimental trends in music were successfully tested, though they were still forbidden by the official censorship.

During the sixty-odd years of its existence, Soviet film music knew soaring flights, lingering crises, and the collapse of its prestige. Now this history is complete: it finished with films very different from that first, still-silent film, which had its own musical accompaniment specially written for it. The distance travelled from the programme-illustrative musical score of *The New Babylon* to the highly complicated sound structure of *The Days of Eclipse* and *The Austrian Field* is great, but at each of its turning-points film music proved its right not only to be styled music, but at the same time to be admired as an integral part of the dramatic conception of film.

NOTES

Part One

1. London, K. (1937) Film Music. Moscow-Leningrad, p. 143.
2. Lissa, Z. (1970) Aesthetics of Film Music. Moscow, p. 33.
3. Bugoslavsky, S. and Messman, V. (1926) Music and Cinema. At the front-line of film music. The principles and methods of film music. An essay in cinema-music composition. Moscow, p. 9.
4. Krakauer, S. (1974) The Nature of the Film. The rehabilitation of physical reality. Moscow, p. 185.
5   Block, D. and Bugoslavsky, S. (1929) Musical accompaniment in the Cinema. Moscow-Leningrad, p. 10,
6. FEKS (The Factory of the Eccentric Actor), an artistic studio organized in 1921 in Petrograd by the directors Grigory Kozintsev and Leonid Trauberg. Interest in modern themes, a search for a new expressive plasticity in silent cinema, and their passion for 'low' genres brought the FEKS members close to the programme manifestos and works of 'the left front', and the post-October artistic experiments of Meyerhold and Mayakovsky.
7. This concerned Meyerhold's trip to France, which was later cancelled.
8. Quoted from N.P. Savkina (1982) 'Sergei Sergeyevich Prokofiev'. Moscow, p. 83.
9. Eisenstein, S. (1964) Selected Works in Six Volumes. Moscow, v. 3, pp. 66,67.
10. Block, D. and Bugoslavsky, S. op. cit., p. 8.
11. Kozintsev, G. (1984) Collected Works in Five Volumes. Leningrad, v. 4, p. 254.
12. D. Shostakovich on his own Times and Himself (1980) Moscow, pp. 20–21.
13. Yu. V. (Vainkop, Yu. Y.) (1929) Music to The New Babylon, Rabochii i Teatr, No. 14, p. 9.
14. Eisenstein, S., op. cit., v. 2, p. 316.
15. Ibid., p. 316.
16. Romm, M. (1981), Selected Works in Three Volumes, v. 2, p. 125.
17. Goléa, A. (1954) Esthetique de la musique contemporaine, Paris, p. 129.
18. Kozintsev, G. (1971) The Deep Screen, Moscow, p. 147.
19. A similar 'transformation' into a sound film was carried out with Yu. Raizman's film The Soil Is Thirsty, first released as a silent film, and then re-made with sound with the help of a composers' 'team' including R. Glier, S. Ryauzov and V. Sokolov.
20. In the early 1930s one more film with Shostakovich's music was released, a newsreel version of A. Macheret Concrete Solidifies. Yet the banality of the poster/slogan idea underlying it resulted in an inexpressive, neutral, background of sometimes openly illustrative 'film music', which the composer chose subsequently to forget.
21. Almost half a century later, fugue was used again by Alfred Schnittke in his music for the tele-serial of M. Shweitser's Dead Souls (1979), not 'within' the picture itself but in the musical postlude during the credits.
22. Cheremukhin, M. (1939) Music in the Sound Film. Moscow, p. 60.
23. Ioffe, I.I. (1938) Soviet Film Music. The Foundations of its Musical Dramaturgy. Leningrad, p. 38.
24. Ibid., p. 39.

25. 'The Vasiliev Brothers' is the pseudonym of two directors bearing the same surname, Georgi Nikolayevich and Sergei Dmitrievich Vasiliev, who have worked together since 1930.

26. The trilogy included the films *Maxim's Youth, Maxim's Return,* and *Vyborg Side.*

27. One of the leading tendencies in Soviet cinema of the 1920s–1930s was that of shooting films on modern material with a linear narrative movement. The peculiarity of this 'prosaic cinema' was its bent for realistic everyday themes, and its interest in the psychological development of the characters. It appeared as a rival to the 'montage-poetic' historical-revolutionary cinema of Eisenstein, Pudovkin, and Dovzhenko, and by the middle of the '30s captured the leading position in Soviet film art. This movement best met the demands of socialist realism.

28. Kozintsev, G. The Deep Screen. Op. cit., p. 175.

29. Frid, E. (1967) Music in Soviet Cinema. Sound and music as elements of film poetics. From the history of Soviet film music. The opera and the cinema. Leningrad, p. 76.

30. Kozintsev, G. The Deep Screen, op. cit., p. 172.

31. Rummel, I. On the history of *Lieutenant Kizhé* (1964) *Sovetskaya Muzyka* 11, 69.

32. Prokofiev, S.S. (1961) Autobiography. *In:* Prokofiev, S.S. Materials. Documents Reminiscences. Moscow, p. 191.

33. Later Prokofiev transformed the music of this film into a suite, and in this state it continued its existence on the concert and ballet stage. In 1958 musical fragments from the film *Lieutenant Kizhé* were used by the English director Ronald Niels in his picture *The Horse's Mouth.*

34. Asafiev, B. (1980) On Choral Art. Leningrad, p. 148.

35. The 'life' of this song was prolonged by the composer himself, who returned to it in Alexander Dovzhenko's film *Michurin* (1949) and in his own operetta *Moskva, Cheremushki* (1958).

36. Dunayevsky, I. (1967) Speeches. Articles. Letters. Reminiscences. Moscow, pp. 30, 31.

37. Quoted from the book of I.I. Ioffe '*Soviet Film Music*', p. 54.

38. The 'Letter-carrier' (pis'monositsa) is an obsolete term. In meaning it is close to 'courier' and 'postman', though neither covers it adequately.

39. The armed conflict between the USSR and Japan is meant, which took place around the Lake Khasan in the summer of 1938.

40. Soon after the release of the film '*A Petersburg Night*', the violin solo *Improvisation* by Kabalevsky was included in *Violinists'* concert programs as an independent virtuoso piece.

41. Eisenstein, S., op. cit., v. 2, p. 192–193.

42. Prokofiev, S.S. (1961) Music to *Alexander Nevsky*. *In:* Prokofiev, S.S. Materials. Documents. Reminiscences, p. 228.

43. Volsky, B. Memories of Prokofiev. *In:* Prokofiev, S.S. Materials. Documents. Reminiscences, p. 530.

44. Yurenev, R. (1988) Sergei Eisenstein. Plans. Films. Method. Moscow, part 2, p. 169.

45. Prokofiev, S.S. (1961) Music to *Alexander Nevsky*, op. cit., p. 229.

46. Eisenstein, S. op. cit., v. 2, p. 198.

Part Two

1. This film was the first produced by the Sverdlovsk film studio.

2. *Niyazi* is the artistic pseudonym of director and composer Niyazi Zulfugarovich Taghi-Zade-Gadjibekov, nephew of Uzeir Gadjibekov.

3. It is curious that in January 1946, that is, seven months before this *Resolution*, the first part of *Ivan the Terrible* was awarded the Stalin Prize, First Class.

4. *On the film 'Great Life'. The Resolution of the Central Committee of the All-Union Communist Party (Bolsheviks)*, 4 September 1946. (1947) *Iskusstvo Kino*, 1, 2.

5. Ibid., p. 2.

6. Sergei Mikhailovich Eisenstein died of a heart attack on the night of 11 February 1948.

7. Volsky, B. (1961) Memories of Prokofiev. *In:* Prokofiev, S.S. Materials. Documents. Reminiscences, p. 536.

8. The decoding of the director's words can be found in the rejoinder of Ivan the Terrible uttered (in part 1) in the cathedral over the coffin of his wife Anastasia: 'Two Romes fell, the third — Moscow! — is still standing. A fourth Rome will never be! And of that third Rome, the power of Moscow, the only master now will be I. Alone!'

9. S.M. Eisenstein's Archive. The film-study collection in the All-Union State Cinematography Institute, No 1455888. The spacing comes from Eisenstein, himself.

10. Kozlov, L. (1967) *Ivan the Terrible.* The musical and thematic structure. *Voprosy Kinoiskusstva*, issue 10, Moscow, p. 255.

11. The History of Music of the peoples of USSR (1941–1945) (1972), Moscow, Volume 3, p. 242.

12. Eisenstein, S. (1964) Non-Indifferent Nature. *In:* Eisenstein, S. Selected works in six volumes, volume 3, p. 424.

13. Eisenstein, S. (1964) On stereo-cinema, ibid., p. 357.

14. Yurenev, R. (1961) Eisenstein. *Ivan the Terrible*, the second part. *Voprosy Kinoiskusstva*, Moscow, issue 5, p. 157.

15. Eisenstein, S. (1964) Some Lectures on Music and Colour in *Ivan the Terrible. In:* Eisenstein, S. Selected works in six volumes, volume 3, p. 553.

16. Eisenstein, S. ibid., p. 591.

17. Eisenstein, S. Non-different Nature, ibid., p. 252.

18. The symbolism of colours in the oprichniks's dance was decoded as follows: gold (yellow) signified power, red meant blood, black was the sign of death.

19. An incredible coincidence: *The Great Life* had the same fate as *Ivan the Terrible*, since its first part was awarded a second class Stalin prize before the war (1940), whereas its second part, shot in 1946, was chosen as a pretext for persecuting the leading directors, was removed from circulation, and collected dust on the shelves of the cinema archives till 1958. Of course, Lukov's picture did not deserve such severe punishment, since it was an unremarkable, standard production of the post-war years. On its return to the screen, it appeared out-of-date. This could not be said about Eisenstein's and Prokofiev's epic, which will for ever remain as one of the chief glories of world film art.

20. *For Bolshevist Principles* (1948) A Collection of the main resolutions of the Central Committee of the All-Union Communist Party (Bolsheviks) and speeches of comrade A.A. Zhdanov on ideological problems. Riga, p. 42.

21. Ibid., p. 42.

22. The usual title of this film comedy by Pyriev and Dunayevsky is *The Merry Fair*.

23. Hanisch, M. (1984) On Songs in the rain. Moscow, p. 80.

24. Dunayevsky, I.O. (1961) Speeches. Articles. Letters. Reminiscences. Moscow, p. 324.

25. At first, music to Dovzhenko's film, entitled at that time *Life in Flower*, was commissioned from G. Popov. But his score was severely criticized for 'formalism and excessive complication of the musical language', the result of which was that 'even correctly reproduced Russian songs were distorted by the harmonic refinements of the composer' (See: Shwarz L. On modern film music. *Sovetskaya Muzyka*, 1948, 3, 6). One could add

that the film *Michurin*, more than any other, suffered from countless alterations and 'corrections', and reached such a degree of ideological sterility that it could have provided clear guidelines on creating reliable, canonic, biographical films. These words could equally be used of music which absorbed the background cliches in model educational films, based on the principles of social realism.

26. Proof of this comes from the article published in the magazine *Iskusstvo Kino*, 1950, 1, where it is said: 'The historical resolution of the Central Committee of the All-Union Communist Party (Bolsheviks) on the opera *The Great Friendship* exerted a beneficial influence upon the composer's creative work. First of all, a considerable tendency should be noted in Shostakovich towards the democratization of his musical language, and the intensification of its emotional content. Shostakovich's music for films... and especially for *Michurin*, makes one glad of its warmth and humaneness.' See: Khrennikov, T. Music in the Cinema. *Iskusstvo Kino*, 1950, 1, 27.

27. It was not until 1991 that the names of the instigators and authors of this article became known. It signalled the beginning of 'purification' among the members of the Composers' Union, and was written by composer Zaslavsky and musicologist Georgi Khubov.

28. However, the composer made a timid attempt to use as a leitmotiv the folk song 'Thoughts, My Thoughts', on which an extensive episode was based, of the punishment with rods and death of a trooper in the regiment where Taras Shevchenko did his service. But this theme, which symbolized the sufferings and tortures of oppressed and hapless people, never received any further development.

29. The initiator of this second *Glinka* was Joseph Stalin; he liked the actor (Boris Chirkov) who appeared as the great Russian composer in an episode of Grigory Alexandrov's film *Spring*.

30. The film *Mussorgsky*, shot at the Lenfilm studio, was the first Soviet full-length colour picture.

31. The melody of *The Song of Peace* was later used by the composer in the final chorus of his *a capella Ten Poems* to texts by Russian revolutionary poets (1951).

32. Karl Baumanys (1838–1905), one of the early Latvian professional composers.

Part Three

1. Naturally, interest in this problem was to a large extent programmed and determined by doctrines of socialist culture — building and education of 'a new type of man'. This 'sudden' burst of fashion for modern film was given impetus by Ivan Pyriev's report, 'On raising the ideologic and artistic level of films on modern themes, and of the tasks of the USSR Cinematographers' Union', delivered by him on 16 February 1960 to the Third Plenum of the Organizing Committee of the Union. In Pyriev's speech, an overriding purpose was also formulated, the achievement of which was to be supported by all Soviet film directors. This consisted of creating 'works, ideologically sound and perfect in form, about our great times-the epoch of the development and building of communism'.

2. From 1974, the music of *The Snowstorm* found a second life as a concert suite — as a 'musical illustration to Pushkin's short story'.

3. The basis of this film, as well as of Kataev's novel, was real historical fact: the construction of the Magnitogorsk metallurgic industrial complex in the South Urals. But neither in the film nor in the novel was there even a hint that the majority of the workers, whose

selfless and heroic efforts made it possible to put into operation this veritable giant of ferrous metallurgy in record time, were prisoners.

4. Some time later, the overture from the film *Forward, Time!* found a second life on TV, where for almost two decades (with a brief interval) it was used as a musical introduction ('call sign') to the state information program 'Time', on the first channel of the Central television.

5. ANS is the first Soviet experimental photoelectronic synthesizer. It was created at the end of the 1950s by the talented acoustic engineer Evgeny Murzin, and it was named by him in honour of the great Russian composer Alexander Nikolayevich Skryabin.

6. The World and Films of Andrei Tarkovsky (1991), Moscow, pp. 14–15.

7. Several years earlier, the device of depicting by sound images the horrors and sufferings which are always the awful bloody traces of war was used in *The Fate of Man* (1959, director S. Bondarchuk, composer V. Basner). In it, a former prisoner of a fascist concentration camp, Andrei Sokolov, returns to his native village after the war, and from time to time suffers from sound hallucinations, which again immerse him in the atmosphere of fear and despair experienced by those people condemned to monstrous suffering and slow death in zones of mass extermination.

8. The History of Soviet Cinema (1952–1967). (1978), Moscow, volume 4, pp. 135–136.

9. Kozintsev, G. (1982) Collected Works in Five Volumes, Leningrad, volume 1, p. 490.

10. A not infrequent result of the use of audio-visual disparity, achieved by instrumental substitution: on the sound-track the harpsichord sounds, whereas Ophelia is dancing on the screen to a lute.

11. Kozintsev, G. op. cit., p. 495.

12. This scene has a lot of analogues in opera, particularly in Prokofiev's works — the scene of Lubka's insanity in *Kotko* and the scene of Andrei Bolkonsky's delirium in *War and Peace*: these may have served as prototypes for Ophelia's madness scene in Shostakovich's *Hamlet*.

13. Dobin, E. (1967) *Hamlet:* Kozintsev's film. Leningrad-Moscow, p. 127.

14. In 1958 Galina Vishnevskaya played Tatiana in the opera film *Eugene Onegin*, where she had the opportunity to acquaint herself with the singer's and actor's specific task in cinema.

15. This title is directly connected with the marvelously beautiful and philosophically deep metaphor leitmotiv in Paradjanov's picture, which appears repeatedly throughout the film: the bloody-scarlet horses in headlong flight, (the association is with the famous Ride of Wagner's Valkyries) carrying away the souls of the dead. Another symbol, not less expressive and, as it were, complementing this metaphor, is the black funeral procession crossing the white frame space: its strictly diagonal movement seems to cross out somebody's life.

16. Mikhalkov-Konchalovsky, A. (1977) Parabola of Design, Moscow, p. 150.

17. Nekhoroshev, L. (1991) *Andrei Rublev:* Salvation. *In:* The World and Films of Andrei Tarkovsky, Moscow, p. 55.

18. According to the composer's note, the performance was carried out as follows: a well-rosined hair from the bow was attached to the string, and the violinist had to slide both his hands along the hair; as the result, the open string emitted a sound resembling *frullato*.

19. All the titles of musical fragments and items are given here according to the composer's own titles, entered in his manuscript score of the film *Andrei Rublev*

20. The noise of rain is a favourite poetic sound metaphor in Andrei Tarkovsky's works, just as the representation of horses is his plastic metaphor.

21. In the film, pictures by the folk artist N. Vasilieva are used. These are painted in a primitivist manner.
22. In the middle part Bibergan, probably wishing to emphasize the revolutionary origin of the march, introduces elements of the famous 'Marseillaise' into it.

Part Four

1. Goszakaz [abbreviated from *Gosudarstvenny zakaz*, the state order] was a system of giving top priority in state film financing to encourage productions which were characterized by a clear thematic tendency, and dealt with topics 'sacred' to Soviet history, those of the revolution, the Civil War, the Great Patriotic War, the restoration of the destroyed economy, collectivization and collective farm movement, and intensive work at state enterprises. The *goszakaz* exerted a powerful pressure upon the cinema, thanks to the state monopoly of film production and hire.
2. The 'industrial' film was a unique outcome of this ideological trend in Soviet film art during the period of stagnation. In films of this sort, the plot was centered around a production conflict and the theme of the personal responsibility of everybody-from the worker to the manager of the highest rank-for the work entrusted to him, and the creative attitude to work and protection of state interests at the state enterprise. But being a still-born genre, whose appearance tried to check incipient corrosion of society and mass misappropriation of national property, the 'industrial' film had many drawbacks. Such, for instance, were the abundant dialogues and monologues, generously spiced with obscure professional terminology and strongly resembling the metaphysical arguments of the radicals and conservatives in the biographical films of the late forties and early fifties. On the other hand, the abundance of verbal text had a negative effect both on the development of the action, which was flaccid and uninteresting, and on the psychological elaboration of characters who were one-sided and affected.
3. Kozintsev, G. (1973) The Space of the Tragedy, Moscow, p. 222.
4. Lipkov, A. (1975) The Shakespearean Screen. Moscow, p. 158.
5. This was one of the main demands made by Kozintsev on the composer. The request to use a modernist musical language was expressed in his letter to Shostakovich written in December 1969, that is, just before starting to work at the film. *In:* Kozintsev, G. The Space of the Tragedy, p. 221.
6. The first screening of the great Russian Writer in the history of Soviet cinema
7. Khaniutin, Yu. The artist is true to his theme. *In:* The World and Films of Andrei Tarkovsky (1991) Moscow, p. 89.
8. The film *Repentance* was shot in 1984 and shelved for two years, appearing on the screen only at the beginning of 'perestroika' in 1986.
9. *Repentance* (1988), Moscow, p. 7.
10. Later Artemyev used the same device, of interpreting classical music in the light of the composer's own world, in Nikita Mikhalkov's *Without Witnesses* (1983), where he derived his material from the famous flute melody from Gluck's opera *Orpheus and Euridice*.
11. The World and Films of Andrei Tarkovsky, op. cit., p. 321.
12. The medieval chant is fully transformed here, and is assimilated to the world of Oriental music-making.

13. Students of Tarkovsky's work frequently remark on the surprising, and not at all accidental, resemblance between the actors who play the roles of Stalker (A. Kaidanovsky), Writer (A. Solonitsyn), and Professor (N. Grin'ko).
14. Two years later, after the death of Larisa Shepit'ko in a car accident, Alfred Schnittke dedicated to her memory his Second String Quartet (1981), which also included the music of *The Ascent*.
15. The history of the opera film certainly did not stop there. But its further development was connected with another variety of screen art-television.
16. Four years later, Gunnar Graps was to appear on the screen again, as a soloist in the vocal-instrumental ensemble in a musical melodrama by director L. Kvinikhidze and composer M. Dunayevsky, *The Place Where We Are Not Present*.
17. Lipkov, A. (1975), 'In One's own person', *Iskusstvo Kino*, 4, 77.
18. Fomin, V. (1985) 'The village was riding past the muzhik', *Iskusstvo Kino*, 2, 70.
19. Ibid., p. 66.

Part Five

1. Lukshin, I. (1991) 'The Mythology of "the black wave"', *Iskusstvo Kino*, 3, 13.
2. Ibid., p. 13.
3. *Taxi Blues* belongs to that rare category of films which were shot with synchronised sound recording.
4. This device, of placing the initial phrase of a song in the title of the film, was borrowed by Solovyev from the Russian pre-revolutionary cinema.
5. Quoted from the article by Dmitry Popov 'The Cosmic Aspect', (1989), *Iskusstvo Kino*, 5, 79.
6. In spite of the seeming originality of this device, it is well known in modern music: as early as 1967 Stockhausen presented his *Kurzwellen*, in which sounds obtained by wandering along the wavelengths of the radio and capturing arbitrarily fragments of broadcasts became the starting point for intuitive instrumental improvisation. However, the use of this same device in *The Days of Eclipse* proved once more the possibility of fruitful interrelation between modern experimental and film music.

FILMOGRAPHY

Abesalom and Eteri, 1967, Georgia-Film, director L. Esakia, composer Z. Paliashvili.

Adomas Wants to Be Human, 1959, Lithuanian Film Studio, director V. Žalakiavicius, composer E. Balsys.

Adventures of a Dentist, The, 1967, director E. Klimov, composer A. Schnittke

Aerograd, 1935, Mosfilm and Ukrainfilm, director A. Dovzhenko, composer D. Kabalevsky.

Aibolit-66, 1967, Mosfilm, director R. Bykov, composer B. Tchaikovsky

Aleko, 1953, Lenfilm, director N. Sidelev, composer S. Rakhmaninov.

Alexander Nevsky, 1938, Mosfilm, director S. Eisenstein, composer S. Prokofiev.

Alone, 1931, Soyuzkino, directors G. Kozintsev and L. Trauberg, composer D. Shostakovich.

Andrei Rublev, 2 parts, 1966, Mosfilm, director A. Tarkovsky, composer V. Ovchinnikov.

Andrus's Luck, 1955, Lenfilm, director G. Rappaport, composer E. Kapp.

Anna Karenina, 2 parts, 1968, Mosfilm, director A. Zarkhi, composer R. Shchedrin.

Answering Move, An, 1981, Mosfilm, director M. Tumanishvili, composer V. Babushkin.

Anton Ivanovich Is Angry, 1941, Lenfilm, director A. Ivanovsky, composer D. Kabalevsky.

Arsenal, The, 1929, Odessa, VUFKU [All-Ukrainian Photo-Cinema Management], director A. Dovzhenko, composer I. Belza.

Arshin Mal Alan, 1945, Bakinskaya Film Studio, directors R. Takhmasib and N. Leshchenko, composer Taghi-zade Niyazi.

Arshin Mal Alan, 1966, Azerbaijan-Film, director T. Taghi-zade, musical editing by F. Amirov.

Ascent, 1976, Mosfilm, director L. Shepit'ko, composer A. Schnittke.

Ashes and Diamonds, 1958, Poland, director A. Wajda, Wroclow Quintet conducted by F. Novak.

Assa, 2 parts, 1987, Mosfilm, director S. Solovyev, composer B. Grebenshchikov.

At Home among Strangers, a Stranger at Home, 1974, Mosfilm, director N. Mikhalkov, composer E. Artemyev.

At 6 p.m. after the War, 1944, Mosfilm, director I. Pyriev, composer T. Khrennikov.

Austrian Field, The, 1991, Video Film Studio Artel-F, Belarusfilm and Lenfilm, the Scientific Production Cooperativ Quant, director A. Chernykh.

Battle Film Collections, 1942, No. 8. Tashkent Film Studio, director L. Lukov, composer N. Bogoslovsky.

Battle of Stalingrad, The, 2 parts, 1949, Mosfilm, director V. Petrov, composer A. Khachaturian.

Battleship 'Potemkin', 1925, Goskino, director S. Eisenstein, composers E. Meisel (1930, Germany), N. Kriukov (1950, USSR).

Before It Is Too Late, 1958, Lithuanian Film Studio, directors Yu. Fogelman and V. Žalakiavičius, composer B. Dvarionas.

Belinsky, 1953, Lenfilm, director G. Kozintsev, composer D. Shostakovich.

Black Rose is a Symbol of Sorrow, Red Rose is the Symbol of Love, The, 2 parts, 1989, Creative Association Krug, director S. Solovyev, songs and their performance by B. Grebenshchikov.

Blue Lightning, 1978, *A. Dovzhenko Film Studio*, director I. Shmaruk,
    composer L. Afanasyev.
Body, The, 1990, M. Gorky Film Studio, the Ladya Studio, director N. Khubov,
    composer E. Denisov.
Boris Godunov, 1955, Mosfilm, director V. Stroyeva, music of M. Mussorgsky.
Bread, Gold, Revolver, 1980, M. Gorky Film Studio, director S. Gasparov,
    composer A. Zubov.
Bridge, The, 1957, Lithuanian Film Studio, director B. Shreiber, composer E. Balsys.
Brief Encounters, 1968, Odessa Film Studio, director K. Muratova, composer
    O. Karavaichuk.
Captain Grant's Children, 1936, Mosfilm, director V. Vainshtok, composer I. Dunayevsky.
Carnival Night, The, 1956, Mosfilm, director E. Ryazanov, composer A. Lepin.
Celestial Slowcoach, A. 1945, Lenfilm, director S. Timoshenko, composer V. Solovyov-Sedoy.
Chapayev, 1934, Lenfilm, directors Brothers Vasiliev, composer G. Popov.
Cherevichki, [The Little Shoes] 1944, Central Association of Film Studios,
    director M. Shapiro, music of P. Tchaikovsky.
Cheremushki, 1962, Lenfilm, director G. Rappaport, music by D. Shostakovich.
Cholpon — The Morning Star, 1959, Lenfilm and Frunze Film Studio, director R.
    Tikhomirov, music by M. Raukhverger.
Circus, 1936, Mosfilm, director G. Alexandrov, composer I. Dunayevsky.
Cities and Years, 1930, Sovkino, director E. Chervyakov, composer D. Astradantsev.
Colour of Pomegranates, The, 1969, Armenfilm, director S. Paradjanov, composer
    T. Mansuryan.
Come Tomorrow, 1963, Odessa Film Studio, director E. Tashkov, composer A. Eshpai.
Come When You Are Free, 1984, M. Gorky Film Studio, director Yu. Mastyugin, composer
    A. Zhurbin.
[*Composer*] *Glinka*, 1952, Mosfilm, director G. Alexandrov, composers V. Shcherbachev and
    V. Shebalin.
Concrete Solidifies, 1931, Moscow Cinema Factory, director A. Macheret,
 composer D. Shostakovich.
Counter Plan, 1932, Rosfilm, directors F. Ermler and S. Yutkevich,
    composer D. Shostakovich.
Crown of the Russian Empire, or the Elusive Ones Again, The, 2 parts, 1971,
    Mosfilm, director E. Keosaian, composer M. Fradkin.
Czar's Bride, The, 1964, Riga Film Studio, director V. Gorikker,
    music by N. Rimsky-Korsakov.
Daisi, 1971, Georgia-film, director N. Sanishvili, music by Z. Paliashvili.
Dawn over the Neman, 1953, Lenfilm and Lithuanian Film Studio,
    director A. Feinzimmer, composer B. Dvarioňas.
Days of the Eclipse, The, 1988, Lenfilm, director A. Sokurov, composer Yu. Khanin.
Dead Season, The, 2 parts, 1969, Lenfilm, director S. Kulish, composer A. Volkonsky.
Dead Souls, The, 3 parts, 1979, Mosfilm, director M. Shweitser, composer A. Schnittke.
Deeds and People [Men and Jobs] , 1932, Soyuzkino, director A. Macheret, composers
    V. Shebalin, S. Germanov, and N. Kriukov.
Deputy for the Baltics, A, 1936, Lenfilm, directors A. Žarkhi and I. Kheifits, composer
    N. Timofeyev.
Devil's Bride, The, 1976, Lithuanian Film Studio, director A. Žebriunas, composer
    V. Ganelin.

Donbass Symphony (Enthusiasm), The, 1930, Ukrainfilm, director Dz. Vertov,
    composer N. Timofeyev.
Don Quixote, 1957, Lenfilm, director G. Kozintsev, composer K. Karayev.
Dummy, The, 1983, Mosfilm, director R. Bykov, composer S. Gubaidulina.
Earthly Love, 1975, Mosfilm, director E. Matveyev, composer E. Ptichkin.
Elite, The, 2 parts, 1983, Mosfilm, director S. Solovyev, music of Mozart, Beethoven,
    Mahler, Shostakovich, Sviridov, Schwarz, Tishchenko, Castro.
Elusive Avengers, The, 1967, Mosfilm, director E. Keosaian, composer B. Mokrousov.
End of the Ataman, The, 2 parts, 1970, Kazakhfilm, director Sh. Aimanov,
    composer E. Rakhmadiev.
End of the Taiga Emperor, The, 1978, M. Gorky Film Studio, director V. Sarukhanov,
    composer E. Krylatov.
Entrust It to General Nesterov, 1984, director B. Galkin, composer K. Volkov.
Evening in Moscow, An, 1962, Mosfilm, director V. Nemolyaev,
Eugene Onegin, 1958, Mosfilm, director R. Tikhomirov, music by P. Tchaikovsky.
Executioner, The, 1990, Russkoe Video Ladoga, attached to Lenfilm Studio,
    director V. Sergeyev, composer E. Artemyev.
Extraordinary Commissar, The, 1970, Uzbekfilm, director A. Khamraev,
    composer R. Vildanov.
Fall of Berlin, The, 2 parts, 1950, director M. Chiaureli, composer D. Shostakovich.
Fate, 1978, Mosfilm, director E. Matveyev, composer E. Ptichkin.
Fate of a Man, The, 1959, Mosfilm, director S. Bondarchuk, composer V. Basner.
Fiddler on the Roof, 1970, USA, director N. Jewison, composer J. Bock.
Fiery Bank, The, 1975, Uzbekfilm, director U. Nazarov, composer R. Vildanov.
First Boxing-Glove, The, 1947, Mosfilm, director A. Frolov, composer V. Solovyov-Sedoy.
First Platoon, The, 1933, Belgoskino, director V. Korsh-Sablin, composer I. Dunaevsky.
Fir-Tree, Queen of Grass Snakes, The, 1966, Lithuanian Film Studio, directors V. Grivickas
    and A. Mockus, music by E. Balsys.
Five-Year Plan (The Plan for Great Works), The, 1930, Soyuzkino, director A. Room,
    composers A. Avraamov, G. Rimsky-Korsakov, N. Timofeyev and N. Malakhovsky.
Flight, 2 parts, 1971, Mosfilm, directors A. Alov and V. Naumov, composer N. Karetnikov.
Following the Wolf's Track, 1976, Moldova Film, director V. Gageau, composer E. Lazarev.
Forget the Word Death, 1979, Odessa Film Studio, director S. Gasparov, composer A. Zubov.
Forward, Time!, 2 parts, 1966, Mosfilm, director M. Shweitser, composer G. Sviridov.
Front without Flanks, The, The Front Beyond the Firing Line, The Front to the Rear of the Enemy,
    1974–1981, Mosfilm, director I. Gostev, composer V. Basner.
Gadfly, The, 1955, Lenfilm, director A. Feinzimmer, composer D. Shostakovich.
Girlfriends, The, 1936, Lenfilm, director L. Arnshtam, composer D. Shostakovich.
Girl No. 217, 1945, Mosfilm and Tashkent Film Studio, director M. Romm,
    composer A. Khachaturian.
Girl Running on the Waves, The, 1967, M. Gorky Film Studio and Sofia Studio of Feature
    Films (Bulgaria), director P. Lyubimov, composer Jan Frenkel.
Glinka, 1947, Mosfilm, director L. Arnshtam, musical composition by V. Shebalin.
Goalkeeper, The, 1936, Lenfilm, director S. Timoshenko, composer I. Dunayevsky.
Go and Look, 2 parts, Belarusfilm, director E. Klimov, composer O. Yanchenko.
Goar Gasparyan Is Singing, 1964, Armenfilm, director G. Melik-Avakyan.
Golden Beak, A, 1929, Sovkino, director E. Chervyakov, music script by D. Astradantsev.
Great Citizen, A, 2 parts, 1937–1939, Lenfilm, director F. Ermler, composer D. Shostakovich.

Great Life, The, 2 parts, 1940–1946, released in 1958, Kiev Film Studio, director L. Lukov, composer N. Bogoslovsky.

Hamlet, 1964, Lenfilm, Director G. Kozintsev, composer D. Shostakovich.

High Title, The, a diptych (film 1, *I am Shapovalov T.P.*; film 2, *For the Sake of Life on the Earth*), 1973–1974, Mosfilm, director E. Matveyev, composer E. Ptichkin.

His Time will Come, 1958, Alma-Ata Film Studio, director M. Begalin, composer E. Brusilovsky.

If a War Breaks Out Tomorrow, 1938, Mosfilm, director E. Dzigan, composers D. and Dm. Pokrass.

I Have Arrived to Say, 1985, Mosfilm, director N. Ardashnikov, composer A. Pugacheva.

Ilyich Gate, The, 1961, Mosfilm, director M. Khutsiev, composer N. Sidelnikov.

Incident in Square 36–80, An, 1982, Mosfilm, director Tumanishvili, composer V. Babushkin.

In the Days of June, 1958, Tallinn Film, directors V. Nevezhin and K. Kijsk, composer B. Körver.

In the Zone of Special Attention, 1977, Mosfilm, director A. Malukov, composer M. Minkov.

Iolanta, 1963, Riga Film Studio, director V. Gorikker, music by P. Tchaikovsky.

Ivan's Childhood, 1962, Mosfilm, director A. Tarkovsky, composer V. Ovchinnikov.

Ivan the Terrible, 2 parts, 1945–1946, Mosfilm, director S. Eisenstein, composer S. Prokofiev.

Jazzman, 1983, Mosfilm, director K. Shakhnazarov, composer A. Kroll.

Karine, 1969, Armenfilm, director A. Manasian, composer T. Chukhadjan.

Katerina Izmailova [*Lady Macbeth of the Mtsensk District*], 1967, Lenfilm, director M. Shapiro, music by D. Shostakovich.

Kendilyar, 1939, Erevan Film Studio, director S. Mardjanov, composer Niyazi Taghi-zade.

Keto and Koté, 1947, Tbilisi Film Studio, directors V. Tabliashvili and Sh. Gedevanishvili, composer A. Keresilidze.

King Lear, 2 parts, 1971, director G. Kozintsev, composer D. Shostakovich.

Prince Igor, 1971, Mosfilm, director R. Tikhomirov, music by A. Borodin.

Kotovsky, 1943, the Central Association of Film Studios, director A. Feinzimmer, composer S. Prokofiev.

Kuban Cossacks, The, 1950, Mosfilm, director I. Pyriev, composer I. Dunayevsky.

Lady with a Dog, A, 1960, director I. Kheifits, composer N. Simonyan.

Last Heyduck, The, 1972, Moldova Film, director V. Gageau, composer E. Lazarev.

Leave-taking, 2 parts, 1983, Mosfilm, director E. Klimov, composers V. Artemov and A. Schnittke.

Leili and Medjnun, 1960, Tadjikfilm, directors T. Berezantseva and T. Valamat-zade, music by S. Balasanyan.

Lenin in 1918, 1939, Mosfilm, director M. Romm, composer N. Kriukov.

Liberation, 5 films, 1970–1972, Mosfilm, director Yu. Ozerov, composer Yu. Levitin.

Lieutenant Kizhé, 1934, Belgoskino, director A. Feinzimmer composer S. Prokofiev.

Life Belongs to Us, 1936, France, director J. Renoir.

Life in a Citadel, 1948, Lenfilm, director G. Rappaport, composer E. Kapp.

Light in Koordi, 1951, Lenfilm and Tallinn Film Studio, director G. Rappaport, composer E. Kapp.

Listopad (Falling Leaves), 1967, Georgia Film, director O. Ioseliani, composer N. Ioseliani.

Living and the Dead, The, 2 parts, 1963, Mosfilm, director A. Stolper.

Longest Straw, The, 1981, Riga Film Studio, director Ritenbergas, music from the works of Albinoni, Reger and Sukhon'.

Love and Hatred, 1934, Mezhrabpromfilm, director A. Gendelstein, composer D. Shostakovich.

Love for Love, 1983, Mosfilm, director T. Berezantseva, composer T. Khrennikov.

Lyana, 1955, Moldova-Film, director B. Barnet, composer Sh. Aranov.

Magic Season, The, 1985, Odessa Film Studio, director G. Youngwald-Hilkevich,
    composer Yu. Chernavsky.

Man Follows the Sun, 1961, Moldova-Film, director M. Kalik, composer M. Tariverdiev.

Man with a Gun, A, 1938, Mosfilm, director S. Yutkevich, composer D. Shostakovich.

Marité, 1947, Mosfilm, director V. Stroyeva, composer B. Dvarionas.

Mashen'ka, 1942, Mosfilm, director Yu. Raizman, music by A. Glazunov,
    arranged by B. Volsky.

Meeting on the Elbe [Banks,] 1949, Mosfilm, director G. Alexandrov,
    composer D. Shostakovich.

Melodies of Veriisky Block, The, 1973, Georgia-Film, director G. Shengelaya,
    composer G. Tsabadze.

Merry Fellows, [Jolly] The, 1934, Moscombinat, director G. Alexandrov,
    composer I. Dunayevsky.

Merry Stars, 1954, Mosfilm, director V. Stroyeva, composers I. Dunayevsky and
    A. Tsfasman.

Michurin, 1949, Mosfilm, director A. Dovzhenko, composer D. Shostakovich.

Mirror, 1975, Mosfilm, director A. Tarkovsky, composer E. Artemyev.

Moor of Venice, The, 1960, Georgia-Film, director and ballet-master V. Chabukiani,
    composer A. Machavariani.

Mountains of Gold [Golden mountains], 1931, Soyuzkino, director S. Yutkevich, composer
    D. Shostakovich.

Mozart and Salieri, 1962, director V. Gorikker, music by N. Rimsky-Korsakov.

Musical Story, A, 1940, Lenfilm, directors A. Ivanovsky and G. Rappaport,
    composer D. Kabalevsky.

Mussorgsky, 1950, Lenfilm, director G. Roshal', composer D. Kabalevsky.

My Friend Ivan Lapshin, 1984, Lenfilm, director A. German, composer A. Gagulashvili.

My Younger Brother, 1961, Mosfilm, director A. Zarkhi, composer M. Tariverdiev.

Naimichka, 1963, A. Dovzhenko Film Studio, Kiev,
    directors I. Molostova and V. Lapoknysh, music by M. Verikovsky.

Natalka Poltavka, 1963, Ukrainfilm, director I. Kavaleridze, music by N. Lysenko.

Nest in the Wind, A, 1979, Tallinn Film, director O. Neuland, composer L. Sumera.

New Adventures of the Elusive Ones, The, 1968, Mosfilm, director E. Keosaian,
    composer Jan Frenkel.

New Babylon, The, 1929, Sovkino, directors G. Kozintsev and L. Trauberg,
    composer D. Shostakovich.

Nine Days of One Year, 1961, Mosfilm director M. Romm.

No Ford in the Fire, 1968, Lenfilm, director G. Panfilov, composer V. Bibergan.

October, 1927, Sovkino, director S. Eisenstein.

Old and the New, The (The General Line), 1929, Sovkino, director S. Eisenstein.

Oliver!, 1968, Great Britain, director C. Reed, composer L. Bart.

One Shouldn't Shoot in a Hurry, 1983, Uzbekfilm, director M. Aga-Mirzoev,
    composer R. Vildanov.

1002nd Night, The, 1965, Tadjikfilm, director M. Makhmudov, composer A. Babaev.

Othello, 1956, Mosfilm, director S. Yutkevich, composer A. Khachaturian.

Others' Patrimony, 1983, Belorusfilm, director V.Rybarev, composer P.Alkhimovich.

Our Dear Doctor, 1958, Alma-Ata Film Studio, director A.Karpov, composer A. Zatsepin.

Parade of Planets, The, 1984, Mosfilm, director V. Abdrashitov, composer V. Ganelin.

Partizans in the Steppes of the Ukraine, 1943, Kiev Film Studio and Ashkhabad Film Studio,
    director I. Savchenko, composer S. Prokofiev.
Pepo, 1935, Armenkino, director A. Bek-Nazarov, composer A. Khachaturian.
Petersburg Night, A, 1934, Mosfilm, directors G. Roshal' and V. Stroyeva,
    composer V. Shcherbachev.
Pirogov, 1948, Lenfilm, director G. Kozintsev, composer D. Shostakovich.
Place where We are not Present, The, 1986, Mosfilm, director L. Kvinikhidze,
    composer M. Dunayevsky.
Polikushka, 1919, Collective Body Russ', director A. Sanin, composer A. Arkhangelsky.
Queen of Spades, The, 1960 Lenfilm, director R. Tikhomirov, music by P. Tchaikovsky.
Radiant Way, The, 1940, Mosfilm, director G. Alexandrov, composer I. Dunayevsky.
Rain in July, 1966, Mosfilm, director M. Khutsiev, songs by B. Okudjava and Yu. Vizbor.
Rainis, 1949, Riga Film Studio, director Yu. Raizman, composer A. Skulte.
Recipe of Her Youthfulness, The, 1983, Mosfilm, director E. Ginzburg, composer G. Garanyan.
Red Square, The (Two Stories about the Workers-and-Peasants Army), 1970, Mosfilm,
    director V. Ordynsky, composer V. Basner.
Relatives, 1981, Mosfilm, director N. Mikhalkov, composer E. Artemyev.
Repentance, 2 parts, 1984, Georgia-Film, director T. Abuladze,
    musical mounting by N. Djanelidze.
Resurrection, 2 parts, 1960–1962, Mosfilm, director M. Shweitser, composer G. Sviridov.
Rich Bride, A, 1938, Ukrainfilm, director I. Pyriev, composer I. Dunayevsky.
Rimsky-Korsakov, 1963, Lenfilm, directors G. Roshal' and G. Kazansky,
    composer G. Sviridov.
Rita, 1958, Riga Film Studio, director A. Neretniek. composer A. Skulte.
Romance about Lovers, A, 2 parts, 1974, Mosfilm, director A. Mikhalkov-Konchalovsky,
    composer A. Gradsky.
Romeo and Juliet, 1955, Mosfilm, directors L. Arnshtam and L. Lavrovsky,
    music by S. Prokofiev.
Romeo, My Neighbour, 1963, Azerbaijan-Film, director Sh. Makhmudbekov,
    composer V. Gadjiev.
Rooks, The, 1982, A. Dovzhenko Film Studio, director K. Ershov, composer V. Silvestrov.
Screen Star, The, 1974, M. Gorky Film Studio, director V. Gorikker, music by A. Eshpai.
Secretary of the District Committee, The, 1942, the Central Association of Film Studios,
    director I. Pyriev, musical mounting by B. Volsky.
Serf Actress, The, 1963, Lenfilm, director R. Tikhomirov, music by N. Strelnikov.
Seventh Bullet, The, 1972, Uzbekfilm, director A. Khamraev, composer R. Vildanov.
Some Days in the Life of I. I. Oblomov 2 parts, 1979, Mosfilm,
    director N. Mikhalkov, composer E. Artemyev.
Sevil, 1970, Azerbaijan-Film, director V. Gorikker, music by F. Amirov.
Shadows of our Forgotten Ancestors, The, 1964, A. Dovzhenko Film Studio, Kiev,
    director S. Paradjanov, composer M. Skhorik.
Shchors, 1939, Ukrainfilm, director A. Dovzhenko, composer D. Kabalevsky.
She Is Defending Her Country, 1943, the Central Association of Film Studios, director
    F. Ermler. composer G. Popov.
Shield and the Sword, The, 4 parts, 1968, Mosfilm, director V Basov, composer V. Basner.
Shore, The, 2 parts, 1984, Mosfilm, directors A.Alov and V. Naumov, music of A. Vivaldi,
    P. Tchaikovsky, G.F. Händel, J.C. Bach, J.S. Bach, J. Strauss.
Siberiade, The, 4 parts, 1978, Mosfilm, director A. Mikhalkov-Konchalovsky,
    composer E. Artemyev.

Siberian Story, 1948, Mosfilm, director I. Pyriev, composer N. Kriukov.

Siege, (film 1, *The Luga Frontline;* film 2, *The Pulkovo Meridian*), 1975–1978, Lenfilm, director K. Ershov, composer V. Basner.

Silva, 1944, Sverdlovsk Film Studio, director A. Ivanovsky, music by I. Kalman.

Simple Story, A, 1960, M. Gorky Film Studio, director Yu. Egorov, composer M. Fradkin.

Sixth One, The, 1981, M. Gorky Film Studio, director S. Gasparov, composer A. Zubov.

Slave of Love, The, 1975, Mosfilm, director N. Mikhalkov, composer E. Artemyev.

Sleeping Beauty, The, 1964, Lenfilm, directors A. Dudko and K. Sergeyev, music by P. Tchaikovsky.

Snowstorm, The, 1965, Mosfilm, director V. Basov, composer G. Sviridov.

Soil is Thirsty, [The Earth Thirsts], 1930, Vostok-kino, director Yu. Raizman; music in 1931 by composers R. Glier, S. Ryauzov and V. Sokolov.

Solaris, 1972, Mosfilm, director A. Tarkovsky, composer E. Artemyev.

Soldiers of Freedom, 4 parts (films 1 and 2), 1977, Mosfilm in collaboration with the film studios Za igralni Film (Bulgaria), Mata-Film (Hungary), Defa (DDR), the Polish film organization Zespoli Filmov (Poland), Bukuresht' (Rumania), Barrandov, Kolliba (Czechoslovakia). Director Yu. Ozerov, composer Yu. Levitin.

Solitary Sailing, 1985, Mosfilm, director M. Tumanishvili, composer V. Babushkin.

Soul, The, 1981, Mosfilm, director A. Stefanovich, composer A.R. Zatsepin.

Sous les Toits de Paris, 1930, France, director R. Clair, composer Moretti.

Spartakus, 1976, Mosfilm, directors V. Derbenev and Yu. Grigorovich, music by A. Khachaturian.

Spring, 1947, Mosfilm, director G. Alexandrov, composer, I. Dunayevsky.

Stalker, 2 parts, 1980, Mosfilm, director A. Tarkovsky, composer E. Artemyev.

Star and Death of Khoakin Murieta, The, 1983, M. Gorky Film Studio, director V. Grammatikov, composer A. Rybnikov.

Steps in the Night, 1962, Lithuanian Film Studio, director R. Vabalas, composer E. Balsys.

Stillness, 2 parts, 1964, Mosfilm, director V. Basov, composer V. Basner.

Stone Guest, The, 1967, Lenfilm, director V. Gorikker, music by A. Dargomyzhsky.

Swan Lake, 1958, The Central Studio of Documentary Films, director Z. Tulubayeva, music by P. Tchaikovsky.

Swan Lake, 1968, Lenfilm, directors A. Dudko and K. Sergeyev, music by P. Tchaikovsky.

Swineherd and Shepherd, The 1941, Mosfilm, director I. Pyriev, composer T. Khrennikov.

Taras Shevchenko, 1951, Kiev Film Studio, director I. Savchenko, composer B. Lyatoshincky.

Taste of Bread, The, 4 parts (films 1 and 2), 1979, Mosfilm and Kazakhfilm, director A. Sakharov, composer Yu. Levitin.

Taxi Blues, 1990, the American-Soviet Film Association Eurofilm and Lenfilm (USSR) MK-2 Production (France), director P. Lungin, composer V. Chekasin.

Terrible Age, The, 1977, Mosfilm, directors V. Derbenev and Yu. Grigorovich, music by S. Prokofiev.

Third Blow, The, 1948, Kiev Film Studio, director I. Savchenko, music from the works of P. Tchaikovsky.

This Summer's Hit, 1982, Tallinn Film, director P. Urbla, composer R. Rannap.

Three Comrades, 1935, Lenfilm, director S. Timoshenko, composer I. Dunayevsky.

Tractor Drivers, The, 1939, Mosfilm, director I. Pyriev, composers D. and Dm. Pokrass.

Train of Extraordinary Destination, The, 1980, A. Dovzhenko Film Studio, Kiev, director V. Shevchenko, composer E. Stankevich.

Trans-Siberian Express, The, 1977, Kazakhfilm, director E. Urazbayev, composer E. Rakhmadiev.

Trembita, 1968, Sverdlovsk Film Studio, director O. Nikolaevsky, music by Yu. Miliutin.

Trilogy about Maxim, A, (*Maxim's Youth* [*The youth of Maxim*], *The Return of Maxim*, *The Vyborg Side*), 1934–1938, Lenfilm, directors G. Kozintsev and L. Trauberg, composer D. Shostakovich.

Troublesome Household, A, 1946, Mosfilm, director M. Zharov, composer Yu. Miliutin.

True Friends, 1954, Mosfilm, director M. Kalatozov, composer T. Khrennikov.

Two Soldiers, 1943, Tashkent Film Studio, director L. Lukov, composer N. Bogoslovsky.

2001: A Space Odyssey, 1968, USA, director S. Kubrick.

Unfinished Piece for Player Piano, An, 1976, Mosfilm, director N. Mikhalkov, composer E. Artemyev.

Unforgettable Year 1919, The, 1952, Mosfilm, director M. Chiaureli, composer D. Shostakovich.

Unlikely Stories, 1983, Lenfilm, director S. Ovcharov, composer I. Matsievsky.

Valeri Chkalov, 1941, Lenfilm, director M. Kalatozov, composer V. Pushkov.

Victory, 2 parts, 1984, Mosfilm (USSR), DEFA (DDR), in collaboration with the All-Union Sovinfilm Organization (USSR) and Sezomen kuvakkasettituotanto (Finland), director E. Matveyev, composer E. Ptichkin.

Volga-Volga, 1938, Mosfilm, director G. Alexandrov, composer I. Dunayevsky.

Volochayevsky Days, The, 1937, Lenfilm, directors Brothers Vasiliev, composer D. Shostakovich.

War and Peace, 4 parts, 1966–1967, Mosfilm, director S. Bondarchuk, composer V. Ovchinnikov.

We are from Kronstadt, 1936, Mosfilm, director E. Dzigan, music and sound effects by N. Kriukov.

Wedding in Malinovka, A, 1967, Lenfilm, director A. Tutyshkin, music by B. Alexandrov.

Where Are You, Love?, 1980, Moldova Film, director V. Gageau, composer A. Mazhukov.

Wind of Freedom, The, 1961, Mosfilm, director L. Trauberg, music by I. Dunayevsky.

Without Witnesses, 1963, director N. Mikhalkov, composer E. Artemyev.

Woman Who Sings, A, 1979, Mosfilm, director A. Orlov, composers A. Zatsepin, A. Pugacheva and L. Garin.

Women's Kingdom, 1968, Mosfilm, director A. Saltykov, composer A. Eshpai.

Yachts Sail Out to Sea, The, 1956, Tallinn Film Studio, director Yu. Egorov, composer G. Ernesax.

Young Guard, The, 2 parts, 1948, M. Gorky Film Studio, director S. Gerasimov, composer D. Shostakovich.

Zangezur, 1938, Armenkino, directors A. Bek-Nazarov and Ya. Dukor, composer A. Khachaturian.

Zaporozhets beyond the Danube, The, 1938, Kiev Film Studio, director I. Kavaleridze, music by Gulak-Artemovsky.

Zaporozhets beyond the Danube, The, 1953, Kiev Film Studio, director V. Lapoknysh, music by Gulak-Artemovsky.

Zhenya, Zhenechka and 'Katyusha', 1967, Lenfilm, director V. Motyl', composer I. Schwarz.

Zoya, 1944, Soyuzdetfilm, director L. Arnshtam, composer D. Shostakovich.

INDEX